Issues in Globalization

Edited by
Stuart Bruchey
Alan Nevins Professor Emeritus
Columbia University

A Routledge Series

ISSUES IN GLOBALIZATION
STUART BRUCHEY, *General Editor*

SOCIAL PARTNESHIPS AND SOCIAL RELATIONS
New Strategies in Workforce and Economic Development
Janet Boguslaw

GENDERING ETHNICITY
Implications for Democracy Assistance
Lori Handrahan

GAY LIFE IN THE FORMER USSR
Fraternity without Community
Daniel P. Schluter

GAY LIFE IN THE FORMER USSR
Fraternity Without Community

Daniel P. Schluter

LONDON AND NEW YORK

Published 2002 by Routledge
2 Park Square, Milton Park, Abingdon, Oxon OX14 4RN
52 Vanderbilt Avenue, New York, NY 10017

First issued in paperback 2018

Routledge is an imprint of the Taylor & Francis Group, an informa business

Copyright © 2002 by Daniel P. Schluter

All rights reserved. No part of this book may be reprinted or reproduced or utilised in any form or by any electronic, mechanical, or other means, now known or hereafter invented, including photocopying and recording, or in any information storage or retrieval system, without permission in writing from the publishers.

Notice:
Product or corporate names may be trademarks or registered trademarks, and are used only for identification and explanation without intent to infringe.

Library of Congress Cataloging-in-Publication Data
Schluter, Daniel P, 1964–
  Gay life in the former USSR : fraternity without community / Daniel P. Schluter.
    p. cm. — (Issues in globalization)
  Includes bibliographical references and index
  ISBN 0-415-93233-5
  1. Gays—Soviet Union—Social conditions. 2. Homosexuality—Soviet Union—History. I. Title. II. Series.
HQ76.3.S653 S38 2001
305.9'0664'0947—dc21   2001034975

ISBN 13: 978-1-138-99186-6 (pbk)
ISBN 13: 978-0-415-93233-2 (hbk)

 Printed in the United Kingdom
by Henry Ling Limited

Contents

ACKNOWLEDGMENTS	vii
A NOTE	
On Translation, Transliteration, Typography, and the Use of Russian	ix
INTRODUCTION	
Fraternity Versus Community in the Soviet Gay World	3
I. Seeking an Understanding of Soviet Gay Life	3
II. Concepts, Goals, and Direction of the Analysis	5
III. Content and Organization of the Book	7
CHAPTER ONE	
Constructing Social Institutions for a Soviet Gay Theory	11
I. Definition and Delineation of Community	13
II. Sexuality and Community Institutions	28
III. Institutions, Community, and the State in the USSR	32
CHAPTER TWO	
Employing Social Research Methods for a Soviet Gay Studies	39
I. Participant Observation	40
II. Unstructured Interviews	40
III. Survey Research & Data Analyses	41
CHAPTER THREE	
The Individual-Level Institutions of Soviet Gay Identity	69
I. Defining Identity and Identification	70
II. The Extent and Types of Identification	75
III. The Development of Homosexual Identities	79

CHAPTER FOUR
Ecological-Level Institutions as Soviet Gay Places 87
  I. Public Places Appropriated for Gay Purposes 89
  II. Semi-Private and Partly-public Places Subverted for Gay Uses 101
  III. Private Places Fashioned to Accommodate Gay Needs 108
  IV. Gay Places in the Soviet Gay World 111

CHAPTER FIVE
Group-Level Institutions and Soviet Gay Politics 117
  I. Legal Restrictions on Homosexual Activity ("Sodomy") 117
  II. Societal Attitudes Toward Homosexuality 124
  III. The Prospects for Gay Political Activism in the USSR 126
  IV. Gay and Lesbian Organizations in the Soviet Union 129

CONCLUSION
Fraternity Without Community in the Soviet Gay World 137
  I. Distinguishing Fraternal Institutions From Communal Ones 139
  II. Secret Individual-Level Interaction Allows for Soviet Gay Fraternity 141
  III. Thwarting Group-Level Interaction Prevents Soviet Gay Community 142
  IV. Constricted Development and the Lack of Soviet Gay Community 146
  V. Directions for Future Research 147

AFTERWORD
On the Development of Fraternity and Community in the Former Soviet Union 149
  I. Some Ecological-Level Institutions Improve, Others Change Form 151
  II. Group-Level Institutions of Community Generally Fail to Thrive 160
  III. Individual-Level Institutions of Fraternity Still Central to Gay Life 170

REFERENCES
  I. English-Language Sources 177
  II. Russian-Language Sources 197
INDEX 201

> ... I am gratified anyway by the hope that this heap of raw materials laying before the reader will give him some sort of impression of the history, daily life, and language of the Russian homosexual subculture and will serve as a starting point for future researchers, who now will not have to start in an empty space.
>
> Владимир Козловский [Vladímir Kozlóvsky],
> *Аргот русской гомосексуальной субкультуры: Материалы к изучению*
> [*The Argot of the Russian Gay Subculture: Materials for Research*]
> p. 5

Acknowledgments

I COULD NOT HAVE COMPLETED THIS STUDY WITHOUT AN IMMENSE AMOUNT OF help and support from several sources, the most important of which were Soviet gay men and lesbians themselves. First and foremost, I must thank my research subjects all across the USSR, hundreds of whom were willing and able to overcome monumental and justifiable fears of disclosure in order to take part in the survey. I am even more indebted to those who were also amenable to discussing their lives openly with me on innumerable occasions and sometimes in dangerous settings.

I must also thank my Soviet cohorts—friends, acquaintances, friends-of-friends, or simply other "kindred spirits"—who took a personal interest in my work and did much to help me gather the data and the other information necessary for this project. The list is long, but I would like to give special mention to: Édik and M. for their aid in developing the questionnaire; Zhénya, Sásha, Vénya, and Alekséy for their help with questionnaire distribution; Géna, Sergéy S., "Sánich", and Ványa for "connections" and "contacts" when I needed them. I am also grateful to Sergéy K. for his persistent friendship throughout the data-gathering process, despite my erratic, sometimes irascible behavior. Special thanks and gratitude also must go to Gálya and Ksénya, who helped me locate Soviet lesbians in a culture that has great difficulty even envisioning the possibility of their existence.

In addition, I am much indebted to Tatyána Semyónovna and Nikoláy Ivánovich, staff members at a cooperative medical facility in Moscow, who were instrumental in helping me obtain access to research subjects and provided a forum for presenting and discussing my ideas about gay life in the USSR. "Hats off!" to them for taking a noble risk in offering public meeting space for Soviet gay men and lesbians when legal measures could have been taken against them for what amounted to "aiding and abetting criminal elements". I am thankful also to Soviet scholars, Ígor S. Kón, Dmítriy D. Isáyev, and Teet Veispak, for their advice and encouragement in carrying out this research.

I must also convey much appreciation to some of my American compatriots in Moscow at that time. Brian Harvey, a fellow American researcher in the USSR, provided much-needed comradeship during the adventurous endeavor. Liz McKeon and Todd Weinberg went well beyond the call of duty as International Research and Exchanges Board (IREX) administrative staff in Moscow by safeguarding my data and other research materials for me when I was detained by the KGB and written up in the Soviet press as a possible "sex spy".

Research for this project was made possible by the fact that I was in the USSR during the academic year 1990–1991 on fellowships from the United States Department of Education's Fulbright-Hays Research Abroad Program and IREX, under the sponsorship of the USSR Academy of Sciences, to study an aspect of the economic reform program then underway. This research was not funded by those agencies, however, and they bear no responsibility whatsoever for it— neither for the way the research was conducted nor for any of the analyses I present here.

Finally, paying homage to those whose work in this area has come before, I am grateful for not having to start in an "empty space."

> Unfortunately, transliteration systems [for rendering Russian words from Cyrillic into the Latin Alphabet] abound: institutions, editorial offices, and authors use their own systems, and the resultant proliferation confuses the uninitiated and promotes sloppiness among the professionals. . . . The U.S. Board on Geographic Names transliteration system is used by most U.S. government offices and publications and is preferred by the Chicago Manual of Style and the author.
>
> Genevra Gerhart,
> *The Russian's World: Life and Language*
> inside front cover.

A Note
On Translation, Transliteration, Typography, and the Use of Russian

IN THE TEXT, NOTES, AND REFERENCES FOR THIS WORK, I WILL USUALLY translate key terms and phrases, titles of books and individuals, and names of organizations, as well as quotations, from Russian into English—where English-language equivalents and near-equivalents exist. In doing so, I will provide the Russian original for clarification (in parentheses and in cyrillic script). When I translate text for quotations, I will also include such Russian words [in square brackets] in cases in which my translation might be disputable.

It is not always possible or desirable, however, to translate all Russian terms into English. I will therefore occasionally use Russian-language words, transliterated into the Latin alphabet and *in italic script*, when it is necessary to indicate or explain a term that is not readily renderable in English. Where I do so, I will use the transliteration system of the U.S. Board on Geographical Names (Gerhart 1974:inside front cover), with a few exceptions to facilitate proper pronunciation among non-Russian-speakers. I will add diacritical marks ("´") to indicate stressed syllables; I will transliterate the Russian "ё", which is always stressed, as "yó" or "ó", depending on proper pronunciation; and I will omit hard and soft (palatalization) signs ("ъ" and "ь"), which are themselves unpronounced.

With these transliterations, I will also provide the Russian-language original (again, in parentheses and in cyrillic script), but only for the first use of the term. These rules will hold for Russian names, titles, and words that have already crossed over into acceptable English, but not for text in quotations, which will be reproduced as in the original. Thus, for instance, the name of the last Soviet President will usually be rendered as "Mikhaíl S. Gorbachóv" rather than the usual "Mikhail S. Gorbachev", indicating that the last syllable in both first and last names is stressed and should be pronounced "il" and "ov", respectively.

In the interest of clarity, I will use **bold script**, rather than the conventional italics, to distinguish my emphasis of certain words and phrases from italicized transliterations. However, I will reproduce emphases made by quoted authors in the style in which they were published and will indicate having done so thusly: (*emphasis in the original*). Sometimes, I will also add emphases to quoted material, in which case I will again use the style of emphasis that is used in the original work quoted —usually the conventional italics—and I will indicate the change: [*emphasis added*].

Finally, the reader will notice my use of quotation marks around Russian words, in both the cyrillic and the Latin alphabets. This is to indicate that the word or expression so set off is not recognized as standard in Russian, but is a slang term.

Gay Life in the Former USSR

The gay world, like other worlds, is a unity of experience. . . . It is perceived by the gay individual as a whole, with a past and future existence independent of his[/her] experiencing of it; [s/]he acts toward that world, and within it, as a member, in certain expected ways.

The gay world itself is not a community of people, a set of relationships, or a spatial entity, although it is usually experienced with others, in special relationships and in particular places. . . .

In general, the gay world has two distinctions. It is almost universally stigmatized, and no one is socialized within or toward it as a child. . . .

. . . This makes the gay experience of stigma particularly significant and sociologically interesting. . . . Belonging to the gay world always entails a choice, often a difficult one.

After that choice comes another one: to be secret and discreditable, or to be open and discredited. . . .

The secret world, especially the world whose secret is a feared stigma, fosters a clear-cut identity as well as a close-knit community.

Carol A. B. Warren,
Identity and Community in the Gay World
pp.3-6, passim

Introduction
Fraternity versus Community in the Soviet Gay World

A GREAT DEAL IS NOW KNOWN ABOUT GAY AND LESBIAN LIFE IN "FIRST WORLD" societies (those of North America and Western Europe) from psychological, sociological, anthropological, historical, and physiological research.[1] In fact, so much interest has been generated on this topic that a new concentration for academic research in the West has emerged within the last decade or two: "Gay Studies" has become a new field of topically oriented, cross-disciplinary area studies.

However, the study of homosexual worlds outside of modern, Western, industrialized countries is a project that is only beginning to attract the attention of academics. Some research has been done on the "Third World" gay subcultures in Latin America, in South and Southeast Asia, in the Middle East, and even in Arab Africa,[2] but there has been almost no scholarly work done on the gay and lesbian populations of Eastern Europe and the USSR or of China and its client states in the region.[3] As a result, very little is known about the lives that homosexuals have led in the East, or communist "Second World."

I. SEEKING AN UNDERSTANDING OF SOVIET GAY LIFE

Such Western accounts of gay and lesbian life in the Soviet Union as do exist (Ebert 1977; "G" 1983; DuCett 1986) have come overwhelmingly from journalists and tourists to the USSR and are of a purely anecdotal character, detailing chance meetings and giving only a shadowy glimpse of the daily lives of the Soviet gay and lesbian population. The works of Western scholars on homosexuality in the Soviet Union were limited to a few papers presented at academic conferences. These reports (von Hagen 1984; Robinson 1991) also chiefly concerned tales of gay contacts made in the USSR while there to study other subjects, and, since these observations were neither systematic nor based on empirical research, their "findings" may not be generalizable. The sociolegal work of De Jong (1982) is exceptional in this regard.

The few works on sexuality and homosexuality in the USSR and Eastern Europe by *émigré* scientists that appeared in the West during the Soviet period were also largely anecdotal in nature (Schuvaloff 1976; Karlinsky 1983) or provided only a quizzical look at the predicaments faced by Soviet citizens in this area of their lives (*e.g.*: Sandomirsky 1951; Stern 1980; Mamonova 1989). One notable exception is the work of a Russian *émigré* linguist (Козловский 1986), which presented a thorough look at Soviet gay slang but, unfortunately, not much insight into the subculture that spawned it. This work did, however, represent original research conducted in the USSR. Another exception is Karlinsky's (1976, 1977, 1989) work on Soviet gay literary history.

To my knowledge, there were neither Soviet sociological data collected on nor ethnographic descriptions of Soviet gay subculture in the anthropological or historical literatures of the USSR largely because the very existence of homosexuals in the Soviet Union was officially denied after the Stalinist "Thermidor" of the 1930s. As the official argument went, Soviet ("Marxist") sociology need not study a behavior that, if it occurred at all, was only a sporadic incidence of a "bourgeois aberration" which would anyhow "wither away." Indeed, the entire field of "bourgeois sociology" was outlawed in the USSR also from that time, and after its rehabilitation in the late 1960s, the disquieting topics of "social problems" research were scarcely broached (Fischer 1966; Shalin 1978, 1990; Shlapentokh 1987). Sex research was conducted only in medical and psychiatric institutions and sexology was treated more as a branch of applied criminology than as an academic interest area (Левин interview 1991). In the USSR, the social-scientific study of homosexuality was, until the final years of Soviet rule, simply taboo.

The first inroads into this void were made only after the relaxation of sociolegal restraints on individual expression (*glásnost*) and several years of political and economic restructuring (*perestróyka*) under Communist Party General Secretary Mikhaíl S. Gorbachóv. Chapters on homosexuality were included in two books on sexuality published in the Soviet Union, one by a noted Soviet sociologist (Кон 1988), the other by a Swiss and a Soviet journalist (Гейгес и Суворова 1990). However, neither book presented any direct research among Soviet gay men and lesbians, and neither offered much in the way of analysis of their daily lives. In addition, a young scholar in a psycho-neurological research institute defended a dissertation for the *kandidátskaya* degree (кандидатская степень)[4] in medicine

Introduction

(медицинских наук) on the topic of homosexuality (Исаев 1989), but this was only allowed under the stipulation that the approach taken was to analyze homosexuality as a mental deficiency (Исаев interview 1991). The first attempt at organizing the study of human sexuality in the Soviet Union was undertaken in early 1991 with the founding of the Soviet Sexological Society (Кон 1991).

In this book, I will address three major audiences for whom the analysis should have relevance. First, I presume that sociologists will be interested in the analysis I present here of a spectrum of institutional development among subcultural groups ranging from undeveloped fraternal-type ties of mutual interest and understanding to the creation of full-fledged community with many formal and informal organizations. This is a more nuanced approach than that taken by many other scholars of community. Second, in demonstrating how this process of development played itself out in the last years of the Soviet regime, I will be contributing to an understanding of the processes involved in the "opening up" of Soviet society to which *glásnost* and *perestróyka* were catalysts. I expect, therefore, that this work will be of interest to scholars in Russian, Soviet, and post-Soviet Studies. Third, I anticipate that scholars in Gay Studies will be academically interested in, as well as "naturally curious" about, my depiction and analysis of a "gay world" outside of the well-known gay and lesbian communities of Western Europe and North America.

As a scholar who has personal experience with, formal education in, and intellectual loyalty to all three groups, I may be in a unique position to demonstrate how each of these areas can benefit and be enriched by the others. In this book then, I will make a special attempt to integrate scholars' thinking on all intellectual areas relevant here: sociological conceptions of community, Sovietology's understanding of the "backwardness" of modern development in the USSR, and the knowledge from Gay Studies of how a homosexual subculture is created and maintained. These are (respectively) the structure, context, and content of the book.

II. CONCEPTS, GOALS, AND DIRECTION OF THE ANALYSIS

One important goal of this work, then, is to document the state of existence of this previously unstudied group, providing broadly based information about the lives of the gay- and lesbian-identified population of the Soviet Union. Issues to be illuminated in a general way are the typical life events of Soviet gay men and lesbians—including opportunities for romantic relationships and sexual liaisons that are open or closed to them, the varying living conditions for homosexuals in different cities and regions of the Soviet Union, and gay and lesbian subculture in the USSR as well as variations in individuals' involvement with it.

From reading such accounts as do exist and from my personal experiences there, but mostly from my original research on this topic in the Soviet Union, I came to appreciate the presence of a fairly well-developed gay identity[5] and a sense of fraternal ties among Soviet homosexuals. I found clear evidence of gay friendship circles and some social networking. I encountered obvious gay street life in the larger cities of the Soviet Union and came across easily recognized gay "stomping grounds."[6] I discovered little in the way of gay and lesbian voluntary associations in the USSR, however, and a complete lack of formal economic, political, societal, or cultural organizations catering to the homosexual population, the likes of which do exist in many other industrialized countries around the world—especially in the modern West.

Although there was certainly a clandestine gay and lesbian subculture[7] in the Soviet Union, organizationally its development had not advanced beyond a sporadically felt sense of "fraternity"[8] of the sort that is often engendered among individuals with a common social position and a commonality of interests. There was nothing in Soviet gay and lesbian life, I found, that could be described properly as a gay "community."[9]

Indeed, the conditions of gay life in the USSR in the late 1980s and early 1990s seemed remarkably similar to the situation described in accounts of gay life in America in about the 1940s and 1950s,[10] when homosexual Americans could make contact with one another safely only in the secrecy of carefully guarded private apartments or in the anonymity of encounters in public places. Because they feared being discovered to be homosexual by heterosexual others (especially by their family members, employers, or the authorities), they did not generally live even a moderately open existence. (See: Leznoff & Westley 1956; Reiss 1961; Hooker 1965; McIntosh 1968; Martin & Lyon 1972; Katz 1976.) In both of these contexts, the idea of gay men and lesbians "coming out of the closet" was incongruous. The very concept of being "out" was simply inconceivable.

The main goal of this work, however, is to put the descriptive information I have gathered about the Soviet gay and lesbian subculture into an analytical framework that distinguishes fraternal social institutions from communal ones by assessing the difference between them in the degree of their institutionalization.[11] In order to do so, it will be necessary to elucidate the developmental processes involved in the elaboration of subcultures generally and then to apply those principles to the analysis of gay and lesbian subcultures and to the Soviet homosexual subculture in particular. In the process, I will present a scheme for determining the types of institutions that must be developed for a subculture to transform itself from being simply a **fraternity** of associating and co-identifying individuals to being a **community** of interconnected institutional actors, roles, places, and relationships as well as individuals.

III. CONTENT AND ORGANIZATION OF THE BOOK

To properly analyze the processes and outcomes of institutional development among homosexuals in the USSR, I have consulted many works in Sociology, Soviet Studies, and Gay Studies. From them, I distilled the basic ideas that form the conceptual framework just outlined. The theoretical approach underpinning this conceptual framework is elaborated in Chapter One. In addition, I gathered both quantitative and qualitative data in a research study carried out expressly for this work. Chapter Two will provide an explanation of the research methods I used in conducting that research along with information about characteristics of the sample subjects I engaged and about data analyses I have subsequently undertaken. The data from these analyses will be proffered throughout the rest of the book in order to provide the documentary evidence needed to meet the descriptive goal set forth above.

It is the main, analytical goal, though, that will dictate the specific content and organization of the work. My analysis will focus on the institutionalization of relations among gay men and lesbians in the Soviet Union in several operational spheres and on at least three levels of analysis, each of which will correspond to a separate chapter.

In Chapter Three, I will describe the **individual-level institutions** that engendered in Soviet homosexuals a sense of fraternity with one another. Among the institutions to be considered are the particular shapes that homosexual identity had taken in the Soviet context, common and uncommon aspects of the Soviet "gay sensibility," and the variety and "types" of gay people that existed in the Soviet gay and lesbian subculture. While these aspects of gay life were certainly institutionalized in the Soviet context, I will argue that the existence of gay and lesbian social institutions on this level was sufficient only for promoting the sense among Soviet homosexuals that they are a distinct "people" ("люди" or "народ"). It was not enough to inspire their coordinated socio-political action or even their public self-identification as homosexuals.

Chapter Four will be a broader, ecological tour of the Soviet "gay world." I will focus on the array and arrangement of **societal-level institutions** that defined the social environment of Soviet homosexuals' everyday life: the bureaucratic rules and demographic patterns that dictated their living conditions and the geographic locales that served as the loci for gay and lesbian social as well as sexual behaviors. In doing so, I will illustrate how Soviet gay men and lesbians were successful in carving out an existence for themselves despite both the generalized and specific oppression they faced in Soviet society. However, I will argue, the ecological conditions under which they lived did not allow for gay community to exist in Soviet society and certainly were no match for the fertile social-ecological context of contemporary Western gay life. Soviet homosexuals were able only to appropriate public spaces for their gay meeting places, redefining them for short-term and secretive use, or to meet privately in their own homes when they could escape the watchful eyes of family members, neighbors, and the authorities. They did not, as a rule, succeed in developing more stable or more original institutional forms that would be recognized as peculiar to the Soviet homosexual world.

In Chapter Five, I will detail the socio-legal situation that Soviet gay men and lesbians had to abide and discuss the few attempts that were made to create both political and social-economic group-level institutions for gay and lesbian people in the USSR. While such institutions are an integral part of Western gay and lesbian subcultures, neither gay and lesbian social-recreational and voluntary associations nor homosexual formal organizations succeeded in establishing themselves in the USSR. Although these types of institutions could lead to the development of a "post-Soviet gay community" at some future time, without them, I will argue, there can be no credible claim of an institutionalized gay community existing in the Soviet Union.

What is more, as I will report in the Afterword to this book, since the general economic, political, societal, and cultural conditions in what is now the former Soviet Union have generally not developed well enough for even the organizations of "mainstream" social groups to function effectively in the post-Soviet era, those of the homosexual minority are not likely to materialize—or at least to be very successful—in the near future.

NOTES

1. For psychological accounts, see: Hooker 1963; Hooker 1965; Weinberg & Williams 1974; Bell & Weinberg 1978; among many others. Sociological studies on gay life in the West abound. See, especially: Humphreys 1972; Adam 1978; Sagarin 1978; Levine 1979; Plummer 1981; Blumstein & Schwartz 1983; Adam 1985; Greenberg 1988. For anthropological work, see: Newton 1972; Callender & Kochems 1983; Grahn 1984; Herdt 1984; Murray 1984; Herdt 1987; Goodwin 1989; *et alia*. Historians of Western gay life have been quite prolific. See: Bullough 1976; Katz 1976; Bèrubè 1983; D'Emilio 1983, 1984; Duberman, Vicinus, & Chauncey 1989; *et alia*. For research on homosexuals and physiology, see: Masters & Johnson 1966, 1979.

2. For references on homosexuality in various parts of the world, see: Dynes 1987.

3. Two recent examples are Lemke's (1991) volume of interviews with East German gay men and Ruan & Tsai's (1987) paper on homosexuality in China.

4. The first of two post-(college)graduate degrees, the Soviet *kandidátskaya* is generally considered to be somewhat higher than the American Master's degree, but less advanced than the doctorate (Ph.D.). (Gerhart 1974:80)

5. The sociological and psychological literatures on "identity" are vast, and definitions of it are nearly as varied as the numbers of scholars seeking to define any particular social identity. While it ultimately will be important to explore and evaluate various scholars'

Introduction

understanding of what identity is, for the moment, Webster's (1970:413) dictionary definition should suffice, being broad enough to encompass many competing conceptualizations. Thus, identity is "the condition of being the same with something described or asserted" and identification, which refers to the process of forming or asserting an identity, is "orientation of the self in regard to something (as a person or group) with a resulting feeling of close emotional association."

6. These places were obvious, at least, to the initiated and were likely well-known to the authorities. (von Hagen 1984)

7. As with the previous concept, extracting the most useful definition of "subculture" from the expansive literature on the subject would not be useful here, when Webster's (1970:874) dictionary definition is adequate to the task at hand, providing as it does a general, orienting explanation. To wit, a subculture is "an ethnic, regional, economic, or social group exhibiting characteristic patterns of behavior sufficient to distinguish it from others within an embracing culture or society." Further explication of what characteristics distinguish a subcultural group from other social groupings will be undertaken in Chapter One.

8. Again, Webster's (1970:332) dictionary definition of "fraternity" seems adequate for the present purpose, though the concept will be developed further in Chapter One. Thus, fraternity is "a group of people associated or formally organized for a common purpose, interest, or pleasure." Alternatively, a fraternity may be "men of the same class, profession, character, or tastes."

9. Yet again, the dictionary definition of "community" provided by Webster's (1983:267) is suitable for the present purposes. Thus, community is "a unified body of individuals: as . . . the people with common interests living in a particular area[;] . . . an interacting population of various kinds of individuals (as species) in a common location[; or] . . . a group of people with a common characteristic or interest living together within a larger society." In Chapter One, I will be concerned with specifying the social dimensions which underlie these geographic and economic characteristics of community and which, in my view, more properly denote its existence.

10. Some scholars have suggested to me that conditions for homosexuals in the last years of the Soviet Union approximated gay life in the West at even earlier periods: the 1920s (Gay Studies scholar, private communication 1992) or the late 19th century (KOH Interview 1991).

11. Webster's (1970:438) defines a (social) institution as "a significant practice, relationship, or organization in a society or culture" and, in a later edition (Webster's 1983:627), the verb "to institutionalize" something is defined as "to incorporate [it] into a structured and often highly formalized system."

> Athens, Sparta, republican and Christian Rome, Jerusalem, Geneva—these are names that are the anchors of Western political thought. Other innumerable communities, villages and towns, feudal manors, monasteries, and shetls [sic: shtetls] also form a historical testament to our ability to create forms of human association that capture a sense of moral cohesion, mutual aid, and intimacy within a place and across time.
>
> Philip Abbott,
> *Seeking Many Inventions: The Idea of Community in America*
> pp. ix-x.

Chapter One
Constructing Social Institutions for a Soviet Gay Theory

SCHOLARLY ANALYSIS OF THE LACK OF COMMUNITY DEVELOPMENT AMONG groups of homosexuals in the Soviet Union, but the presence there of social interaction and an awareness of fraternal bonds between individual Soviet gay men and lesbians, requires an understanding of theoretical schemes and operational measures for evaluating the development of "community" and "fraternity" in general. Yet, the academic literature on community provides no widely accepted definition of the term and no unambiguous measure of its development (or lack thereof); there is, literally, no academic literature on the concept of fraternity as I use it here (in the broadest sense). Clearly, definitions and measures of both community and fraternity must be put forward in order to proceed. To that end, I have devised a theoretical framework for this analysis that combines and reformulates several conceptions of community drawn from the disciplines of sociology, anthropology, philosophy, and urban studies and also provides for the differentiation of fraternity from community on the basis of the different levels of analysis appropriate for analyzing these distinctive forms of social organization.

My reformulation stresses the "institutional basis" of community. While recognizing that people are the "natural resources" necessary for all forms of human social organization, I will insist, as Park (1952) did, that it is the social institutions created by people through interaction that are the building blocks of community. Hoult (1969:165) defines an institution as:

> A process or an association that is highly A) organized (i.e., there is a careful specification of the roles and role relationships of those involved), B) systematized (i.e., there is a careful specification of what can and should be done by those involved), and C) stable (i.e., relative to any given group or process, there is no dependence upon the presence of any particular individuals, and the organization and systematization tend to remain relatively unchanged over time).

Instead of assuming a well-understood or predefined notion of community, as is common in these literatures, I will give substance to Effrat's (1973) conception of "communityness" as a **measurable variable** rather than a static condition. For indicating this variable, Breton's (1964) concept of the "institutional completeness" of a community fits well with the institutional approach. His rough, quantitative operationalization of the measure, however, is inadequate for the task at hand. I will argue that this quality of extensive institutional development is not a variable among different community types, as Effrat (1973) applied it. Rather, from the perspective I develop here, extensiveness of institutional completeness is a defining characteristic of community itself.

This redefinition of "the community concept" can be achieved by adopting Berger & Luckmann's (1966) social-constructionist approach to the development of "social institutions," which defines them as recognizable patterns of habitualized actions. This is combined with Abbott's (1987) depiction of communities as creative "inventions" developed by individuals and adopted by similar others as a means of solving some life-problem or satisfying some commonly felt need among a segment of the population in a society. The combined conception allows for the reformulation of one of the standard components of many problematic community definitions. This required characteristic is usually termed "the **number of functions** provided to individual members by the community" or "the **number of ties** connecting individual members to the community." Adding a qualitative element to this characteristic, I will consider both "the **number and type of functions** provided to individual members by the community" and "the **number and type of needs met** for individual members by the community."

Differing needs may be met by different communities, of course, as well as by families, the state, an industry, volunteer associations, churches, and many other social formations that are not communities. Some needs can also be met by other individuals without any supporting organization. Discussion of the needs that are met by community as a form of social organization will be enhanced through consideration of a philosophical theory of just what it is that "human needs" are. (Doyal & Gough 1991)

After combing through competing conceptualizations and definitions of "community" and specifying what I believe to be a better way of defining it, I will discuss works from the Gay Studies literature that can help to determine the "completeness" of such institutional development in the gay and lesbian communities of the West. This will provide a basis for implicit and explicit comparisons with the institutional arrangements I describe as typical of Soviet gay and lesbian life.

Finally, I will make use of analyses of the "constricted development" of non-state institutions in Soviet society from the annals of Sovietology to form the backdrop for detailing, in the rest of the book, why the forms of social organization I observed among the homosexual population of the Soviet Union do not meet the definition of an institutionally complete community put forth in this framework.

I. DEFINITION AND DELINEATION OF COMMUNITY

Perhaps the most difficult and enduring problem associated with community research is the lack of clarity about the concept of "community" itself. One dictionary of sociological terminology, defines it as: "A concentrated settlement of people in a limited territorial area, within which they satisfy many of their daily needs through a system of interdependent relationships." (Theodorson & Theodorson 1969:63) Yet there is little agreement among social scientists about just what constitutes a community or what are its essential components—and this lack of consensus is nothing new. Indeed, as early as the mid-1920s, Gillette (1926:677) remarked that:

> in our casual reading we would likely discover quite distinctly dissimilar usages [of the term "community"], ranging all the way from the small country district up to national and international situations, indicating that there is more or less confusion of thought about it.

From a sampling of 61 publications on issues of community, he found a considerable array of definitions of the concept.

Three decades later, Hillery (1955:117) found 94 distinct definitions of the term in the sociological literature and determined that among them the only area of unanimity was that "all of the definitions deal with people. Beyond this common basis, there is no [universal] agreement." Nonetheless, he did find it possible to isolate three characteristics common to many of the community definitions: the existence of a substantial amount of intimate social interaction among members, many and varied "ties" linking members to the community, and a territorial coherence.

It seems that this specification was not enough to resolve the problem, however, for almost twenty years thence, another student of community (Effrat 1973:1–2) was incited to declare that:

> Trying to study community is like trying to scoop up jello with your fingers. You can get hold of some, but there's always more slipping away from you. When we talk about community research, we can—and often do—refer to material on community organizing, action, and planning as well as more traditional research on interaction patterns, institutions, norms, and roles within phenomena characterized as communities.

> Not only is the range of subject matter broad but it is also divided into differing camps, whose debates with one another continue heatedly and underlie much of the work being done. . . . in the process of debate [over community] the controversial issues have become mixed together in a gelatinous mess of hypotheses, research, and value judgment. It is difficult, then, to differentiate these issues, and to see what positive and negative implications do in fact derive from emphasis on one or another point of view.

Yet, in spite of this longstanding conceptual confusion, further clarification can be attained with a careful typological approach.

A. Typology of Community

From a grounding in the community research literature, Effrat (1973) developed a typology of "traditions of research" on community that stresses two of the three key features Hillery (1955) had detected in many community definitions. Her scheme, presented in Table 1.0, arranges the approaches to studying community based on the number of "functions" a community provides for its members (which accounts for the number of "ties" a person has to the community)[1] and on whether or not a territorial grounding is seen as a necessary component of community. (She apparently assumes that the third factor, the existence of significant and sustained social interaction—which Hillery (1955:118) had found to be the most important for community definitions—is invariable: a "given" for all communities.)

Table 1.0: Four Major Traditions of Research on Community*

		Number of Functions Provided by the Community	
		Few	Many
Territorial Grounding	Necessary	The Community of Limited Liability	The Compleat Territorial Community
	Not Necessary	Personal Community	Community as Society

*Modified from Effrat (1973:5).

Scholarly works falling into the category of analyses termed "the compleat territorial community" describe small, locally-based, tightly-integrated social groups which may or may not be ethnically homogeneous. Effrat (1973:5) explains:

> In other words, it is assumed that the residents [of such places] comprise a community that is a relatively self-contained social environment supplying its members with a wide range of services. . . .

Constructing Social Institutions for a Soviet Gay Theory

> ... All such studies have proceeded more or less on this assumption that "true" communities are relatively autonomous social systems.

She cites works in this tradition that have analyzed as "communities" towns, villages, and small cities in industrial society (Lynd & Lynd 1929; Warner & Lunt 1941; Vidich & Bensman 1958); the human ecology of large-city neighborhoods and ghettoes (Wirth 1929; Zorbaugh 1929); rural folk-groups (Redfield 1941); groups of powerful social elites in a city (Hunter 1953; Hawley & Wirt 1968); and networks of local social organizations (Warren 1963; Hillery 1969; Stacey 1969).

Scholars working in the tradition of "the community of limited liability," following Janowitz's (1952) introduction of the term, have focused on describing the workings of territorial groupings that are not characterized by multi-faceted interconnections between individuals in a given area, but rather those in which area residents have limited ties to one another, usually based on only one or a few commonalities. From this perspective, researchers focused on analyzing the social interactions that took place within any given urban, geographically-defined area. Thus, according to Effrat (1973:15–18), city streets or blocks (Shaw & McKay 1942; Whyte 1955; Lorimer & Phillips 1971), distinctive residential neighborhoods (Greer 1956; Bell & Boat 1957; Young & Willmott 1957; Keller 1968; Lee 1968; Suttles 1968), and even local election districts or public utility service areas (*conferre* Keller 1968) were studied to determine how they functioned as "communities."

Works categorized as analyses of "personal community" focus on the close personal relations individuals have with others in their environment. Henry (1958:827), from whom the term was adopted, describes personal community as "the group of people on whom an individual can rely for support and/or approval." Listing a reliance on one another, the number of people involved, the constancy (or frequency) of direct interaction, and the type of involvement (or obligation) between individuals as the important properties of personal communities, Henry (1958:831) insists that "the personal community is the core of [psychic (or perceived)] security." Viewing community in this way has led to the study of individuals' involvement with social, political, or economic voluntary organizations (Phillips 1969) and to the study of personal social networks (Craven & Wellman 1973) as "communities."

The "community as society" tradition of theorizing treats communities as small-scale versions of the larger society, analyzing each as a functional system of interdependent social institutions. Effrat (1973:20) explains that:

> Within the tradition of community as society, "community" refers to segments of the population who [sic: individual members of which] are differentiated from others because of their common participation in specific institutions and their interaction with one another in friendship and kinship relationships. Calling a

group a community in this sense also usually implies the group's consciousness of kind, a shared subculture or set of values, and internally shared norms based upon them.

By defining communities based on the solidarity their members share (Neuwirth 1969), in this tradition, ethnic and racial groups (Breton 1964; Kramer 1970), "deviant" and disabled groups (Sagarin 1971), and occupational and professional groups (Goode 1957) have been studied as "communities."

While Effrat (1973) intended this scheme as a guide to understanding the focus of sociological and anthropological research into the nature of community, the terms she used to classify three of the four cells in the table reveal an urge to identify as different types the very communities that each of these traditions seeks to understand. In fact, it seems likely that these traditions of research into the nature of community have differed in their approach and focus because each is actually attempting to understand a different set of social formations, some of which are not communities at all. Reconceptualized with this in mind, I believe the scheme can be useful both in differentiating community from other forms of social organization and in distinguishing among various types of communities. To do so, it will be helpful first to note the flaws in some of these community definitions and to point out the basic inaccuracy of defining others as "communities" of any sort.

1. What Is Community and What Is Not

"Compleat territorial community" studies have been criticized for many reasons, but the most damning when it comes to defining community is Effrat's (1973:14) own observation that:

> ... the community investigated is often such by predefinition rather than by empirical research. By not leaving "communityness" itself completely open to investigation, researchers make it difficult to ever completely characterize the fundamental components of a community, and hence to clearly tell a community from a noncommunity, other than on the basis of size.

Thus, a large part of the ongoing conceptual confusion in the sociological literature on this topic may stem from the fact that studies of the traditional, localized community have not adequately contrasted it with other, discrete forms of social organization. Community has sometimes been declared to exist where researchers expected it to be, whether or not it is actually there.

The studies of "community of limited liability" attempted to make such a contrast. However, the social formation they chose to differentiate from the traditional, local community falls short on two of Hillery's (1955) three key features of community definitions: the large number of ties a person has to the community (or: the many functions a community provides its members) and significant, ongoing social interaction. Thus, these places of "limited liability" are termed "communities," it seems, solely on the basis of their territorial characteristic—sometimes one defined by the researchers themselves—while they involve neither strong affective ties nor much sustained social interaction. Without an affective or interactive basis of integrity though, such social forms as the typical urban neighborhood, police precinct, voting district, and political ward cannot qualify as "communities" in a very meaningful sense. They are merely aggregates of individuals who may or may not identify with the territorial area they inhabit, may or may not interact with other area residents, and may or may not share personal or cultural traits or political or economic interests. The problem is basic: interaction requires some form of communication and, as Webber (1964:110) has rightly pointed out, "It is clearly no linguistic accident that 'community' and 'communication' share the Latin root communis, [meaning] 'in common.' Communities comprise people with common interests who communicate with each other." Thus, varieties of community cannot be distinguished by the presence or absence (or large or small amount) of close, personal, and sustained social interaction, but different forms of social organization can be so differentiated. (I am therefore inclined to agree with Effrat (1973) on one point: social interaction must be present for community to exist. It is, indeed, a "given" for all communities.)

Worse yet, what is being called "personal community" (an oxymoron), entails none of the features important for definitions of the community concept. It has neither a territorial grounding nor members who provide one another with a wide range of functional benefits or ties. Moreover, while this kind of social organization surely involves a form of bonding between individuals engendered by personal interaction with the central figure in the array, many "members" will have little knowledge of, and little or no interaction with, others also tied to that person. Such groupings are actually **networks** of self-interested actors or interconnected circles of friends which simply do not come together often enough as a group to cohere as a "community." The individuals who make them up interact for the purpose of obtaining whatever personal, **individual** benefit they derive from (or whatever benefit they provide through) mutual contact—whether that benefit is material, social, spiritual, or emotional. Ego-centered networks are focused on addressing the "personal problems" of individual members, not the "social issues" of shared communal life. (Mills 1959)

"Community as society" studies, on the other hand, do analyze social formations that exhibit both substantial social interaction and significant affective ties among, or functions provided to, members. They may only lack a territorial basis.

2. Forms of Community

It seems that territoriality cannot be utilized as a means of differentiating between community and non-community, since communities can be of either sort. However, territoriality can distinguish between communities of the traditional, local type and modern types of community not necessarily defined by physical proximity.

a. Community Without Propinquity

The assumption that a territorial grounding is fundamental to "communityness" is understandable. It is one of the things that can most clearly demarcate such important and competing social formations as churches, schools, municipalities, ethno-linguistic groups, and nation states one from another. The connection between community and territory, however, is more and more a spurious one, as Webber (1964:108–109) makes clear:

> Both the idea of city and the idea of region have been traditionally tied to the idea of place. Whether conceived of as physical objects, as interrelated systems of activities, as interacting populations, or as governmental dominions, a city or a region has been distinguishable from any other city or region by the fact of territorial separation.
>
> The idea of community has similarly been tied to the idea of place. Although other conditions are associated with the community—including "sense of belonging," a body of shared values, a system of social organization, and interdependency—spatial proximity continues to be considered a *necessary* condition.
>
> But it is now becoming apparent that it is the accessibility rather than the propinquity aspect of "place" that is the ne\cessary condition. As accessibility becomes further freed from propinquity, cohabitation of a territorial place—whether it be a neighborhood, a suburb, a metropolis, a region, or a nation—is becoming less important to the maintenance of social communities. [*emphasis in the original*]

This decreasing significance of a common location or territoriality is vital for understanding the difference between traditional and modern forms of community. By providing greater access to more and more different sorts of people, modernity has created new forms of communities.

Yet, even a quarter-century later, Mayhew (1990:297) noted that many scholars of community—as well as non-academics—still have not understood this:

> ... common thinking about modernity and change have [sic: has] not always shaken the ... assumption that authentic community must rest on natural bonds: kin, clan, and community [*sic!*], supported in the last analysis by inescapable common fate and reinforced by traditional cultural forms and ceremonies.

For those who do not assume that community must be a localized phenomenon, the opportunities for close, affective ties and social interaction based on mutuality of interests and/or identification with one another is not (any longer) limited to those in immediate geographic proximity. Webber (1964:110–111) notes that, while still important in modern society, "... the place-community represents only a limited and special case of the larger genus of communities, deriving its basis from the common interests that attach to propinquity alone." In the modern age, at least, it is possible to have "community without propinquity."

b. Community of Interest

This modern kind of "placeless," "aspatial," or "nonspatial community" (Effrat 1973; Tilly 1973) is based on common interests. The development of modern, Western social mores has encouraged the increased salience of individuals' own interests in determining their associations in life. The greater availability of education and access to information that modern, urban life affords played a role in this as well. Technological developments increasing the ease of transportation and communication are also advantages in terms of personal development and self-expression, and these have had an effect on the nature of the ties individuals have to communities. Webber (1963:29) explains:

> As the individual's interests develop, he is better able to find others who share these interests and with whom he can associate. The communities with which he associates and to which he "belongs" are no longer only the communities of place to which his ancestors were restricted; Americans are becoming more closely tied to various interest communities than to place communities, whether the interest be based on occupational activities, leisure pastimes, social relationships, or intellectual pursuits.

Common interests which generate such non-territorial ties are developed, of course, through individuals' communicating one with another and, as Mayhew (1990:297) put it: "The key [to the creation of modern forms of community] . . . is the idea that solidarity is or can be created by communication." For determining with whom individuals can communicate, and thus with whom they can choose to interact, the effects of urbanization and technological advancement have no rivals.

B. Community Isn't Everything (and Vice Versa)

This does not mean, however, that all sets of people with common interests are communities. All forms of social organization involve ties between individuals, whether these are affective or utilitarian, personal or impersonal, weak or strong, *et cetera*. Most such ties require interaction with others in order to be meaningful. To create and maintain some ties, social intercourse in the form of direct, face-to-face contact is necessary. To constitute a community, a group of people must engage in direct or indirect, predictable, regular, and sustained social interaction, and this implies that they must have some shared form of communication. Through such interaction they must come to share a common group-identity, a sense that they have an important commonality in their shared interest or condition.

Before going any farther, it will be helpful to make an important distinction between different types of aggregations of people, only some of whom form groups and may create community. As a relatively concise explication of the difference between a "category" of people and a social "group," I know of none better than this by Goffman (1963:23-24):

> Here . . . there is a common conceptual confusion. The term "category" is perfectly abstract and can be applied to any aggregate, in this case persons with a particular stigma. A good portion of those who fall within a given stigma category may well refer to the total membership by the term "group" or an equivalent, such as "we," or "our people." Those outside the category may similarly designate those within it in group terms. However, often in such cases the full membership will not be part of a single group, in the strictest sense; they will neither have a capacity for collective action, nor a stable and embracing pattern of mutual interaction. What one does find is that members of a particular stigma category will have a tendency to come together into small social groups whose members all derive from the category, these groups themselves being subject to overarching organization to varying degrees. And one also finds that when one member of the category happens to come into contact with another, both may be disposed to modify their treatment of each other by virtue of believing that they each belong to the same "group." Further, in being a member of the category, an individual may have an increased probability of coming into contact with any other member, and even forming a relationship with him as a result. A category, then, can function to dispose its members to group-formation and relationships, but its total membership does not thereby constitute a group.

It is also crucial to note that many kinds of social formation can be found among many groups of people who, before the modern period, would not have been considered solidary enough even to form groups.

> There is no novelty in noting that members of professional groups are members thereby of limited-interest fraternities. Similarly, it is commonly recognized that members of churches, clubs, political parties, unions, and business organizations, and that hobbyists, sportsmen, and consumers of literature and of the performing arts are thereby also members of limited-interest groups whose spatial domains extend beyond any given urban settlement. (Webber 1964:110- 111)

This differentiation of professional groups, churches, clubs, political parties, unions, and business organizations from communities seems logical and obvious when one considers it. Similarly, the difference between a community and a category of people such as hobbyists, sportsmen, book readers, and movie-goers is clear and unmistakable, if one takes note of it.

Nonetheless, both in common parlance and in scholarly work, various social formations are indiscriminately described as "communities" despite their diverse histories, structures, and functions. It seems to have become fashionable (in the United States at least) to describe nearly any set of individuals with similar backgrounds, interests, or activities as a "community," even though there are other, common, and more apt words to describe those associations or categories of people. Common examples of this abound: the "disabled community," the "law-enforcement community," the "bodybuilding community," the "woodworking community," the "scientific community," the "sociology community," the "financial community," the "AIDS community," the "prison community," the "relief community," the "international community," and the "Internet community." The distinction between community and other forms of social organization do not seem all that "common" to me, and Berger (1988:51) suggests one reason why:

> the invocation of the concept of community may more often be like an incantation than a precise reference; its rhetorical use taps the magic and mystery of culture and frames it in a gauzy halo, rather like soft-focus photography. It emphasizes the familiarity and comfort that secure membership is supposed to bring—that sense of "we" that we congratulate ourselves that we "need" and which community provides.

Unfortunately, although Webber (1964) began by extolling this differentiation among types of social formations, he too succumbs and also uses the term "community" too loosely. If community is really to be conceived of as a multi-faceted set of ties among somewhat heterogeneous but interdependent people pursuing their special group interests, then the limited ties connecting individuals with professions, hobbies, confessions, or consumption patterns in common cannot also be so construed. They can only amount to something less than community. Webber (1964) does not follow through on the distinction he himself makes between community and "fraternity."[2]

Whatever else it is, community is a set of interconnected social institutions created by people who interact with one another by communicating, have some significant commonality, and share a certain "consciousness of kind." Park (1952:66) made this stipulation about institutions quite strongly:

> A community is not only a collection of people, but it is a collection of institutions. Not people, but institutions, are final and decisive in distinguishing the community from other social constellations.

What is lacking, then, from Webber's (1963, 1964) analyses is consideration of the institutional basis of community.

C. Institutionalization, Community, and Human Needs

The sociological term "social institution" is another concept that is neither clearly defined nor consistently used in the social-science literatures. One such definition, though, seems particularly apt for the theoretical argumentation I am constructing here. This is because it focuses on individuals, who are communicating their shared interests or concerns, in their interactions with others and, by those very acts, creating and maintaining social institutions. In fact, Berger & Luckmann (1966) argue convincingly that the whole of social order is a product of human efforts and that therefore, even our notion of reality is itself "socially constructed." One real, or "reified," aspect of this social order is the phenomenon of social institutions.

Berger & Luckmann (1966:48) reason as follows: because important biological developments take place in our species after birth, "the process of becoming [hu]man takes place in an interrelationship with an environment." That is why *homo sapiens* have an underdeveloped biological instinct system, as compared with that of animals and most other mammals (including other primates). Moreover, since we humans do not have the guidance of instinct to structure our lives, we have evolved to develop a "social structure." This social structure is born of the need to reduce the number of decisions required and the variety of options available for the performance of any given behavior. The sheer complexity of human life demands that our regular actions be limited to repeatable, patterned "conduct"[3] that can be easily apprehended by others and readily comprehended in terms of its meaning and the response it is intended to elicit. Thenceforth go humans to the creation of social institutions. Berger and Luckmann (1966:53) explain:

> Any action that is repeated frequently becomes cast into a pattern, which can then be reproduced with an economy of effort and which, *ipso facto* is apprehended by its performer *as* that pattern." [*emphasis in the original*]

This is institutionalization.

Institutionalization of individuals' actions, then, allows for the establishment of patterns of shared actions, since individuals can recognize each other's behavior and interact with one another on the basis of the shared meanings that those actions are intended to convey. It also makes it possible for shared meanings to be applied to those patterns. This process creates and defines a regular "way of doing things," which allows for anticipation of the expected behaviors of others. By clarifying the definition and allocation of roles in social groups and in interpersonal relationships, making actions habitual—institutionalizing them—permits people to predict who can be expected to do what. Thus, social institutions—whether they are roles (such as "husband" or "bureaucrat"), groups (churches, families, or communities, for instance), affective behaviors (such as insolence or obeisance), activities (like running a race or raising a child), or relationships (such as friendship, love, or subservience)—are social constructions that develop out of the need to reduce the number of decisions required and the variety of options available for satisfying any particular human need. Community is a social institution constructed to a greater or lesser degree, depending on the needs of groups of individuals and on the possibilities for the satisfaction of those needs open to the groups of individuals within their broader economic, political, societal, and cultural environment.

1. Institutional "Inventions" to Satisfy Human Needs

Since institutions are socially constructed, they are not created randomly. The habitualization of behavior patterns Berger & Luckmann (1966) described as social institutions are the creations of socially motivated actors in response to the specific conditions of their lives. Abbott (1987) asserts that it is appropriate to see institutions of all sorts as "inventions" of individuals or groups of individuals who see a particular need for an innovation in technology or in social relations.

According to his scheme, a problem is first discovered with (or "constructed from") the circumstances in which people find themselves. This discovery implies a "use community" that could benefit from the invention of a solution to their problem, it inspires an invention that will resolve the difficulty, and it usually mobilizes a "promotion group" to expound on the merits of the thing invented. If the invention is successful and catches on, a procedure is implemented to replicate it for use by other groups or in other places and linkages are created to tie it into the system of other institutions which are already operative in society. In this way, Abbott (1987) sees social institutions like "motel sex," the pieced quilt, and evangelism—just like technological inventions such as the telephone, air travel, and the penitentiary—as inventive solutions to problems posed by living conditions in the era of their creation. In this sense, community, as an invention, is also an institution that changes with the differing needs and opportunities of a given society over time.

2. The "Basic Human Needs" met by Community

Social institutions exist in a multitude of specific types on several different levels of social interaction, each depending on the particular needs it is intended to satisfy and on the conditions in which it is required to operate. This seems true to most people, prima facie; yet, scholars in the social sciences and humanities have spent years, even decades, bickering over the source of those needs. The relevant question, to which each of two sides in this debate feel they have the answer, is as follows: Do people create the social structures of our societies because we have an innate compulsion to do so or simply because we have the capacity for it and are born into such structures, which tend to perpetuate themselves? Another way to pose the question, on a lower level of analysis, is: Are some basic needs and the specific social institutions developed to meet them somehow essential to human beings or are they figments of our collective imagination, artifacts of the form of social organization we **constructed** by choice?

"Essentialists" have generally lost these skirmishes, given the enormous evidence contrary to their position. Most scholars, in most cases can easily see that the social institutions regarding childhood education, for example, are created differently in all societies that educate their children and that some societies choose not to educate their offspring in any formal way at all. Many "social constructionists," however, in their academic battle with essentialists, make the error of assuming that even the most basic of human needs are established only through societal conditioning. Really, both essence and construct (both nature and nurture) play an important role in shaping individuals and their societies. To insist on a strict, "either/or" position is logically and scientifically unsound. Doyal & Gough (1991:54) have identified at least two such basic needs that must be attended to for the survival of individual humans to be assured:

> ... since physical survival and personal autonomy are the preconditions for any individual action in any culture, they constitute the most basic human needs—those which must be satisfied to some degree before actors can effectively participate in their form of life [in order] to achieve any other valued goals.

Physical survival and personal autonomy are needs that can only be satisfied in interaction with others, in society, but how well are those needs met by the overall society? The less well they are met, the more people will need to create a different form of social organization (to invent a different type of social institution) in order to meet them. Community is one social institution that may or may not satisfy individuals' and groups' needs. It is also an institution that, as I detailed above, can be created by those individuals or groups based on common interests in the modern age rather than only on the basis of location—if they have the opportunity to do so.

Autonomy, the ability to participate in one's society, according to Doyal & Gough (1991:60) is dependent on three things:

> Three key variables affect levels of individual autonomy: the level of *understanding* a person has about herself, her culture and what is expected of her as an individual within it; the *psychological capacity* she has to formulate options for herself; and

the objective *opportunities* enabling her to act accordingly. [emphasis in the original]

Without such opportunities, individuals are unable to participate in "their form of life." That is, they are disabled and cannot fully "assume the mantle of persons" (Doyal & Gough 1991:69). They are not autonomous, but what level of autonomy is required to be truly "human"? Doyal & Gough (1991:73) have a ready answer:

> The optimum level of autonomy can be specified in two ways. . . . The lower optimum entails the *minimisation of social constraints* on a person's participation in socially significant activities coupled with access to as much cognitive understanding as is necessary successfully *to pursue their chosen form of life*. The higher optimum will further entail access to knowledge of other cultures coupled with the critical skills and the *political freedoms to evaluate their own [culture] and to struggle to change it* if they choose. [emphasis added]

Making changes in society so that one can choose to live according to his/her own particular needs is a tall order and one that many individuals cannot fulfill. Yet, the responsibility for making it possible for individuals to take such action does not rest with them alone. Individuals can make such strides only in interaction with others in their society. Once again, from Doyal & Gough (1991:78):

> . . . the opportunity to express individual autonomy requires much more than simply being left alone—more than negative freedom. If we really were ignored by others, we would never learn the rules of our way of life and thereby acquire the capacity to make choices within it. . . .
> In other words, to be autonomous and to be physically healthy, we also require *positive freedom*—material, educational and emotional need satisfaction. [emphasis in the original]

So, in order to be fully human, through participating in their chosen way of life, individuals whose needs are not satisfied by the social institutions of their society require the autonomy (knowledge, ability, and opportunity) to change their condition for the better. They must be able to replace existing social institutions in their society with ones that will meet their needs (or at least be able to "opt out" of participating in them). Moreover, to create a separate community for themselves would require the development of such social institutions that would provide not only for their autonomous functioning, but also the opportunity to meet many and all manner of their other needs as well. In other words, to create a community for themselves, a group of people whose needs are not met by their society must develop so many special institutions to satisfy those needs that their particular social group could be said to be "institutionally complete."

D. Institutional Completeness of Community on the Group Level

Breton (1964) describes the "institutional completeness" of an (ethnic) subcultural community as the degree to which it can provide all of the services that might be needed by its members. His (Breton 1964:194) definition of this spectrum of institutional development takes into account a variety of social organizations and encompasses several levels of developmental variation:

> Ethnic communities can vary enormously in their social organization. At one extreme, there is the community which consists essentially in a network of interpersonal relations: members of a certain ethnic group seek each other's companionship; friendship groups and cliques are formed. But beyond this informal network, no formal organization may exist. . . .
>
> . . . Many [communities], however, have developed a more formal structure and contain organizations of various sorts: religious, educational, political, recreational, national, and even professional. Some have organized welfare and mutual aid societies. Some operate their own radio station or publish their own newspapers and periodicals. The community may also sustain a number of commercial and service organizations. Finally, it may have its own churches and sometimes its own schools. Between the two extremes much variation can be observed in the amount and complexity of community organizations. . . .
>
> Institutional completeness would be at its extreme whenever the ethnic community could perform all the services required by its members. Members would never have to make use of native institutions for the satisfaction of any of their needs, such as education, work, food and clothing, medical care, or social assistance.

Breton operationalized his concept of institutional completeness as the number of a community's formal organizations. He then ranked communities, rather crudely, as either "high" or "low" in institutional development.[4]

Breton's concept of "institutional completeness" has been challenged on both of its components. Some (Craven & Wellman 1973; Effrat 1973; Goldenberg & Haines 1992) object to the concept because it focuses on a simply enumerative definition of institutional development within a subcultural community, rather than a "relational" one, which would allow for analysis of the reach, size, range, density, and "multiplexity" of the ties that individuals have to the institutions that are a part of their subcultural community. In fact, they see these institutions as merely an outgrowth of the social networks that make up "community." Others (Rosenberg & Jedwab 1992) charge that Breton's concept does not distinguish between types of institutions developed in a subcultural community, only assessing the level of development of formal organizations. Because of this, they argue, it misses the importance of (ethnic) "organizational style" which is characteristic of a specific subcultural group and leads to the development of peculiar institutional forms, especially informal ones.

At base, these scholars are justified in their criticism. Variations in kinds of sociocultural institutions, whether they are seen as differing relations among people or as different types of institutions, really ought to be taken into consideration when assessing the level of development of a subcultural group. Unlike their authors, though, I do not see these critiques as devastating to the concept of institutional completeness, particularly since Breton himself felt that its definition could be extended to include at least voluntary associations (Breton 1964:195, note 5). These shortcomings, however, can and should serve as guides to better operationalization of the term.

Yet, what is more important is that these critics miss the point about "community" when they call for abandoning the concept of institutional completeness altogether. By over-focusing on the qualities of the individual-to-individual ties, or relations, among members of a subcultural group, network theorists, too, fail to appreciate the **institutional** basis of community. In calling for a reconceptualization on the basis of subcultural uniqueness, or "style," cultural theorists wrongly dismiss the notion of degree, or **completeness**, of institutional development.[5] What Effrat (1973)—and Nisbet (1953) before her—refers to as the "number of functions provided by a community" and what Wellman (1979; Craven & Wellman 1973) calls the "density of network ties" are really no different from Breton's (1964) concept of "institutional completeness." Indeed, they are simply different aspects of it: they refer to the completeness of the "coverage" subcultural institutions offer (their reach, size, range or variety, density, and multifacetedness) in performing the functions for which community members have a need.

E. What is Meant by "Fraternity"

Institutional completeness is, of course, a relative concept. No subcultural group can provide absolutely all of the services its members need, for if a group does so— or very nearly does so (as with Native American tribes or the Old Order Amish in North America, for instance)—it is not properly called a "subculture," since it does not constitute a sub-unit of the larger society. Rather, it is an isolated group (largely) disconnected from and (almost) unaffected by the national society on the territory of which it happens to reside. Up to that point, however, the extent to which a subcultural group does provide services alternative to those of the larger society (and the extent to which the group sets this as a goal) determines its level of institutional completeness.

Unfortunately, while Breton's (1964) analysis of institutional completeness is useful as a measure of social organization among a particular population, he too errs in his exceedingly broad use of the term "community." To label as community the first of his extreme cases of (ethnic) subcultural organization—that "which consists essentially in a network of interpersonal relations"—must be judged inaccurate. At best, I contend, such a social formation could be described as "fraternity" among those individuals. Thus I will define fraternity as a category of people who share some common interest or condition and do identify themselves as members of that category, but do not interact as a group often or consistently enough to develop (or "construct" or "invent") group-level social institutions specifically designed to satisfy the needs of that segment of the population to which they belong.

II. SEXUALITY AND COMMUNITY INSTITUTIONS

If community can be built simply on the communication of common interests and ongoing and significant social interaction among a category of people in modern society, then all manner of population segments should be able to create communities for themselves. Even people whose only commonality, and therefore single defining characteristic, may be their "deviant" sexual orientation ought to be able to form a community. In order to understand how precisely this has happened among the gay and lesbian populations of modern, Western countries, it will be helpful to examine works in the Gay Studies literature that relate to the forms of social organization, the development and continued existence of social institutions, and the relative institutional completeness of gay community there.

A. The Social Construction of Sexuality

According to the "social constructionist" view of reality, sexuality is not different from other aspects of human social life. Sociologists of the constructionist school have applied Berger and Luckmann's (1966) scheme to the analysis of human sexual behavior, asserting that sexuality—like the rest of social life—is entirely a human creation rather than an inherent instinct or "biological drive" (Gagnon & Simon 1973; Weeks 1986; Foucault 1986). As such, it is argued, the forms and content that human sexual relations take on are constructed in the same manner as are all other manifestations of human culture and society. That is to say, certain habitualized actions become institutionalized and imbued with special sexual meaning that can be apprehended and comprehended by others as being "sexual." This formulation has led constructionist scholars of sexuality to explore the varieties of sexual expression institutionalized in various human communities. In Gay Studies, it has led them to see gay life as the social construction of a homosexual "way of doing sexual things" that is different from that of the dominant heterosexual society, taking homosexuality as a distinct "way of being in the world" (*conferre*: Greenberg 1988).[6]

One core concept of Gagnon and Simon's (1973) theoretical treatise on sexuality is that action taken with sexual meaning is, in fact, sexual "conduct." In their formulation they emphasize the shared meanings, rituals, and "dramas" involved when humans behave sexually, employing the dramaturgical metaphor for social life made popular by Goffman (1959). They have developed their ideas in the same line of thinking as Berger and Luckmann (1966) had, and from an identical theoretical orientation. Indeed, the suggestion for their work on the social construction of sexuality may have come from passages such as this one from Berger & Luckmann (1966:49–50):

> The plasticity of the human organism and its susceptibility to socially determined interference is best illustrated by the ethnological evidence concerning sexuality.... It is not only relatively independent of temporal rhythms, it is pliable both in the objects toward which it may be directed and in its modalities of expression. Ethnological evidence shows that, in sexual matters, man is capable of almost anything.... At the same time, of course, human sexuality is directed, sometimes rigidly structured, in every particular culture. Every culture has a distinctive sexual configuration, with its own 'anthropological' assumptions in the sexual area. The empirical relativity of these configurations, their immense variety and luxurious inventiveness, indicate that they are the product of man's own sociocultural formations rather than of a biologically fixed human nature.

Following this lead, I intend to look at the social construction of Soviet gay and lesbian life as a way of defining who is expected to do what, in gay circles in the USSR.

1. The Social Construction of Homosexuality

Historians of sexuality have charted the path of the development of a "homosexual identity," which is said to have emerged fully only in the late 19th century with the rise of modern medical practice and Freudian psychoanalysis. (Foucault 1986; Weeks 1985, 1986) Before that time, they argue, there were neither homosexual nor heterosexual people, as such—that is, as social categories—there were only people who acted homosexually or heterosexually, and quite often, they insist, people acted in both ways. The growing preeminence of the medical model at that time along with the imposition of legal sanctions for such behavior forced such a homosexually-acting person, according to the constructionist view, to start thinking of him- or herself as a separate kind of individual.

Later, the advent of modern capitalism in the West gradually allowed for the development of social and economic institutions directed by and operating for this new category of people, D'Emilio (1983a, 1983b) has argued. In the twentieth century—and especially after the conclusion of World War II—the social forces of migration and economic expansion opened up many and varied social spaces in large cities, making room for all sorts of new communities to develop, among them communities of homosexuals. In the wake of other more-or-less successful movements for recognition of human rights (such as the Black Civil Rights Movement) and for political and social equality (like the struggle of the Women's Liberation Movement), political activism on the behalf of homosexuals also developed.

2. "Inventing" the Homosexual Community

From Abbott's (1987) perspective, the social construction of the homosexual world can be seen as the creation of a system of social institutions invented to satisfy the needs of one part of the population which were not met by already existing social institutions. Individual homosexuals have had to innovate, inventing social (and technological) institutions for their own use as a means of adapting to the difficulties of life imposed by their (different) status in society. Successful individual adaptation implied a general usefulness of these innovations for many homosexuals, targeting them as a "use community." Groups of homosexuals have then acted as "promotion groups," spreading these new inventions, and, over time, they have been integrated into a system of gay social institutions known variously as "the gay subculture," "the homosexual lifestyle," or "the gay world."

If the scheme is accurate, this scenario should be true of the Soviet gay world as well as the Western one. Indeed, it should be true of any gay lifestyle wherever there are homosexuals who can innovate, promote their creations, and develop a system of institutions which will help them adapt to their status as sexual minorities.

It is important to note here that the Soviet gay and lesbian world of the late 1980s and early 1990s was not simply an invention of native innovators. It was composed of a mixture of indigenous social inventions and social constructions imported from the West. The utilization of imported institutions can be seen either as "borrowing" from Western gay subculture or as "cultural imperialism" on the part of Western gay and lesbian activists, whose influence on the development of Soviet gay activism was integral and exuberant. Although this distinction is important to the analysis since it relates directly to the issue of comparative development of the Soviet and Western gay worlds, theoretically, it can be subsumed under the framework of innovation presented here. It is not really important for this scheme whether an innovation is actually the invention of a particular individual or is "picked up" somewhere by that individual because it is interesting or because s/he feels it might be useful in his/her native context. What is important is how it is received by the group—whether the innovation actually does serve the needs of the "use community"—and by the success or failure of its institutionalization—that is, whether it can be integrated into the previously-existing institutional structure of the group that "borrows" or is "colonized" by it.

B. Institutional Completeness and Gay Community

Up to and throughout the 1960s and 1970s, most American scholars studying homosexuality clung to a view of gay life as "culturally impoverished" (Gagnon & Simon 1973; Karlen 1978) without actually investigating the operative conditions and interpersonal relations among people participating in the gay world for evidence of its institutional development. Most psychological researches on the subject either explained homosexuality as a sexual psychopathology (Bieber 1962; Socarides 1968) or focused on assessing individuals' (positive and functional) psychological adaptation to their homosexuality (Hooker 1963; Weinberg & Williams 1974; Bell & Weinberg 1978). Much of the sociological work on the topic either analyzed homosexuality as a form of social and sexual "deviance" (Gagnon & Simon 1967, 1973; Goode & Troiden 1975) or examined homosexual behavior and its institutionalized relations only in their more sensationalistic aspects (Humphreys 1970, 1971; Weinberg & Williams 1975; Delph 1978), failing to examine the full range of organizational structures or social institutions of the gay world.

In the late 1970s however, a few scholars began to look at the social structure of Western gay life and applied the concept of institutional completeness to the study of homosexual populations. In their studies, Harry & DeVall (1978), Lee (1979), and Murray (1980) all found the homosexual worlds of large, North American cities to be highly "institutionally complete," since gay men and lesbians there had developed all of the types of community institutions Breton (1964) used to construct his operational index—as well as many that he had left out. This was true despite continuing legal sanctions against homosexuality[7] and extraordinary social opprobrium directed at gay people in the cities investigated, including the use of physical violence. Indeed, as Murray (1980) pointed out, by Breton's (1964) criteria, the activities and organizations of the homosexual populations in North American cities of the late 1970s (with that of Toronto as a special case study) would have to be judged more institutionally complete than those of many minority ethnic groups.

Timing is of the essence here. Murray's (1980) chief point is that it was the dramatic developments in economic, political, societal, and cultural institutions which took place in the American homosexual subculture only in the late 1960s and 1970s (Katz 1976; D'Emilio 1983b; Adam 1987) that allowed for the legitimate designation of the social organization of the gay world in the West as "community." Although there were individual-level institutions for making contact with one another, for defending oneself and harboring fellow homosexuals when discovery or physical harm was possible or imminent, for integrating one's personal identity and recognizing other gay "types," and for distinguishing "us" (gays) from "them" ("straights"), the lack of group-level institutions before the "me decade" meant that there had been no gay community in the West in previous historical periods. Of course, this incomplete elaboration of such subcultural institutions is another reason that earlier studies (Leznoff & Westley 1956; Reiss 1961; Hooker 1965; McIntosh 1968) did not discover a great deal of institutionalization in the (male) homosexual world—there was not much to be found.

It is for this reason that I take issue with conclusions like Leznoff & Westley's (1956:263) that: "it is [only] the casual and promiscuous sexual contacts between the members of different categories of [social stigma] evasion (i.e. the secret and the overt [homosexual]) which weld the city's homosexuals into a community." In fact, it is because the (New York City) gay subculture was not institutionally elaborate at the time they studied it that it seemed "excessively focused on the sexual behavior of its members" (Leznoff & Westley 1956:258) and appeared to be "impoverished" culturally. I maintain that, while a "fraternity" of homosexuals may be knit together by sexual contacts, such a loose and informal social configuration cannot accurately be called "community."

III. INSTITUTIONS, COMMUNITY, AND THE STATE IN THE USSR

In the Soviet political culture, almost all spontaneously formed social groups were considered undesirable because of the threat they might pose to the regime. Therefore, all activities that the state/Party authorities deemed worthy of organization (those that were sufficiently "proletarian," "Leninist," etc.) were scripted and directed by one or another wing of the Communist Party. Those activities that were considered harmful to the Soviet regime or to "socialist morality," including homosexuality, were often ruthlessly repressed. What was more problematic, though, was the arbitrary nature with which activities could be declared contrary to social and moral norms in the USSR: "anti-Soviet." In the Soviet Union's absolutist state structure, the Party was the *de facto* sovereign and a "dictatorship over the needs of citizens" was affected in its ideologically rigid society as a means of establishing and ensuring the implementation of "the will of the people"—the will of the people, that is, as dictated by Party ideologists and government leaders. Fehér, Heller, & Márkus (1983:161–162) put it this way:

> All absolutist states make attempts to totalize society, in other words, to homogenize a system of values, patterns of behaviour and institutional procedures according to the will of the state, society's sovereign ruler. Absolutist kings always crushed religious dissent ruthlessly, for the state religions were the state ideologies of their times. They either tamed or liquidated all social forces and institutions which attempted to remain relatively independent of the state—the self-organizations of the estates no less than the first germs of civil society.

Yet, this is not quite right. In fact, not only absolutist states but all states and societies seek "to homogenize a system of values, patterns of behaviour, and institutional procedures" that members should follow. The distinction is really in the means and methods that a state uses to garner the submission of citizens to its rules and regulations and also in the official definition of those imperatives.

A. Constricted Development of Non-State Institutions in Soviet Society

This limitation on the social and political activities of Soviet citizens imposed and policed by the state has led to the condition that Field (1988) called "constricted development" of all modern socioeconomic institutions in the Soviet Union, and to the phenomenon generally referred to as Russia's "backwardness."[8] Thus:

> Soviet culture and society have become differentiated [as do all modern societies], but incompletely so. At least as seen on a comparative and evolutionary scale, that society falls short of other, more advanced, pluralistic social systems. The process of differentiation is slowed by the totalistic nature of the value system and the orientation of the Communist Party, the guardian of the Soviet *Weltanschauung*. (Field 1988:126)

Only under Communist Party General Secretary Mikhaíl S. Gorbachóv in the late 1980s did the Soviet leadership begin to allow the (guarded) expression of citizen initiative, which would bring about the emergence of a new "civil society" in the USSR (Lapidus 1989).

Gorbachóv's exhortations about "new thinking" (новое мышление) in political discourse, "speeding up" the process of economic reform (ускорение), and "speaking out" about social problems to be tackled (*glásnost*)[9] were all launched at the corrupt, indolent, and servile Soviet bureaucracy as parts of his general campaign for "reconstructing" the Soviet economy (*perestróyka*). Yet, to the Soviet citizenry this sounded like a call to action and, when they overcame the skepticism which was a natural response to such an unusual, even extravagant invitation,[10] there could be no stopping them from thinking in a new way about, speaking up about, and trying to speed up the process of reform in other areas as well.

This new permission to "make a difference" allowed Soviet citizens to discover the diversity of their interests in all spheres, not just economic ones, and the response to Gorbachóv's "call to arms" against the Soviet bureaucracy became a boisterous outcry against the entire Soviet system (Lapidus 1989). It led to the open expression of unorthodox ideas in all aspects of life, from the desire for more variation in social roles to demands for change in the legal, political, and social systems as well as in the economy. Homosexual rights groups were among the first of legions of new associations to spring up in the USSR, ready to be heard.[11]

Ultimately, these processes of "civilizing" Soviet society are what tore apart the Soviet Union itself—and despite many setbacks in their efforts to organize, Soviet homosexuals, individually and as a group, were there on the barricades in August 1991 resisting the *coup d'état* attempted against Gorbachóv by outraged political and military leaders. (Gessen 1991b)

Of course, the success of subcultural institutionalization does not depend only on lessening government repression. Social opposition to their efforts also held back the processes of institution-building among gay men and lesbians in the Soviet Union, as discrimination, stigmatization, and "gay bashing" (ремонт) still force most post-Soviet homosexuals to live a secretive existence. By examining the Soviet gay and lesbian subculture in a comparative perspective, then, I will show how the specific political dynamics of the Soviet system, as well as public opposition and social stigma, "constricted" its institutional development. Analysis of the successes and failures of attempts at social organization among Soviet gays and lesbians over the last decade will clarify how moves toward political pluralism, new concepts of civil liberties, and "the rule of law" can aid in the processes of subcultural institutionalization. It should also allow me to predict the future course of institutional development among homosexuals in the former Soviet Union.

B. The Possibility of Soviet Gay Community

Institutional development is difficult for a subcultural group to manage when it is a "stigmatized minority" (Goffman 1963; Plummer 1975; Adam 1978), and it is next to impossible when group members are subject to political repression simply for engaging in group activities. Harry & DeVall (1978:149) list several ways in which political authorities in North America have sought to limit homosexual interaction:

> Typical powers that have been used to prevent the development of gay institutions have been zoning powers; prohibiting persons unrelated by blood or marriage from living together in certain areas; differential use of police power, as in the cases of raids on gay bars; power over liquor licensing (or at least pressures on state alcohol control boards); and uneven enforcement of loitering ordinances. A further power that has been used to suppress the growth of gay institutions has been the selective and arbitrary refusal of permission for gay groups to utilize public meeting places.

In the Soviet context, the absence of generally accepted notions of the desirability of social and political pluralism or of the inviolability of "the rule of law" meant that the Soviet government did not need the legal arguments of liquor licensing boards, anti-loitering ordinances, or zoning laws to repress the institutionalization of homosexual activities. The sanctity of individual civil rights (as the right to privacy) was never guaranteed by the Soviet Constitution, much less the civil rights of minority citizens, and simple existence of a law prohibiting sodomy (мужеложство—literally: "men lying together") in the Soviet Penal Code was enough to condemn any homosexual association, whether for sexual or social purposes. Therefore, equal treatment as regards civil liberties was never something for which Soviet homosexuals could fight.

Although the Tsarist prohibition of sodomy was reversed in 1917 after the Bolshevik Revolution, with the rise of Stalin to the leadership of the Communist Party and of the state, new, repressive social legislation as well as repressive political and economic policies were put into effect. Thenceforth seen as a "bourgeois aberration," homosexuality, which would not produce new citizens for the Soviet state, was outlawed in 1934 (as was abortion in 1936). Homosexuality was seen as "anti-proletarian," came to be associated or even equated with the old ruling order, and was therefore counterrevolutionary. (Lauritsen & Thorstad 1974; Greenberg 1988; Karlinsky 1989)[12]

Significantly, Soviet gay men and lesbians did not have a term for describing such a subcultural institution as "gay community." Though they did speak of "gay people" ("голубые люди") and hear rumors of "gay places" ("наши места"), they did not conceive of a set of subcultural organizations or of institutional arrangements developed specifically by and for them. Even some familiar with the phenomenon of gay community in the West are not sure whether it should be translated into Russian as "community" (общность), as "commune" (община), as "society" or "social organization" (общество), or as "public" or "social sphere" (общественность), all of which terms are very close linguistic cognates. (Russian sociologist interview 1991)

It is my conclusion, then, that gay community was not in existence in the USSR. In the rest of this book, I will demonstrate that, in fact, the limited extent to which forms of social organization could be developed among the gay and lesbian population there, was that of homosexual "fraternity."

NOTES

1. Equating Hillery's (1955) "number of ties a person has to the community" with Effrat's (1973)—and before her Nisbet's (1953)—"number of functions the group serves for its members" makes sense if one takes either a "functional" or a "rational action" approach to interpersonal "ties." The functional approach is commonly assumed throughout most of the early sociological works on community and argues that people are "tied" to a community by the fact that it serves certain, necessary functions for them, such as helping in the provision of food, clothing, and shelter. The rational action approach is axiomatic to the more recent literature on community and asserts that people maintain "ties" to a community because it provides the best opportunity for satisfaction of at least some of their immediate needs.

2. Instead, he focuses on his concept of the "nonplace urban realm" (defined as "communities of interest-communities") as a counterpoint to the "place community" (Webber 1964).

3. Action performed in regard to such shared meanings and institutions is not merely random behavior but intentional, directed social conduct. "Conduct is behavior as prescribed or evaluated by the group. It is not simply external observable behavior, but behavior that expresses a norm or evaluation." (Burgess 1949:153)

4. Breton seems to have conceived of social institutions only in a formal way, as "an organized social group." (Theodorson & Theodorson 1969:207) I will employ the term "institution" in a broader sense, as when Webster's (1970:438) defines it as "a significant practice, relationship, or organization in a society or culture." Specifically, an institution is socially "significant" because it consists of "Any traditional cultural pattern or interrelated complex of social norms." (Theodorson & Theodorson 1969:207)

5. I am utterly unconvinced that Rosenberg & Jedwab's (1992) "organizational style" is anything more than a misunderstood structural variable—in this case, one related to the religious affiliations distinguishing the ethnic subcultural groups they studied.

6. The introduction of this paradigm into Gay Studies has also engendered a hotly-contested debate over the causes and origins of homosexuality roughly following the "nature versus nurture" debate. Those who hold to the belief that sexual orientation itself, regardless of its forms of expression, is somehow biologically determined or otherwise innate to human (as to animal) nature are referred to as "essentialists." "Social constructionists," on the other hand, believe that sexual orientation, like all other aspects of human sexual expression, is itself a social construction, and they locate the beginnings of homosexuality, as a separate sexual identity, in the historical medicalization and illegalization of homosexuality in the late 19th century. (Foucault, 1986; Weeks, 1985; Greenberg, 1988)

7. In 1991, there were still anti-sodomy statutes in effect in 24 of the 50 United States, as well as in the District of Columbia, and the US Supreme Court upheld the constitutionality of such laws as recently as 1986 in the case of Bowers versus Hardwick. (Amnesty International USA 1994)

8. The continuities between the Tsarist and the Soviet periods in Russian history in this regard have been noted by many scholars, among them Pipes (1968) and Szamuely (See: Fehér, Heller, & Márkus 1983: 162). Both regimes are generally regarded to have been at least absolutist if not also totalitarian.

9. Although the Russian word *glásnost* (гласность) has most often been rendered in English as "openness," this translation does not convey the vocative component of the Russian term. It does not make use of the word's root "*gólos*," which means "voice." To "voice oneself (or one's opinions)" and to "speak up" or "speak out" about something are all better translations. I will use the latter two translations interchangeably.

10. The following joke, often told during the first few years of *perestróyka*, was an unmistakable signal of this trepidation. It acutely expresses the consequences Soviet citizens expected they would face if they were to do publicly anything that went against the Soviet system. "Вопрос: Что проследует перестройку? Ответ: Перестрельку." (Question: What comes after reconstruction? Answer: Re-execution.)

11. Although gay groups had been organizing since 1985, the first year of Gorbachóv's rule, none were allowed to register their existence officially as informal organizations (неформальки) until after the break-up of the Soviet state. (The irony of formal registration for "informal" association was lost to routine on the gay activists I met.) Despite the reform movement, members of the first gay group were arrested or exiled for their "anti-Soviet behavior" and later groups were forbidden to operate, first by local authorities, then by the courts. Though there were "behind the scenes efforts" to repeal the anti-sodomy statutes in the RSFSR (articles 121.1 and 121.2 of the criminal code)—and, under Soviet law, such repeal would likely have been duplicated in all of the former Soviet Republics—repeal did not take place under the Soviet regime. (See Chapter Five for information on gay political activism and on gay and lesbian organizations in the Soviet Union and see the Afterword for information about the current legal status of homosexuals in the newly independent states created by the dissolution of the USSR.)

12. See Chapter Five for a more-detailed analysis of the legal restrictions on homosexual behavior in pre-Revolutionary Russia and the Soviet Union.

> The idea of a method that contains firm, unchanging, and absolutely binding principles for conducting the business of science meets considerable difficulty when confronted with the results of historical research. ...
> ... To those who look at the rich material provided by history, and who are not intent on impoverishing it in order to please their lower instincts, their craving for intellectual security in the form of clarity, precision, 'objectivity', 'truth', it will become clear that there is only one principle that can be defended under all circumstances and in all stages of human development. It is the principle: anything goes.
>
> Paul Feyerabend,
> *Against Method: Outline of an anarchistic theory of knowledge*
> pp.23, 27–28.

Chapter Two
Employing Social Research Methods for a Soviet Gay Studies

THIS WORK REPORTS ON THE STUDY I MADE OF THE PEOPLE, PLACES, AND activities that were a part of gay life in the Soviet Union as it existed during the period of social, political, and economic reform (*glásnost*, "new thinking" (новое мышление), and *perestróyka*) introduced by General Secretary of the Communist Party of the Soviet Union and Soviet President, Mikhaíl Gorbachóv. Inspiration for conducting this research came from my experiences with Soviet gay men and lesbians and the knowledge of their subculture that I gained during summer-long visits to the Soviet Union in 1988 and 1989. Data serving as evidence for the theoretical argument laid out in Chapter One come from three research methods I employed for this study while on a year-long research trip to the USSR from August 1990 to August 1991.[1]

First, I used participant observation techniques throughout my research stay to explore and comprehend as many of the social institutions of the Soviet gay and lesbian subculture as I could. Second, I conducted formal but unstructured interviews with gay and lesbian activists operating in the Soviet Union during that time and with academic and medical professionals and paraprofessionals there who have a special interest in the topic. Third, I devised and implemented survey research (N=421) among the Soviet gay and lesbian population during the spring and summer of 1991.[2] All of the research for this project was conducted in Russian, a language in which I am fluent.

I. PARTICIPANT OBSERVATION

I began my study by acting as a participant observer in many activities in which my research subjects engaged—both exceptional and unexceptional ones—as a part of their participation in Soviet gay and lesbian life. During my stay in the USSR, I became acquainted with many Soviet gay men and lesbians and got involved with them on a friendly basis in most aspects of their lives. As a gay man, I became well-acquainted with the vicissitudes of the Soviet gay and lesbian world. I went alone and with friends to gay "cruising places" and was invited to numerous private parties and other social events hosted by and comprised of Soviet gay men and lesbians. I heard many stories of common problems faced by Soviet homosexuals relating to the disclosure of one's sexual identity, to relationship issues, to finding a sexual partner, to social and political persecution they faced, *et cetera*. Indeed, as my informants often saw me as a new member or potential member of their social group, they spent much time educating me about their ways of life and giving me practical advice so that I would be both safe and successful in negotiating my own position in the Soviet gay world and in my own personal relationships there.

Information from these experiences cannot always be equated with that which might have been gathered through strict participant-observation methods, however. I sometimes did not follow a rigorous procedure of sampling people, places, and timings of events that occurred among Soviet gay men and lesbians and did not always take consistent and comprehensive field notes after each encounter with some aspect of Soviet gay life. Nonetheless, the fact that I *lived* as much as possible in that world and took part in as many activities of that life as I could during the year I spent in the USSR provided me with a profound understanding of the circumstances that Soviet gay men and lesbians faced in their country and of the dynamics at work in shaping the institutions of their "world." This "closeness to the data" was particularly important for providing insights and intuitions about the population under study, and I took my "sociological imagination" (Mills, 1959) with me everywhere I went. This aspect of my work also allowed me access to more potential subjects for my survey research than would have been possible otherwise, since it went a long way toward enhancing my subjects' trust in me as a human being.

II. UNSTRUCTURED INTERVIEWS

These observational data will be enhanced by information I gathered from formal and informal unstructured interviews with several Soviet professionals and paraprofessionals who have a special interest in the topic of homosexuality. I interviewed eight gay and lesbian activists about their activism, the organizations they have formed, the tactics they use, and the likelihood of their success.[3] Five of these interviews were tape recorded and transcribed.

I interviewed five therapists and clinicians who worked to better the health of Soviet homosexuals and to promote prophylaxis against Acquired Immune Deficiency Syndrome (AIDS). They answered questions about the nature of their clinical work and how they were drawn into it as well as what they expect their clients to get out of their relationship and what responses they had gotten from gay and lesbian clients.[4] One of these interviews was tape recorded and transcribed.

I interviewed five Soviet scholars who had been doing some academic work on the situation of gay men and lesbians in Soviet society, soliciting their opinions on the activities of gay and lesbian activists and information about government deliberations on the rumored repeal of Soviet anti-sodomy statutes.[5] I met with two of them repeatedly to discuss their academic work and attended meetings and one conference at which presentations were made on the subject.

Finally, I interviewed a Soviet journalist who wrote for a Western gay newsmagazine about gay life in the USSR and a former gay activist who was working to publish a gay-themed magazine. These interviews were aimed at finding out what information these two felt was of interest to Soviet gay men and lesbians and how successful they thought they could be in making such information available to their readers.

In addition to interviews with professionals and paraprofessionals, I spent several months talking with many "regular" Soviet gay men and lesbians whose acquaintance I made for purposes of the research. In these interviews, none of which were tape recorded, I attempted to get at the personal problems and private meanings that are a part of the daily life of Soviet homosexuals. Topics of discussion included such issues as relations with family members, negotiating sexual liaisons, and friendship and other interpersonal relations that occurred among Soviet homosexuals.

III. SURVEY RESEARCH & DATA ANALYSES

A. The Questionnaire

The Russian-language survey questionnaire I developed for this project consisted of 84 closed- and open-ended questions on a broad range of topics related to gay life in the USSR. Since the nature of my research agenda was quite sensitive, I judged it better to use a self-administered questionnaire, rather than doing in-person interviews with an interview schedule. Respondents are freer to express themselves more honestly when they are answering questions completely anonymously and without coaching, whereas they are more likely to be put off by a face-to-face interview on "touchy subjects." (Sudman & Bradburn 1983; Rossi, Wright, & Anderson 1983:295)

Unfortunately, using a self-administered questionnaire also meant that I had little chance of correcting any misunderstandings respondents might have had about the questions asked, since with this format one usually cannot probe for clarification of answers given. There is always a "trade-off" between these two potential problems in relation to the validity of survey data. I chose to err on the side of possible misunderstanding, since respondents often had very grave misgivings about answering the questions at all, and I felt that overcoming the alternate problem of an inadequate response rate was paramount. Moreover, since I tried as much as possible to have people fill out questionnaires while I was present, I did have some opportunity to make myself available for answering questions respondents had about the questionnaire. Given the social and organizational circumstances under which the survey was distributed, though, this was only sometimes possible. In these instances, and when respondents did feel comfortable enough to inquire about any particular issue, I clarified the questions and made a note of their confusion. This fact will allow me to consider the possible problems with the *prima-facie* validity of certain responses.

An introductory paragraph was included at the top of the first page of the questionnaire to present the topic of homosexuality in a benevolent way and to instruct respondents on how to fill out the questionnaire properly. Strong recommendation for such an introduction comes from Sheatsley (1983:295): "Whatever the mode [of surveying], the introduction is crucial. If the survey task sounds overly demanding, if its purpose seems trivial or threatening... they [potential respondents] will probably refuse to participate." The plea for participation was as follows:

> The question of sexual preferences is each person's private affair. However, since it is unknown how people who belong to so-called "sexual minorities" actually live and with what problems they are confronted, a survey is being conducted "About the lives of gays, lesbians, and bisexuals in the USSR." We ask that you take seriously the questionnaire on "our theme." Fill it out without hurrying, not omitting questions. Each question has several possible answers. Your task is to select those answers which are, in your opinion, fitting, and mark them with a check-mark to the left of the proposed answer. In the tables, mark the column that corresponds to your answer also with a check-mark. In a few instances, you will need to write in an answer. The survey is being conducted anonymously. Please be as open as you can in your answers. Without such information, changing the situation of "our people" for the better is impossible.

In preparation, the questionnaire was pre-tested, and on the advice of initial informants, expanded to include a few issues that seemed important to them but that I had not anticipated. These informants also helped to ensure that the survey was grammatically correct and that its tenor and question order seemed appropriate to the native Russian speaker.[6] This was no small task since Soviet citizens were generally unaccustomed to being surveyed on any matter and were certainly not used to answering questions on a topic as sensitive as their homosexual experiences. In addition, most of the open-ended questions I had initially included were replaced with closed-ended ones, as initial respondents were extremely uncomfortable with the open-ended format. They did not want to chance being found out by the authorities by divulging any "extra" information that might reveal their personal identity.[7]

The survey instrument asked for general demographic information about the respondent's sex, age, educational attainment, profession, nationality (ethnicity), party membership, marital status, possible parenthood, place of residence, living situation, place of origin, and family of origin. These questions were necessary to provide general descriptive information about the sample; to gauge its representativeness in comparison with Soviet national statistics; and, with careful generalization, to extrapolate those findings to the homosexual population as a whole.

The survey requested information on respondents' personal history. This involved questions about their childhood, about their age at the time of their first sexual experience, and about the social relations surrounding that event. Respondents were asked for information concerning their attitude about and adjustment to their homosexuality, their openness with others about their sexuality, and their current and past relationship status. These questions were asked in order to get at issues of individual sexual identity and at the character of the relationships they have with both homosexual and heterosexual others.

The survey queried respondents about living conditions for homosexuals in the USSR, both past and present, eliciting specifics about meeting places, information about gay life that they might get from communications media, locations for particular types of encounters (both sexual and nonsexual), and other aspects of the "social space" they inhabit. Questions were also asked about responses to their homosexuality from non-homosexual others in their social environment. These included issues of discrimination and oppression as well as experiences of verbal and physical threat or abuse against them on the part of either Soviet officials or private individuals.[8] This line of questioning was intended to gather information about the "social ecology" of the Soviet gay and lesbian world that could provide a basis for assessing the possibility of institutional development among homosexuals there and a basis for comparison with gay communities in Western countries.

Finally, the survey inquired about respondents' sexual behaviors, questioning them about the number of sexual partners they had had; about specific sex acts that they engage in; about precautions they take against contracting AIDS; about their sexual, erotic, and romantic attractions; and about their sexual self-identification. This most intrusive set of questions was placed at the end of the questionnaire[9] and was intended as a check on the continuity between stated "sexual-role" and "sexuality identities."[10] Some of these questions were also intended to provide information about the likelihood of an expanding AIDS epidemic in the Soviet Union in the near future.

The best results from survey work are achieved when questions are worded in a straightforward manner and employ the language that members of the target population themselves use. Sudman & Bradburn (1983) insist that such practices are important so that misunderstanding is avoided. My experience in developing the survey questionnaire confirms this assertion. Early responses to the questionnaire from initial informants revealed that there were several questions that were misinterpreted or unclear in their meaning because respondents were unfamiliar with what I had thought were readily-understood terms.

Some initial informants misunderstood the terms "homosexual" and "heterosexual" ("гомосексуальный" and "гетеросексуальный") as applied to themselves, the terms "oral sex" and "anal sex" ("оральный секс" and "анальный секс") in terms of their sexual behaviors, or the concepts of "active" and "passive" identities ("актив" and "пассив") as applied to their possible roles in sexual activity. Therefore, such common and sometimes vulgar terms as "gay" and "straight" ("голубой" and "натураль") and "sucking" and "fucking" ("брать/дать в рот" and "трахать") had to be used in conjunction with the more academic terminology of some questions in order to facilitate understanding. Also, employing uniquely Russian gay slang terms such as "our people" ("наши (люди)"), "one of us" ("наш (человек)"), and "on the (or our) theme" ("по (нашей) теме") was critical for "personalizing" the survey and gaining the trust of respondents. Speaking with subjects in their own terms undoubtedly made them more amenable to participating in the study and probably made them more likely to provide accurate responses to my survey questions.

B. Sampling and Representativeness

When studying a "difficult" population (Sudman & Bradburn 1983) such as almost any highly-stigmatized group, gathering a broadly-representative, random sample from which the researcher can generalize to the target population as a whole is not possible. (Martin & Dean 1990) This is the case when one aims to study gay men and lesbians anywhere in the world, in the USA as well as in the USSR.[11] This is so because there is in existence no complete or unbiased listing of any nation's gay and lesbian population from which to draw a representative probability sample. Given the oppression historically faced by the homosexual population of almost every country, if one imagines the opportunity for universal repression that would be given by such a listing, one might well be thankful for its absence. From the point of view of social scientists interested in studying the lives of gay men and lesbians, however, the lack of such a helpful tool is a significant handicap.[12]

Therefore, less-representative methods of non-probability sampling must be used to collect survey data from homosexual respondents (Martin & Dean 1990; NOGLSTP 1990). Although such sampling methods necessarily limit the generalizability of the data obtained, there is simply no other way to proceed. Recruiting subjects for non-probability samples of the gay and lesbian populations in Western countries is typically accomplished in one of two ways: with either "snowball" or "targeted" (purposive) sampling.

In a snowball sample of homosexuals, the researcher contacts one or more gay men and lesbians (by whatever means), surveys them, and then asks to be referred to others who would be suitable subjects for the study. Of course, just who is to be considered an appropriate subject for such a study is a matter of great concern. As with all populations that do not have a well-defined, objective criterion for inclusion in their ranks, determining who should be considered homosexuals for research purposes is more problematic than one might think. (Bell 1975, Bell and Weinberg 1978, Martin & Dean 1990) Since it has not been clearly established in scientific or any other literature just what homosexuality is—whether a "natural" "sexual orientation" or an (inborn or acquired) "sexual preference," much less a vice, sin, illness, genetic anomaly, hormonal imbalance, or (acceptable or objectionable) "lifestyle choice"—recruitment of subjects has to be a matter of personal self-identification and, therefore, one of partial self-selection.

Once put in contact with these other potential subjects, the researcher repeats these steps and the sample "snowballs" as he or she reaches further and further into the subject pool.[13] Normally, one would want to be as systematic as possible in gathering the snowball sample by limiting the number of other potential subjects each respondent names (three or five usually), so that one does not end up with "bunches" of friends or with only a few sets of highly interconnected people in the sample. (Babbie 1973) If researchers do not have any direct contacts in the gay and lesbian population or if they wish to broaden the sample being gathered (to access a more diverse subset of the target population), respondents can be recruited by contacting them through gay and lesbian organizations in various localities and starting another "snowball." Typically, several such recruitment nodes must be utilized in the creation of a single snowball sample (Sudman 1976).

For targeted sampling, subjects are recruited by querying or advertising in publications (newspapers, magazines) catering to a gay and lesbian readership. Subjects can be sampled from the (published or purchased) membership roles of gay and lesbian organizations or from subscription lists to gay- and lesbian-oriented publications. Finally, subjects can be recruited by canvassing them directly in the places where they gather. In the West, such places include gay- and lesbian-oriented social events, recreational areas that homosexuals utilize, meetings of gay and lesbian political and professional organizations, business establishments catering to the specific needs of a gay and/or lesbian clientele, or simply among inhabitants of areas with a well-recognized, highly-concentrated population of homosexual residents (in the "gay ghetto" (Levine 1979)).

C. Sample Recruitment & Data Collection

In the sociopolitical climate of the time, Soviet gay men and lesbians feared for their families, their friends, their jobs, their freedom, and their lives because of the consequences they might face if they were to be open about their homosexuality. Given this oppressive situation, I expected that many potential subjects would be wary of participating in such research—however they were sampled—and so my primary concern was to recruit as many subjects as possible to the study, putting few restrictions on means and recruitment criteria. In order to obtain the largest and broadest sample possible, I was eager to have everyone fill out my questionnaire who would consent to do so. I made a pitch for potential subjects' participation in the study as soon as they came into my purview and seemed to be, or were presented as, gay or lesbian.

Even so, it proved so difficult to get enough respondents to answer even an anonymous questionnaire on gay and lesbian issues in most parts of the USSR that I had to use both snowball and targeted sampling methods in every venue that I could think of where it would be generally safe to do so in order to get an adequate sample. Although they trusted me enough to reveal a great deal of information privately and on a personal basis, many Soviet gay men and lesbians were cautious about answering any questionnaire which they could not be absolutely certain would not "fall into the wrong hands." A large number refused to answer the questionnaire under any conditions, fearing that any involvement with the project would be taking a bigger risk than they could afford. The only feasible method of sampling and subject recruitment for such a study under these conditions was "catch as catch can." (Schluter 1991)

For the purposes of this study, the target population was all self-identified gay men and lesbians in the Soviet Union, plus some self-identified bisexuals who also see themselves as, at least marginally, "one of us." The subject pool from which research subjects were drawn was that of self-identified gay men, lesbians, and bisexuals living in the USSR and somehow participating in gay life there. Respondents may have been recruited through friendship networks, through a habit of "cruising" gay "pick-up" spots, or because they took part in a gay-related event made possible by the new opportunities available for those with homosexual interests under the newly-relaxed socio-political regime.

Wherever I found subjects suitable for the study, then, and whenever they were willing to participate, I included them in the sample and coaxed them to provide me with further leads. As a practical matter, because gay and lesbian life in much of the Soviet Union at that time was so hidden (or "closeted"), the only way to recruit a sample of a size and "reach" suitable for even unrepresentative survey research on sexual minorities in the USSR was to use all possible sampling methods when distributing questionnaires. Each is discussed here in detail.

1. Snowball Sampling

a. Through Friends and Acquaintances

For the survey, I started out distributing questionnaires to my immediate friends who are homosexual—and who self-identify as such—and through them to friends and acquaintances of theirs. At each stage of recruitment, I asked respondents to take several questionnaires with the goal of handing them out to a number of their friends to expand the "reach" of the sample. I felt it important not to limit them in the number of additional questionnaires they were asked to distribute among their friends, since that would limit the pool of potential subjects. In any case, most of those to whom I gave additional questionnaires said that they only knew two or three others of whom they could safely request this on my behalf. They were willing to take the risk of introducing me to only their very closest friends.[14] I then gathered the completed questionnaires at later meetings from the friends to whom I had given them, through other mutual acquaintances, or, in some limited cases, I received them through the mail.[15]

Though my base of operations for this study was in Moscow, I managed to take several trips on my own to other cities and regions of the USSR to gather data through friends and acquaintances there, despite restrictive Soviet travel regulations for foreigners.[16] The places I visited included Leningrad (now once again Saint Petersburg), in the north of Russia; Tallinn, capital of Estonia; Riga, capital of Latvia; Vilnius, capital of Lithuania; Tbilisi, capital of Georgia; Sochi, a resort city on the Black Sea in the south of the Russian Soviet Federated Socialist Republic (RSFSR); and, in the Soviet Far North, Ukhta, the largest city in the Komi Autonomous Soviet Socialist Republic (ASSR).

From such "snowball sampling" through homosexual friends and acquaintances, 123 subjects were recruited to the study over a 6-month period.

b. Through Gay and Lesbian Organizations

When it became clear to me that gathering a sample solely through friendship networks would not allow me to recruit enough subjects to the study, I began also distributing my questionnaire through the few, and very new, gay and lesbian organizations that had formed in various Soviet republics. I contacted the groups' leaders (as listed in the few gay and lesbian publications that existed) independently, or established contact with them through mutual acquaintances, often through members of other organizations. Although the procedure I followed in recruiting subjects from these organizations varied, the approach I took was similar and paralleled that used when recruiting them through friends and acquaintances.

In Leningrad, I attended meetings of the only nascent organization to meet on a regular basis, Banks of the Nyevá (River) (Невские Берега) as it was called at that time.[17] To these meetings I brought copies of my survey for members to fill out "on the spot," if they agreed to do so. In addition, I gave each of the members who would take them several copies of my questionnaire to give to their friends and acquaintances—as many as they thought they could reasonably distribute and retrieve. I gathered the responses at subsequent group meetings and at separate meetings with some individual members.

In Moscow, I met separately with several of the nine founding members of one organization, the Association for the Equal Rights of Homosexuals, or ARGO (Ассоциация за Равноправие Гомосексуалистов, АРГО), because it had already split into two, mainly-inactive factions by the time of my survey. I got most of them to fill out the questionnaire at our meetings and to take several copies to pass out to their friends. These survey responses I gathered later at subsequent meetings with the same individuals or they were passed to me through other members or former members of the organization.

Without success, I attempted the same recruitment strategy with the remaining gay and lesbian organizations in Russia's two largest cities: The Moscow Union of Lesbians and Homosexuals (Московский союз лесбиянок и гомосексуалистов),[18] and the Chaykóvskiy Fund for Cultural Initiatives and the Defense of Sexual Minorities (Фонд культурных инициативов и защиты сексуальных меньшинств, имени П.И. Чайковского). The "membership" of these groups was limited to two or three individuals each, none of whom were willing to fill out a questionnaire themselves, or to pass any on to friends, collaborators, or acquaintances.

Despite my requests, I was not permitted to attend any meetings of the only gay organization in Latvia (The Latvian Association for Sexual Equal Rights, or LASR (Латвийская Ассоциация Сексуального Равноправия ЛАСР), but through a mutual friend in Riga I was able to meet individually, on two separate occasions, with the group's most consistent leader.[19] After a lengthy first-meeting interview, he agreed to take several copies of the questionnaire to distribute among the group's membership, and I convinced him to take twice again as many so that members could pass them along to their friends. At our second meeting these were returned to me, all completed, and I gave him more to distribute, should the opportunity arise. Additional completed questionnaires did come in from this channel through our mutual friend.

I did not have such good luck in Lithuania. The one, shadowy Lithuanian gay and lesbian organization of which I had heard rumors remained incognito during my trip there and its reputed leaders in Vilnius and Kaunas remained incommunicado, despite attempts to make contact both on my own and through friends. At the very end of my research stay in the USSR, however, I did come in contact with the leader of another, new Lithuanian gay organization—the Lithuanian Gay and Lesbian Information Bureau—to whom I gave several questionnaires. Unfortunately, I was to leave the Soviet Union shortly thereafter and was unable to meet with him again to collect any completed questionnaires. This gay activist did not make use of any of the alternate contact information I gave him as routes for returning the surveys to me and contact was thus lost. Through later efforts, I found out that he had been forced to flee his home by neighbors and local authorities angered by his open advocacy of gay rights. No one knew of his whereabouts.

Having obtained a copy of the introductory issue of a gay-oriented newspaper put out by a group in Barnaul, in the Altai region of Siberia, I wrote to the editors at the post-office-box address given in the masthead. One of the founders of the group, The Siberian Union of Homosexuals and Lesbians (Сибирьский союз гомосексуалистов и лесбиянок), then contacted me, and we arranged to meet on his upcoming trip to Moscow. When we met, I was informed that the group had ceased to exist, and that, in any case, it had only consisted of two members, whose main goal was to put out the broadsheet SV ("СВ"). However, I was able to meet with the former group's founder on a few trips he made to Moscow, and convinced him to take several questionnaires home with him to distribute among his friends and acquaintances. He returned them both by mail and on subsequent visits.

I met the leader of a gay and lesbian support group (at the time unnamed) in Minsk, Byelorussia on one of my sporadic trips to Leningrad. He took several questionnaires and returned them through various routes: in person, through mutual friends, and through other organizations with which he maintained contact.

From "snowball sampling" through nascent gay and lesbian organizations, 58 subjects were recruited to the study over 5 months.

2. Targeted Sampling

a. By Canvassing in Gay Meeting Places

As a means of sampling more widely, I considered distributing my questionnaires in the most widely used public meeting places of Soviet gay men in Moscow and Leningrad, that is: at night, on the streets that are well-known gay "cruising places" ("на плешке") and in certain public bathhouses popular with gay men in the evening hours. Recognition of the personal and professional risk I would have been putting myself in and the potential political consequences that such an open canvassing likely would have had on subjects led me to abandon the idea of gathering data in these locations, however.

Under different conditions though, I thought I would probably be safe and successful with this means of questionnaire distribution: in a less-public place and during daylight hours. Several friends and research subjects had informed me about the existence of (unofficial) nudist beaches frequented by gay men and lesbians, more or less exclusively, in several locations: on the Moskva River in Moscow, just outside of Leningrad on the Gulf of Finland, on the Lithuanian Baltic-Sea coast, on the Bay of Riga, and near two major resort cities on the Russian and Ukrainian Black-Sea coast. I felt that canvassing in these locations would be a more feasible option.

Two of the three beaches I visited (the one in Moscow and one on the Black Sea) proved to be good sources of subjects. Unfortunately, I was only able to visit the third gay beach, outside Leningrad, in very late spring when few homosexuals were congregated there. On these beaches, in appropriate attire (or lack thereof), on my own or in tandem with some friends who had agreed to help me with questionnaire distribution, I approached individuals directly, asking them to fill out questionnaires as they sunned.

In an attempt to reach friends and acquaintances of these beachgoers, in "snowball" fashion, I gave extra questionnaires to individuals who acknowledged being frequent visitors to that particular beach and asked them to return completed ones to me on my next visit, which I tried to schedule with them. In other cases, I gave out additional questionnaires if respondents indicated that they could return questionnaires to me by some other means. Neither of these attempts to combine targeted with snowball sampling was very successful.

I was unable to visit a fourth gay beach (in the Crimea) myself but sent numerous copies with some friends of mine who went, and they brought me many responses upon their return.

From targeted sampling at secluded beaches where Soviet gay men and lesbians gather to relax and socialize undisturbed, 65 subjects were recruited to the study over a period of about 2 ½months.

b. By Direct Appeal

In February 1991, a group of medical doctors and psychiatrists had begun to see several young gay men and lesbians at their offices in a newly-opened, private (cooperative) sexually-transmitted-disease (STD) clinic in Moscow, and over the next few months, the doctors held bi-weekly group meetings with them. These were generally open discussions on issues of concern to Soviet homosexuals. Gradually, their meetings began to attract more and more people. One group grew from about 5 or 10, mostly young, gay men in the early Spring to over 100 in May and early June. A separate group with lesbians, which went from 6 or 7 to about 20 attenders over the same period. At that point, I decided that it would be beneficial for me to try to recruit those in attendance to my study sample. The last four times that the groups met that spring (the doctors called a break for the summer months) I brought with me copies of my questionnaire and distributed them to attenders.

On these occasions, I was given "the floor" for the first five minutes to introduce my project and pass out the questionnaires. I requested that individuals fill them out during the meeting and return them to me at the close of the evening or, if they did not succeed in doing this, that they take them home and bring them back next time. Requiring that they all complete the questionnaire immediately was not reasonable, since the doctors leading the discussions were not willing to give me that much time (it would have taken 20–30 minutes to complete). Even my compromise request that attenders fill out the questionnaire during lulls throughout the course of the evening was not always appropriate, since one of these meetings was devoted to a lecture by a noted sexologist and another to presentations by the doctors on sexually transmitted diseases of particular interest to gay men (syphilis and AIDS).

So as to retrieve as many completed questionnaires as possible, then, and to encourage those who had started but not finished filling one out to do so before leaving, I stationed myself at the door when people were exiting. Probably because this was a sort of "captive audience," a large proportion of questionnaires distributed at these meetings were returned completed (about 80% overall). Again, although I surmised that loss would be high if questionnaires went out the door, I continued the practice of asking subjects to take extra questionnaires to their friends and return them to me at the next group meeting. Only a few actually did so.

From targeted sampling among Soviet gay men and lesbians gathered for the gay-oriented discussion group, 88 subjects were recruited to the study over a period of 8 weeks.

In late July and early August of 1991, a conference on "Human Rights and AIDS" was held in Leningrad and Moscow, by the International Gay & Lesbian Human Rights Commission (IGLHRC), then a fledgling organization that had been started in Moscow the previous year by one Russian and two American gay activists. That first-of-its-kind event attracted a few hundred Soviet gay men and lesbians and included several practical presentations and workshops on various issues of concern to potential Soviet gay and lesbian activists as well as showings of several Western films with gay-related themes. Over the eight days of the conference (four in each city), I handed out questionnaires to conference participants before and after sessions and to movie-goers before and after screenings, as I could catch them. I collected the questionnaires immediately after their completion.

From targeted sampling among attendants at the gay and lesbian conference, 100 subjects were recruited to the sample in a two-week period.

c. Through a Gay-Oriented Publication

In addition to the above-mentioned recruitment efforts, I also arranged with the editor of the magazine *RISK* ("РИСК"), the Moscow-based gay-oriented publication that was the mouthpiece of the group ARGO, to send questionnaires along with the latest issue to individuals who had written to him requesting a copy. Only a small number of these people actually returned completed questionnaires, however.

From this special solicitation from new gay-themed-magazine subscribers, 13 subjects were recruited to the study.

D. Risks and Precautions in Questionnaire Distribution

In the ideologically capricious Soviet legal system, simply agreeing to participate in this study would have been ample grounds for suspicion of violating any of the anti-sodomy statutes that were a part of each Soviet republic's penal code and might by itself have been used as evidence for criminal indictment, regardless of the circumstantial nature of the evidence. It would also likely have led to social persecution should subjects' identities be discovered by friends, family, coworkers, or the authorities. Many people later told me that they had decided, after taking a copy, that the questionnaire was "too personal" or "too risky" and that they therefore would not be returning it to me.

Since I was well aware of the potential danger I might be putting my subjects in simply by asking them to participate, I took several precautions to protect them and to encourage their involvement despite the risk. I made and kept promises to keep the identity of all of my contacts absolutely confidential. I made sure that questionnaires were completely anonymous by making it impossible for anyone to tell who had filled them out: I did not keep track myself. Indeed, there is no list at all of subjects' names, with or without indication of their respective ID numbers. Of course, I maintained that participation in the study was strictly voluntary at all times, and I never tried to force potential subjects to become involved against their better judgment.

What is more, the sensitive nature of the study questionnaire—especially the explicitness of the questions asked about sexual behaviors—meant that even having such a suggestive document in one's possession could be damning evidence for any of my respondents, and they feared that a completed questionnaire could be seen as an admission of guilt in violating the anti-sodomy statutes. It was likely, therefore, that many potential respondents would feel compelled simply to discard the questionnaire or otherwise destroy it if they were liable to be found with it on their person, rather than risk the penalty of a prison sentence of up to five years for consensual (male) homosexual sex.[20]

Of course, my practice of giving each individual respondent several copies to pass on to his or her friends multiplied the risk. Given this danger, I tried as far as possible to set up personal and private meetings with potential respondents—individually or in a group, in neutral, public places as well as at gatherings hosted by my trusted friends who were the initial contacts. Whenever possible, I tried to make it convenient for subjects to fill out and return the questionnaire to me during the course of a single meeting. This also protected against questionnaires being lost due to lack of further contact.

On the issue of the safety of canvassing on (gay and/or nudist) beaches, my optimism regarding risk was unfortunately proven wrong. While in Sochi, I was detained and subjected to harassment and recruiting efforts by the Soviet Committee on State Security (KGB) for "impersonating a Soviet citizen" and "distribution of illegal materials." Subsequently, I was written-up in a local as well as a national newspaper as a possible "sex spy" ("сексуальный шпион").[21] (Ермаков 1991; Черноморская здравница 1991) I am confident that this incident did not bring harm to any of my research subjects as I successfully safeguarded all completed questionnaires during and after this crisis—both those that I had been gathering on that trip and those that were in my Moscow apartment, having been gathered there and elsewhere.[22] Two of my accomplices in Sochi and another friend were questioned by KGB operatives, however, and might well have suffered more serious consequences if the Soviet "secret service" had not been in serious disarray at the time.

Despite these precautions and necessary mechanisms for safeguarding completed questionnaires, the potential risk to subjects was clearly substantial, and I therefore expected a very high nonresponse rate.

E. Sample Characteristics

1. By Recruitment Source

In all, 800 surveys were distributed through the various sampling methods described above and 447 of those (55.9%) were completed and returned.[23] Each of the two recruitment methods contributed a substantial amount of subjects to the study total in about a 40/60 ratio (snowball to targeted sampling). Through both processes of snowball sampling, 181 subjects were recruited to the study over a period of six months (February through July), that is, 40.5% of those who returned questionnaires. A total of 266 subjects were recruited through the various means of targeted sampling over four months (April through July), which is 59.5% of all questionnaires returned.

A number of questionnaires that were returned had to be excluded from the study since they were drastically incomplete, improperly completed, or because the respondent was judged unsuitable for inclusion in the study. For example, there were several respondents who, having started to fill out the questionnaire, felt that they could not continue, fearing possible negative consequences. They indicated as much either on the questionnaire itself or to me in person when they returned the questionnaire uncompleted. Some others surveyed filled in nonsensical responses, for whatever reason. Finally, some respondents were excluded from the study because answers to the questionnaire revealed that they were clearly heterosexual (had little or no homosexual experience and no sexual self-identification as homosexual or bisexual). Such individuals had usually been recruited on nudist beaches or at the gay and lesbian conference, where a number of non-homosexuals were in attendance.

After excluding these cases, the sample size was reduced to 421 respondents, which resulted in a 52.6% "usable" response rate. The overall profile of the sample was not substantially changed in the process. However, because all of the responses that were excluded had been recruited through targeted sampling, the ratio of usable responses from each method of sampling was evened somewhat: 43.0% from snowball sampling versus 57.0% from targeted sampling. Sampling results by recruitment source are reported in Table 2.1.

Table 2.1: Number and Percent of Respondents in the Survey Sample by Recruitment Source

	surveys returned #	surveys returned %	surveys excluded #	surveys excluded %	survey sample #	survey sample %
Recruitment Method						
1. Snowball Sampling:	181	40.5%	0	—	181	43.0%
a. among friends acquaintances	123	27.5%	0	—	123	29.2%
b. through gay & lesbian groups	58	13.0%	0	—	58	13.8%
2. Targeted Sampling:	266	59.5%	26	5.8%	240	57.0%
a. on beaches	65	14.5%	9	2.0%	56	13.3%
b. i. at gay discussion group	88	19.7%	2	0.5%	86	20.4%
ii. at gay & lesbian conference	100	22.4%	15	3.4%	85	20.2%
c. among gay magazine subscribers	13	2.9%	0	—	13	3.1%
Totals:	447	100.0%	26	5.8%	421	100.0%

While most methods of recruitment were reasonably effective (recruitment from gay-themed magazine subscribers being an important exception), snowball sampling was more effective than targeted sampling, in that it yielded 100% usable questionnaires. This was probably because, with snowball sampling, I could count on the recommendation of trusted friends or organization members for references to other suitable and willing respondents. The direct-appeal approach of targeted sampling left me more vulnerable to "mistakes" in sampling (recruitment of inappropriate subjects), to unusable responses (incomplete questionnaires or "joke" answers), and to nonresponse (failure to return questionnaires or refusals by potential respondents). On the other hand, targeted sampling appears to have been more productive, in that approximately 1½ times as many subjects were recruited by that method than by snowball sampling—and in about two-thirds the time.

2. By Place of Residence and Origin

The geographical range of respondents either living in or native to (родом из) all of the Soviet Republics was not representative in terms of relative population distribution. Respondents were from only 13 of the 15 Soviet republics. (See Table 2.2.) Respondents from several republics were over-represented in the sample (those from the Russian Federation, Estonia, Latvia, and Georgia) and those from others were under-represented, sometimes drastically (especially those from the Ukraine, Azerbaijan, and the Central Asian Republics).

Table 2.2: Number and Percent of Respondents in the Survey Sample Living in and Native to Each of the Soviet Republics, Compared to the Soviet Population (1991).†

Republic:	Living in #	Living in %	Native to #	Native to %	Soviet Population #	Soviet Population %
Russian Federation	298	70.8%	262	2.2%	148,543,000	51.2%
Ukrainian SSR	17	4.0%	28	6.7%	51,944,000	17.9%
Byelorussian SSR	12	2.9%	19	4.5%	10,260,000	3.5%
Estonian SSR	6	1.4%	6	1.4%	1,582,000	0.6%
Latvian SSR	46	10.9%	46	0.9%	2,681,000	0.9%
Lithuanian SSR	2	0.5%	3	0.7%	3,728,000	1.3%
Moldavian SSR	4	1.0%	5	1.2%	4,367,000	1.5%
Georgian SSR	13	3.1%	15	3.6%	5,464,000	1.9%
Armenian SSR	2	0.5%	2	0.5%	3,376,000	1.2%
Azerbaijanian SSR	0	—	4	1.0%	7,137,000	2.5%
Kazakh SSR	2	0.5%	4	1.0%	16,793,000	5.8%
Uzbek SSR	2	0.5%	4	1.0%	20,708,000	7.1%
Kirgiz SSR	1	0.2%	2	0.5%	4,422,000	1.5%
Turkmenian SSR	1	0.2%	3	0.7%	3,714,000	1.3%
Tajik SSR	0	—	1	0.2%	5,358,000	1.9%
Outside the USSR	—	—	3	0.7%	—	—
unknown	15	3.6%	15	3.6%	—	—
Totals:	421	100.1%‡	421	100.4%‡	290,077,000	100.1%‡

† Soviet population statistics are from Госкомстат СССР (1991:67).
‡ Totals do not add to 100.0% due to rounding error.

Nevertheless, the representation of subjects from the Russian Federated Soviet Socialist Republic (RSFSR), which was by far the largest and most diverse of the Soviet Republics with 76.2% of the nation's land surface and 51.2% of its population in 1991 (Госкомстат СССР 1991:68–73), was quite broad. Although not all areas of the RSFSR were definitely represented by residents in the sample—only 16 of the 49 Provinces, or *Oblasts* (Области); 4 of the 6 Territories, or *Kráys* (Края); 1 of the 16 Autonomous Republics (ASSRs); none of the 5 Autonomous Provinces (Автономные Области); and none of the 10 Ethnic (Native) Districts (Народные Округа) are represented—the coverage is still quite wide-ranging.[24] Even more so is the coverage by those who are native to the various areas (31 Provinces, 5 Territories, 6 Autonomous Republics, and 1 Autonomous Province).

3. By Ethnicity

The geographic disparities are reflected in similar distortions in the representation of "nationalities" (ethnicities), but this does not mean that Soviet ethnic groups (with or without a dedicated ethnic territory) were not widely represented in the sample. In fact, most of the largest ethnic groups of the Soviet Union are represented, albeit not proportionately to their distribution in the Soviet population. (See Table 2.3.) Of course, respondents of some ethnic groups were over-represented in the sample (particularly Russians, Latvians, Georgians, and Poles) and those of other ethnic groups were under-represented (especially Ukrainians, Azerbaijanis, Uzbeks, and Tatars).

Table 2.3: Number and Percent of Respondents in the Survey Sample by Ethnicity, Compared to the Soviet Population (1989).†

	Survey Sample		Soviet Population	
Ethnicity	#	%	#	%
Russian	292	69.4%	145,155,000	50.8%
Ukrainian	23	5.5%	44,186,000	15.5%
Byelorussian	16	3.8%	10,036,000	3.5%
Estonian	3	0.7%	1,027,000	0.4%
Latvian	25	5.9%	1,459,000	0.5%
Lithuanian	1	0.2%	3,067,000	1.1%
Moldavian	2	0.5%	3,352,000	1.2%
Georgian	15	3.6%	3,981,000	1.4%
Armenian	2	0.5%	4,623,000	1.6%
Azerbaijani	0	—	6,770,000	2.4%
Kazakh	1	0.2%	8,136,000	2.9%
Uzbek	3	0.7%	16,698,000	5.8%
Kirgiz	0	—	2,529,000	0.9%
Turkmen	1	0.2%	2,729,000	1.0%
Tajik	0	—	4,215,000	1.5%
Tatar	4	1.0%	6,649,000	2.3%
Polish	6	1.4%	1,126,000	0.4%
Jewish	4	1.0%	1,378,000	0.5%
German	3	0.7%	2,039,000	0.7%
Greek	2	0.5%	358,000	0.1%
other/unknown	18	4.3%	16,330,000	5.7%
Totals:	421	100.1%‡	285,743,000	100.2%‡

† Soviet population statistics are from Госкомстат СССР (1991:77–80).
‡ Total does not add to 100.0% due to rounding error.

4. By Age

Respondents ranged in age from 16 to 64, with an average age of 27.4 years (sd=7.4 years). Respondents were overwhelmingly young, with over 40% being under age 25 and over 80% under age 35. (See Table 2.4.) Heavily over-represented in the sample were those aged 20 to 30 years; grievously under-represented were those over 50 years old. Although I made every attempt to make contact with and survey older Soviet gay men and lesbians, they are particularly difficult to locate since the chief outlets for homosexual interaction in the USSR are amenable to use only by the relatively young and daring. Gay and lesbian friendship circles are also rather age-homogeneous, which made it difficult to reach those who were much older than those already contacted.

Table 2.4: Number and Percent of Respondents in the Survey Sample by 5-Year Age Group, Compared to the Soviet Population Aged 15 and over (1990).†

Age Group	Survey Sample #	%	Soviet Popultion aged 15+ #	%
15-19	39	9.3%	21,627,000	10.1%
20-24	136	32.3%	20,064,000	9.4%
25-29	103	24.5%	23,700,000	11.1%
30-34	77	18.3%	23,816,000	11.2%
35-39	34	8.1%	21,200,000	9.9%
40-44	17	4.0%	16,010,000	7.5%
45-49	8	1.9%	12,747,000	6.0%
50-54	3	0.7%	18,671,000	8.7%
55-59	1	0.2%	14,039,000	6.6%
60-64	1	0.2%	15,311,000	7.2%
65+	0	—	26,436,000	12.4%
unknown	2	0.5%	—	—
Totals:	421	100.0%	213,621,000	100.1%‡

† Soviet population statistics are from Госкомстат СССР (1991:74).
‡ Total does not add to 100.0% due to rounding error.

Reflecting this skewness, the median age of respondents in the sample was 26 years while the modal age was 22.

5. By Educational Level

The sample survey is also highly skewed as regards respondents' level of educational attainment. Sample subjects are more highly educated than the Soviet population as a whole, despite their youth. (See Table 2.5.) Over three times more respondents had a higher education (32.3%) than did Soviet citizens aged 15 years and over in general (10.8%). What is more, 61.3% of those with an uncompleted higher education are currently of college age (18-24)[25] and may well be currently enrolled. It is likely that many of these will ultimately complete their higher education, further exacerbating the disparity between the sample and the Soviet population in this regard. Conversely, while fully half of the Soviet population

(50.6%) has only a secondary or uncompleted secondary school education, only about one-fifth (20.0%) of sample respondents are so basically educated.

Table 2.5: Number and Percent of Respondents in the Survey Sample by Level of Educational Attainment, Compared to Soviet Population Aged 15 and over (1989).†

Education Level	Survey Sample #	%	Soviet Popultion aged 15+ #	%
"Illiterate"*	—	—	4,300,000	2.0%
Uncompleted Secondary	11	2.6%	42,400,000	20.0%
Secondary	73	17.3%	64,600,000	30.5%
Specialized Secondary	126	29.9%	38,600,000	18.2%
Uncompleted Higher	75	17.8%	3,600,000	1.7%
Higher	136	32.3%	23,000,000	10.9%
unaccounted for*	—	—	35,568,000	16.8%
Totals:	421	99.9%‡	212,068,000	100.1%‡

† Soviet population statistics are from Госкомстат СССР (1991:74,209).
‡ Totals do not add to 100.0% due to rounding error.
* Although the source cited does not indicate as much, presumably those labelled "illiterate" have no formal education and those unaccounted for have only primary-school education or some other form of education not reported.

6. By Gender

Finally, and very importantly, respondents were overwhelmingly male. While the Soviet population aged 15 and over was 46.0% male and 54.1% female (Госкомстат СССР 1991:75),[26] 367 men, but only 54 women were recruited into the sample. These figures represent 87.2% and 12.8% of respondents, respectively. Although I took every possible opportunity to recruit women to the study, Soviet lesbians remain much less visible (being much less a part of the largely gay-male subculture) and have much more tenuous social networks than do Soviet gay men, despite less legal persecution.[27] They were much more difficult to sample and the data obtained from them are even less likely to be representative of Soviet lesbians. I will, therefore, generally limit my presentation of statistical data to those collected from Soviet gay men. I will also, on occasion, report data obtained from lesbians when these are substantially different in an important way from those of the gay men. Of course, I will include in the analysis discussion of information I gathered from observations of and interviews with Soviet lesbians.

In general, individuals more likely to be drawn into the sample were those who were somehow connected to my particular social circle—directly or through one or more "weak ties" (Granovetter 1973) such as through acquaintance with a member of a gay organization whom I had contacted, who frequented beaches known to be gathering places of homosexuals, or who were intrigued enough by the recommendations of their friends to attend meetings for gay men and lesbians at the newly-opened health center in Moscow. Those who actually answered the questionnaire were more likely to be individuals who either felt that they had less to lose by risking involvement, those who were less afraid of the possible repercussions of their participation, and/or those who were convinced of the anonymity of the research and of my ability to maintain their confidentiality.

F. Data Modifications

It is common in all survey research for the data collected to be incomplete and, therefore, not entirely representative. There are at least three ways in which this can come about. Some people in the target population—usually most of them—are not selected for the study sample. They are simply **not surveyed**. This is the essence of survey sampling, but also the crux of one sampling problem: "noncoverage." Another reason surveys may reap "incomplete" data is that some individuals who are selected for recruitment into the sample are **not willing** to comply. That is "unit (case, subject, or individual) nonresponse." In addition, even those subjects successfully recruited into the sample sometimes give **no answer** to some questions, which means that the researcher will have "missing data," or "item nonresponse."

It is usually desirable to compensate for these flaws in the research and Kalton (1983:5–6) delineates three possible solutions: "When missing data compensations are made, noncoverage and unit nonresponse are generally treated by weighting adjustments while item nonresponse is treated by imputation."

1. Weighting Data to Compensate for Noncoverage & Unit Nonresponse

The proper weight for respondents in any sample "is the inverse of respondents' probabilities of being selected into the sample" (Babbie 1973:127). Thus, for each variable on which the sample is to be weighted, the value of each respondent's weight, "w," is given by the formula:

$$w = 1/(ng/pg)$$

where "g" is a sub-group of the variable on which weighting is to be done and of which the respondent is a member (*exemplar gratius*: males when weighting by sex), "ng" is the number of respondents selected from that sub-group, and "pg" is the probability of a person in that sub-group being selected into the sample. This probability is a function of the method and means of respondent recruitment as well as of the proportion of such individuals in the overall population from which the sample is drawn.

Since there was no way for me to determine the probability of any respondent's selection into my sample, however, and since there existed no

Employing Social Research Methods for a Soviet Gay Studies

accurate national statistics on the incidence of homosexuality in the USSR—much less on the ratio of male versus female homosexuals, or on any other variable on which it might be desirable to weight a sample—no accurate weighting could be done.

Although I considered substituting the percentages of men versus women, each of the relevant age-groups, *et cetera*, in the overall Soviet population as a proxy value, doing so would have involved making several assumptions, none of which could be readily justified. For example, it would mean assuming that the percentage of homosexuals in the Soviet population is knowable and known. This is certainly not the case. Using the corresponding figure generally quoted for the U.S. population, about 10% (which statistic is, one must recognize, also not known to be accurate), and assuming that it would also fit the Soviet Union would have been possible, but it would also have been a huge "stretch." Another necessary assumption would be that the percentage of gay men to lesbians in the sampling pool was the same as it is in the Soviet population. Yet, as I have already mentioned, I believe my sample under-represents lesbian women because I sampled from the mostly male-oriented gay world in the USSR and because lesbians are more difficult to reach. For all of these reasons, then, I judged weighting to be inappropriate for use on these data.

2. Imputing Values to Compensate for Item Nonresponse

In a number of instances, respondents to my survey did not fully complete the questionnaire: they either left out answers to whole groups of questions or failed to answer a question here and there. Sometimes these questions went unanswered because respondents did not know the correct response; in many other cases, they failed to answer questions for which the answer was surely known, probably out of a concern for maintaining their privacy or by simple oversight. At the same time, some respondents answered certain questions when it was inappropriate for them to do so. For example, young respondents frequently provided opinions about the conditions of life for homosexuals in the Soviet Union during time-periods (now, five years ago, ten years ago, and 20 years ago) before they had had homosexual experiences or even during the years before they were born.

When enough non-contradictory information was available from responses to questions logically related to these unanswered or inappropriately answered ones, "deductive imputation" (Kalton 1983:68–69) was employed to recover the missing data or to delete that which was inappropriate. In the example just mentioned, for instance, respondents were reassigned answers of "not applicable" if they gave answers to the question "How would you evaluate the situation of gays/lesbians in the USSR (relative to your experience and age)?" for time periods prior to the time of their age at first homosexual contact or age when they first recognized that they had "homosexual tendencies" (which were assessed in separate qustions). In another instance, it was deduced that the most probable answer to an omitted item in the question about the frequency with which respondents engaged in each of ten different sex-acts was "never" when other items in the list were answered, and none of those answers was "never." This allowed me to recover answers from respondents who were probably failing to answer simply by oversight: they probably didn't notice the optional answer "never." Yet, I did not impute answers for respondents who had answered "never" to other items in the question, because I reasoned that those respondents were aware of the option, but may have purposely left the item blank (whatever their reason).

Of course, my subjective judgments about what and how much other information was "enough" to impute any particular value to a question with a missing or inconsistent response may not always have been accurate. However, it is reassuring that, in Kalton's (1983:121) judgment:

> A decision to be made with any multiple imputation procedure is the number of replications, c, to employ ... with unrestricted sampling ... the choice of c=2 goes a good way towards removing the imputation [error] variance. ... Thus with regard to the reduction of the imputation variance, most of the gain of multiple imputations can be achieved from a small number of replications, even the minimum of 2.

I did not impute any values using less than two stipulations (or "replications").

G. Data Analyses

Decisions must also be made about the proper use of the data gathered for this study, both because they are drawn from a population whose general characteristics are unknown and because two different methods of sampling were combined and subjects were recruited in several different ways.

Since the data are drawn not from a probability sample, but from snowball and targeted sampling, they are, properly speaking, not appropriate for analysis by statistical techniques that base their validity on assumptions of the random distribution of subjects in the population. What is more, because there is no reliable information on the make-up of the gay and lesbian population in the USSR (or in any other country), it is not possible to make anything more than an educated guess about the representativeness of the sample obtained.[28]

However, Martin and Dean (1990) provide one example of a non-probability sample of homosexual men that "measures up" to others gathered by more-nearly representative sampling methods. Their sample was about equal to others gathered by random digit dialing and cluster sampling of households in measuring standard attribute variables (age, race, education) as well as "degree of closetedness."

Indeed, Martin and Dean (1990:548) argued, "the use of certain types of nonprobability samples does not preclude the estimate [sic: estimation] of population parameters." Although my sample was not gathered as systematically as that of these researchers, the means I employed were quite similar: initial recruitment from a variety of sources to guarantee that a wide range of gay people and lifestyles would be represented, and then chain-referral of friends and acquaintances to the study in order to extend the "reach" of the sample to less-readily-accessible subjects. (Martin & Dean 1990:550)

For most of my analyses, I will report only descriptive statistics and whatever generalizations from them that I make to the overall population under study will always be very cautious ones. In those circumstances when I will use inferential statistics to buttress a point, I will report coefficients as indicative of a relationship but not conclusive, and will report probability values as only suggestive of the strength of that possible relationship in the Soviet gay and lesbian population as a whole. For tests of my theoretical hypotheses about the level of development of subcultural institutions, statistical significance is less important anyhow than the general patterns of relations that the data show.

NOTES

1. Although I will make educated inferences about the situation of Soviet gay men and lesbians in periods prior to and following on this research "window of opportunity" (and will also analyze other scholars' previous and subsequent studies of this population), my assertions on those matters can only be claims that require greater substantiation than I can provide here. They will be, in fact, theoretical predictions that would require further research into the institutionalization of relations in pre-reform and post-Soviet gay life.

2. While such preliminary work on an unstudied population might have more traditionally confined itself to participant observation methods, I felt that the experience I gained from living as a gay man in the USSR before beginning this research (coupled with the expertise I had already acquired on gay and lesbian populations of other countries) provided enough background information to serve as a sound basis for informed survey research. Moreover, my participant observation work, which was ongoing throughout the survey and interview processes, provided not only further material to augment my contentions, but also checks on the veracity of the survey and interview data.

3. The activists interviewed were from the Association for the Equal Rights of Homosexuals (ARGO), from Banks of the Nyevá, from The Moscow Union of Lesbians and Homosexuals, from the Siberian Association of Homosexuals and Lesbians (Сибирьская Ассоциация Гомосексуалистов и Лесбиянок), from the Lithuanian Gay and Lesbian Information Bureau, and from the Latvian Association for Sexual Equal Rights (LASR). (For more information on these ativist organizations, see Chapter Five.)

4. The therapists/clinicians interviewed were from the Diagnostical-Treatment Center "Medicine and Reproduction" or "MIR" (Лечебно-диагностический Центр «Медицина и репродукция», "МИР"), a cooperative health-care clinic in Moscow; from the Moscow telephone hotline "Anti-AIDS" (горячая линия «Анти-СПИД»); from the Lithuanian AIDS Prevention Center (*Lietuvos AIDS profilaktikos centras*) in Vilnius; and from the Center for

the Formation of Sexual Culture (Центр формирования сексуальной културы), a health center of Moscow's Main Health Administration.

5. The scholars interviewed were: Professor Ígor S. Kón, a sociologist and sexologist at the Institute of Ethnography, Soviet Academy of Sciences; Dr. Borís M. Levín, a criminologist at the Institute of Sociology, Soviet Academy of Sciences; Professor Teet Veispak, a historian at the Institute of History, Estonian Academy of Sciences; Dmítriy D. Isáyev, a psychiatrist at the Leningrad Psychoanalytic Scientific-Research Institute; and a student from the Sociological Center at the University of Ufa, Bashkiria, whose work was sponsored by the Soviet Ministry of Internal Affairs (MVD).

6. For example, initial informants suggested that the questions about precautions taken to avoid contracting AIDS should come directly after that asking whether respondents had had any sexual contact with foreigners, since it was a common perception in the Soviet gay and lesbian world that AIDS was a threat largely for those who have had sex with foreigners (especially Americans). Otherwise, the questions about AIDS precautions seemed to them to come "out of nowhere." Whether or not it is true that foreigners were bringing AIDS to the USSR, it is likely that putting these questions together elicited a higher response rate since the pairing of the ideas is in accordance with, rather than being dissonant to, subjects' own logical reasoning.

7. My experience in this regard parallels that of the only other survey research being conducted on the homosexual population of the Soviet Union: a comparative study of the gay male populations of three major cities neighboring each other on the Baltic Sea's Gulf of Finland. Those cities were Helsinki, capital of Finland; Tallinn, capital of the Estonian Soviet Socialist Republic of the USSR; and Leningrad, the second-largest city in the Russian Soviet Federated Socialist Republic (RSFSR), which was itself the largest and most populous, by far, of the Soviet Union's constituent members. That study was being undertaken by a joint Finnish-Estonian research team at the same time as I was carrying out my work. The questionnaire those scholars used was a translation of parts of Weinberg & Williams' (1974) survey of American homosexuals, which contained mostly open-ended questions asking for paragraph-long responses to broadly-worded questions on all aspects of gay life. The principal Estonian researcher on that project revealed to me that they were lucky to get a full sentence from their Russian respondents in answer to most of their open-ended questions. They were most likely to get only a single-phrase response and rarely got the in-depth, descriptive information that they were seeking. Estonian subjects were usually more forthcoming, and Finns were very comprehensive in their answers. (Veispak 1991 interview)

8. In English slang, physical abuse by private citizens vehemently and violently opposed to homosexuality is termed "gay bashing." In Russian slang, the corresponding term used is "*remónt*" ("ремонт"), which means, literally, "renovation." This has a connotation similar to the English-language threat: "I'll rearrange your face!"

9. Placing the most sensitive questions at the end of a survey is standard procedure in sociological survey methods (Sudman & Bradburn 1983; Rossi, Wright, & Anderson 1983). In America, such questions are most likely to be demographic ones, such as age and income. In the former Soviet Union, however, as in the Russian Empire that preceded it and the Russian Federated Republic that followed it, such basic demographic information is not considered to be privileged with privacy. In fact, under the centuries-old internal-passport system, almost all such information was noted in every Soviet citizens' internal passport which was scrutinized in many official and unofficial circumstances. The information listed there included individuals' name and birthdate (and therefore calculable age); their parentage and nationality (ethnicity); their education, profession, and place of employment (including

educational and employment histories); their party affiliation; their marital status and parenthood (with number and age of children); as well as their residence permit and place and type of residence. Because questions requesting this information were likely to be common and familiar to most respondents, I chose to use them at the beginning of the questionnaire, saving the most personal and intimate questions for last.

10. By "sexual-role identity" I mean the "active/passive" dichotomy or "top/bottom/versatile" trichotomy of sexual role-oriented identities that are often found in both male and female homosexual subcultures. These sexual relations and their corresponding identities are based on the heterosexual model of active-male/passive-female sexual roles prominent in society generally. This concept is distinguished in my usage from "sexuality identity," which refers to individuals' concept of themselves as heterosexual, homosexual, or bisexual in any or all of three relational realms: sexual behavior, erotic attraction, and romantic interest. "Sexuality identities" are not role-related, but behaviorally or affectively oriented. Neither of these terms should be conflated with the more common concepts of "sexual identity" and "gender identity" that are based, respectively, on male or female anatomy and on sex-role or gender-role socialization in society.

11. There can be little doubt that it is much easier to put together a sample of members of the gay and lesbian population of any Western country (despite considerable obstacles) than it is to do so in the USSR. There are vastly more social and political organizations, homosexually-oriented publications, and cultural activities among and for gay men and lesbians in Western countries than there were in the Soviet Union (Schluter 1992a) —and most study samples of gay men and lesbians must be drawn from the ranks of such gay and lesbian groups for lack of any other, more-reliable method of *entrée* into this sub-population. (Leznoff 1956; Weinberg 1970; Gagnon 1988) This does not mean, of course, that such a sample will necessarily be representative of the particular (American, say) gay and lesbian population from which it is drawn. The peculiarities of the specific source(s) from which subjects are recruited pose their own difficulties in this regard.

12. From the point of view of gay and lesbian socio-political activists, eager to defend their fellows against stereotyping, harassment, and discrimination, or hoping to enlist them as a basis for popular support (both political and financial) and to mobilize these "constituents" to their common cause, not being able to locate other homosexuals readily is also a problem to be overcome. (For more information on gay and lesbian activism in the USSR, see Chapter Five.)

13. Good examples of studies on the American gay and lesbian population that used this sampling method are Blumstein & Schwartz (1983) and McWhirter & Mattison (1984).

14. There is considerable agreement among Sovietologists on the restrictive nature of friendship relations in Soviet society. Most of the explanations of this fact center around the illicit aura surrounding many social relations under the communist system. Only the closest of friends could be trusted with covert aspects of one's life, and in a "totalitarian" system, many facets of everyday life had legal or political restrictions placed on them by the government. The circle of trusted others that could be counted on not to reveal one's secrets was therefore exceedingly small. (Fehér, Heller, & Márkus 1983; Кон 1980)

15. The Soviet postal system was notoriously inefficient. Internal mail in the USSR routinely took about two weeks to reach its destination and was subjected to random as well as targeted censorship. Therefore, most Soviet citizens did not trust it for sensitive correspondence, preferring to send such things with friends and acquaintances who were traveling to a particular location where the recipient would make arrangements to collect it.

Though I left the mail option open to respondents, I received many more survey responses via friendly "courier" than through the Soviet mail.

16. At the time, foreign scholars in the USSR on an academic (учебная) visa, were allowed travel to three cities or academic institutions other than the place where their sponsoring institution was located. Doing so required the approval of the Soviet Visa and Registration Office (OVIR) in each of those places before entering the country. It also required a written explanation of the purpose of the visit and its relation to the scholar's government-approved research agenda, which had to be co-signed by the scholar's assigned academic adviser (usually a member of the Soviet Academy of Sciences) and approved by their Western financial and organizational sponsor for the research stay.

Yet, after a month-long visit with a friend at the beginning of my year in the Soviet Union, visa officials neglected to switch my documents from a "guest" (гостевая) visa to an academic one when I began my officially-sponsored research on another topic. Instead, they simply extended the existing visa well beyond its legal limit. That impropriety made my research triply illegal: I was conducting unsponsored research, which was not allowed; I did so while in the country on a guest visa, which was prohibited; and I was officially in the USSR on a (three-month) guest visa for the entire year, which was unlawful under Soviet regulations. I rightfully reckoned that, if that much deviation from the rules was overlooked, further subversion on my part (such as traveling more freely) would likely go unnoticed or unpunished for some time.

17. Aside from the legal and juridical obstructions to formal registration this group encountered, the issue of names created a petty stumbling block. The group was barred from registering its existence —and thereby from legitimizing its operations— under that name. Since group members were determined to organize legally, they had to re-form themselves under another name and repeat the attempt at registration. The group's second name was Nyevá Perspectives (Невские Перспективы) under which, incidentally, official registration was again denied. (For more information about the evolution of this group and its struggle with local authorities, see Chapter Five on politics and gay activism.)

18. This group previously had been called the Association of Sexual Minorities (Ассоциация сексуальных меньшинств). I am unaware of the reason for this name change.

19. At the time of my research, most of the gay and lesbian organizations in the USSR were very disorganized. In the case of LASR, even informal leadership positions were shifting and undefined —based, apparently, on who was able to provide the group with the most and best resources (funds, publicity, meeting places) at any given time.

20. For more information on the legal condition of homosexuals in the former USSR, including discussion of the relevant article of the Russian Federation's Penal Code, see Chapter Five on social-environmental institutions surrounding the Soviet "gay world."

21. I later learned from well-connected friends there that a KGB informant had been "planted" on the beach in Sochi to keep the authorities abreast of any unusual activities and to provide the names of gay men and lesbians who went there for possible future prosecutions and/or recruitment to the ranks of KGB informants. I was told, but have no way of confirming, that one very effeminate young man, a local resident, had been coerced into acting as a KGB informant as a means of procuring the unofficial protection he needed from the harassment he suffered at the hands of others in town. The KGB seems to have been more than willing to exploit this young man's vulnerability to societal oppression and expressly offered to do the same in my case, offering me "connections" to the benefits of elite life in the USSR in return for my "cooperation." (Actually, the KGB agents who interrogated me used

the term "collaboration" ("сотрудничество") and insinuated that it was really a kind of "research collaboration" they were after.) Then they offered to keep quiet about my research and about my homosexuality, and finally offered to "wine and dine" me, before I demanded that they either arrest and deport me or release me. I was ultimately fined for a violation of travel regulations and released.

22. Although I was caught "red-handed" with a number of completed questionnaires in my possession at the time I was detained, when allowed to go free for two hours, I managed to rid myself of them before being questioned further. Cognizant of the likelihood that I was being followed during that time, I made an effort to steer clear of my cohorts but did succeed in having a new but trusted acquaintance mail the data I had collected to a third-party address in a major city in another part of the country for safe-keeping. Of course, the package was sent by registered mail and sealed for protection. A month or so later, when back in Moscow, I received the data package through another friend, with the seals intact.

Data that had been gathered elsewhere and stored in Moscow was made inaccessible to authorities by an urgent phone call to a friend there who had access to my apartment. With the help of another building resident, she gathered all of the completed questionnaires and all other material related to my research on the topic (as well as my address book, personal papers, and even my answering machine tape) and removed them to the home of a third person in another part of Moscow for security. Since there was no identifying information on the questionnaires, in most cases it would have been impossible for the Soviet authorities to identify my respondents. However, the fact that some individuals might have been traceable due to their peculiar professions (especially in conjunction with age and ethnicity information about them), I felt these measures were necessary so as to be "on the safe side."

23. While there is no strong agreement as to what constitutes an acceptable response rate for survey research, it bears noting that one eminent survey research methodologist (Babbie 1973:165) feels that "a response rate of at least 50 percent is *adequate* for analysis and reporting," while "A response rate of at least 60 percent is good" *(emphasis in the original)* —for a mail survey. In comparison, one study of American gay men and lesbians sampled from among the membership of gay and lesbian organizations and in places where gay people commonly go for recreation and relaxation (bars and clubs) achieved a 30% response rate. (Weinberg 1970:313)

24. It should be emphasized that 192 (fully 64.4%) of the 298 respondents living in the Russian Federation and 114 (43.5%) of those 262 who were native to it did not indicate what region of the Republic they were from. They may or may not add even more to the geographical "reach" of the sample. What is more, since Autonomous Provinces and Ethnic (Native) Districts can be located within the expanse of Provinces and Territories, it is not clear that they are not better represented here than these data show. Respondents from such areas may have simply indicated that they live within the boundaries of the larger area.

25. In the Soviet educational system, a standard higher-education consisted of five or six years (курсы) of schooling, the last of which was chiefly devoted to completing a thesis (дипломная работа).

26. The reason for this divergence from the usual sex ratio of about 50:50 between the genders in most societies, has to do with the great number of men killed in the Soviet Union during World War II, which leaves a gender imbalance among Soviet citizens over age 60.

27. The Soviet Penal Codes did not penalize lesbian sex. This does not mean, however, that lesbians were not oppressed in Soviet society and repressed by the Soviet state apparatus. Indeed, lesbian women were often committed to psychiatric hospitals for "treatment"

(usually with psychotropic drugs and/or electroshock therapy). (Amnesty International USA 1994; Gessen 1994)

28. Even the landmark studies of sexual behavior in American males (Kinsey, Pomeroy, & Martin 1948) and females (Kinsey, Pomeroy, Martin, & Gebhard 1953), which included a sub-focus on homosexuality, were not taken from a random sample. Although their findings have been often (mis)read as being generalizable to the U.S. population as a whole, they cannot claim to be statistically representative. Comparing the results of these studies with the results of mine is particularly apt, it seems to me, because these studies were conducted at a time in which the American homosexual subculture was at a similar (uninstitutionalized) state of subcultural development.

> Society establishes the means of categorizing persons and the complement of attributes felt to be ordinary and natural for members of each of these categories. Social settings establish the categories of persons likely to be encountered there. The routines of social intercourse in established settings allow us to deal with anticipated others without special attention or thought. When a stranger comes into our presence, then, first appearances are likely to enable us to anticipate his category and attributes, his "social identity" ...
>
> Erving Goffman,
> *Stigma: Notes on the Management of Spoiled Identity*
> p.2.

Chapter Three
Individual-Level Institutions of Soviet Gay Identity

HOW IS IT THAT SOME PEOPLE ARE HOMOSEXUAL? THIS IS A QUESTION ASKED countless times in the 130 years since this term for individuals with a clear and persistent sexual interest in others of the same sex was coined in 1869 by Kertbeny.[1] (Bullough 1976:637; Dynes 1987:13; Greenberg 1988:409) It has probably been asked throughout much of human history in one form or another, using other terms such as "sodomite," "pederast," "bugger," "pervert," "invert," "gay," "faggot," "queer," "sissy," and "Molly" (or the equivalent slang terms in other languages). To date, the question has not been definitively answered in scientific terms—not by genetics, biology, physiology, psychiatry, psychology, or sociology. Speculatively, homosexuality tends to be seen in pairs of incompatible ways: as "sexual orientation" versus "sexual preference"; as a part of one's essence, or "being," versus a socially constructed set of activities which one can be socialized into doing; and, ultimately, as determined by "nature" or "nurture." The origin(s) and cause(s) of homosexuality are puzzles that will not be resolved in this book either.

Rather, since being homosexual commonly involves an individual's self-identification as such (as well as identification of the individual by others as homosexual), it is more expedient to focus on defining "homosexual identity" and examining its relation to Soviet homosexuals. Homosexual identity is an important and incontrovertible manifestation of homosexuality as a phenomenon,[2] whether homosexuality is, in fact, determined either by bio-chemical (genetic or hormonal) influences or by socio-psychological factors. In this chapter, I will first explicate just what the social institution of "identity" is. This will involve differentiating between the prerequisites of identity and its various aspects, and then delineating the forms that identity can take. Then I consider a popular explanation of how homosexual identities may be formed and describe what can be termed "Soviet gay identity."

I. DEFINING IDENTITY AND IDENTIFICATION

Unfortunately, even deft sidestepping of the "nature versus nurture" controversy by focusing on identity does not provide an unambiguous basis for analysis of homosexual identity (Soviet or otherwise) for, as Troiden (1988:3) points out:

> Theorists disagree sharply about the nature and meaning of homosexual identities. Do homosexual identities represent a confusion of being with doing, the mistaken belief that one is what one does, the equation of the entire self with one form of behavior? Do homosexual identities represent one of several major interests constructed socially and defined as reflecting essential facets of personality? Are homosexual identities inevitable, unambiguous outgrowths of a specific kind of sexual orientation present at birth, the outcroppings of an essential, inherent, and inescapable facet of personality?

There are several sources for this confusion about what homosexual identity is. To be sure, it is partly a result of the persistent uncertainty and ardent controversy over competing conceptualizations of homosexuality itself. However, a substantial amount of the disagreement over what constitutes homosexual identity stems instead from imprecise use of the term "identity"—both in common practice and in scholarly works (Cass 1983, 1984; Troiden 1984). Both theoretical and empirical scholarship have suffered from this lack of definitional clarity, some serious consequences of which I will address straightaway.

A. Prerequisites for Identity

Troiden (1988:1-2) described a set of preconditions he considered necessary for the assumption of any social identity (with special reference to homosexual identity):

> People are not born with perceptions of themselves as homosexual, ambisexual (bisexual), or heterosexual. Before they can identify themselves in terms of a social condition or category, they must learn that a social category representing the activity or feeling exists (e.g., homosexual preferences or homosexual behavior); discover that other people occupy the social category (e.g., homosexuals exist as a group); and perceive that their own socially constructed needs and interests are more similar to those of persons who occupy that social category than they are different.

This all seems simple and true, *prima facie*. As awareness is logically prior, one cannot identify with a social group or category which is unknown to him or her. It is also clear that identification with a group of people will not occur if one does not perceive a similarity to them. Yet, there are at least three problems here.

First, similarity is not a sufficient basis for self-identification. Identity is not just a state of being like someone else in some way, but of being exactly like, or identical to, him or her in that respect. In relation to a group, it means being one of them. This is a condition for defining identification more stringent than that applied in common practice, but one to which I believe it is well to adhere. Erroneously, people say: *"I really identify with him/her. I've been in a similar situation myself.,"* when what they really mean is that they sympathize or empathize with the individual. Truly to identify, one would have to assert being in a position not just similar, but identical to that of the person to whom one is comparing oneself. Many people of either gender can sympathize with a woman who is beaten by her husband, for instance, but only another (woman) in that same situation can identify (herself) as a "battered wife."[3]

Second, it is also problematic to define the "discovery that other people occupy a social category" as a prerequisite for identification with that category. It overstates the case. Although it does seem clear that in order to identify with someone or as some thing one must relate oneself to a recognized social category or group, this point was already made by explaining that one "must learn that a social category representing the activity or feeling exists" in order to identify him or herself as a member of that category. There are numerous ways individuals can find out that a socially-defined category or group exists without actually having someone who embodies the category as an example. Many people come to identify themselves with fictional characters, for instance, which cannot be said to exist except in the novels, plays, and films they inhabit. Socially stigmatized categories, since they are not likely to be disclosed easily or often, are especially likely to be learned of through written, verbal, or visual depictions, which also are likely to convey negative cultural attitudes and stereotypes, for that is how the stigma is maintained. (Goffman 1963; Adam 1978) It is not a "living, breathing example" then, but the very idea of a social category or group that allows individuals to identify themselves as that particular kind of person. Knowing (of) actual incumbents in the category cannot be required to make such a judgment.

Third, it is an additional problem of overstatement to insist that "perceiving one's own socially constructed needs and interests as more similar to those of persons who occupy that social category than they are different" is a precondition for identification. The act of comparing one's own situation to that of others is certainly required for identification to take place, but the perception of similarity (actually, **identity**) that may result from such comparison cannot be a prerequisite. It is, in fact, the **determinant** of identification. Wherever they get the knowledge on which to base their judgment, when individuals recognize that a social category or group is defined by certain characteristics which they realize that they themselves possess, they are identifying with that category or group.

Restating Troiden's (1988) propositions more accurately then, the three basic preconditions for identification are: 1) recognizing that some condition applies to oneself; 2) learning that a category of people with that condition exists; and

3) comparing oneself to those in the category or group. If the comparison is apt, then identification results. The basic logic contained in this cognitive process is reflected in the following syllogism with reference to homosexual identity: 1) I am erotically attracted to others of the same sex; 2) people who are erotically attracted to others of the same sex are homosexuals; therefore, 3) I am homosexual.

B. Aspects of Identification

Having blithely equated similarity with identity, mistaken the power of an example for that of an idea, and confused comparability with the act of comparison, Troiden (1988:2) made himself vulnerable to additional misconceptions. Continuing with his enumeration of prerequisites for identification, he only made matters worse by declaring that:

> In addition, they [who would identify] must begin to identify with those included in the social category; decide that they qualify for membership in the social category on the basis of activities and feelings in various settings; elect to label themselves in terms of the social category (i.e., define themselves as "being" the social category in contexts where category membership is relevant); and incorporate and absorb these situationally linked identities into their self-concepts over time . . .

This involved two errors. The first was a lapse into tautology caused by stating that "beginning to identify . . ." is a precondition for identification. A thing cannot be a precursor for itself. The second error was to list the acts of "deciding that one qualifies as . . . ," "electing to label oneself in terms of . . . ," and "defining oneself as being [a member of] the social category [to which one feels a similarity]" as necessarily occurring before identification can take place. In fact, these are not prerequisites to identification. They are interrelated aspects of identification itself.

1. Identification as the Application of Labels

One of the confounding issues here is that of labeling. Many scholars of homosexual identity, especially those sociologists working in the traditions of symbolic interactionism and labeling theory (*conferre* Plummer 1975; Troiden 1979, 1988; Weeks 1985), see identity formation as "coming to label oneself as something," in this case, as a homosexual. Basically, they use the term "identity" and the verb "to identify" as synonyms for "label" and "to label." Yet, a label is not an identity; it is only a referent to an identity. This distinction may seem picayune, but it is not inconsequential. Without distinguishing between a label and its referent identity, one is apt to overlook the institutionalized nature of identities, for, although labels can be applied and denied at will, identities are not so easily taken on or shed.

A label can be applied honestly, wishfully, erroneously, facetiously, or in any manner of other ways which may or may not indicate that personal identification is actually taking place. Although identification requires at least some degree of acceptance of the designation, labeling is surely not always a willing act of self-definition. Sometimes, it is an act of imposing, or attempting to impose, an identity on someone, but that label may or may not be recognized as appropriate by others who are witness to the labeling. That is, a label may or may not be accepted as truly "fitting" the individual(s) being labeled.

Name-calling is one obvious example of this disputable aspect of labeling. The epithets that people hurl at one another (*"You creep!," "Liar!," "Faggot! Hey, look at the sissy faggot!"*) are unabashed attempts to label someone in a negative way. People do this, often in public, in order to fend off someone they feel is (about to be) harming them or to point out someone from whom they wish to distinguish themselves. One aspect of identification, then, can be thought of as the institutionalized application of a label. It is the act of categorizing or defining someone or something (signified by a label) by designating them as such in certain groups or circumstances. Here Berger & Luckmann's (1966) treatise on institutionalization is especially pertinent. We say: "*I am white.*" or "*She is a model.*" and—if only for the moment and only in one respect—we have identified someone **as that thing.**

Another example is the legal system in a country, which is charged with the task of determining whether the label alleged by an accuser ("thief," "rapist," *et cetera*) is indeed applicable to a particular individual. Until this is determined, the individual is temporarily labeled the "accused" or the "defendant." For the trial period, everyone involved agrees that these temporary labels, at least, do apply. Whether such attempts at labeling are successful in producing a lasting identity for the individual in question—*id est,* whether the label "sticks"—is often not just a matter of public acceptance and use of the designation as found appropriate by the jury in a trial or by onlookers who witness a name-calling incident. It also requires the (subsequent) self-perception by the individual so labeled that s/he is, indeed, such a person. As most wrongly-convicted felons are eager to point out, for instance, though they may be successfully labeled "convicted criminals" by a prosecuting attorney as determined by a jury, they do not identify themselves as "criminals"—that is, as actual perpetrators of a crime.

2. Identification as both "Being" and "Doing"

Troiden (1979, 1988), among others, has argued that a critical error which leads to the confusion about (homosexual) identity is the equation of "being" with "doing." Such theorists maintain that not enough attention is paid to the distinction between what one is (social identity) and what one does (social behavior). Recall Troiden's (1988:3) pointed distrust of defining homosexuality as a thing that one "is": "Do homosexual identities represent *a confusion* of being with doing, *the mistaken belief* that one is what one does, the equation of the entire self with one form of behavior?" *(emphases added)*.

While there is something to be learned from this distinction between what one is and what one does, this dismissive line of argumentation strikes me as rather disingenuous. After all, many identities are formed around behavioral patterns. One would not say that to label someone a "dancer," for instance, is to confuse that person's "being" with his/her "doing," or that it is overstated to propose that being a "dancer" could be one's primary identity because it is only one aspect of his/her behavior. In modern society, we typically give much weight to people's profession or avocation as an identifying aspect of their personality. In fact, we tend to see their (chosen) profession as an important part of what it means to be "them." Sexuality is a similarly strong behavioral identifier.

Weinberg (1978) takes a more illuminating stance in attempting to understand just what it is that allows people to "convert doing to being" and why they might desire to do so, rather than disparaging the equation of behavior and identity. His (Weinberg 1978:154) research finding is as follows:

> The social context became a critical factor in the development of a homosexual self-identity for a number of the men [in the interview sample who had engaged in homosexual activity before they came to label themselves homosexual (usually in mid-to-late childhood)] when they began to perceive it changing.... They began to examine their own motivations and to compare and contrast them with those of their friends. "Appropriate" sexual interest was now defined by their friends as sexual interest in girls rather than in boys.... These changes caused the[se] respondents to reevaluate the meaning of their own feelings and behavior.

In fact, far from being dubious about equating doing and being, he (Weinberg 1978:155) contends that: "The stability of a person's conception of what he 'is' depends upon the stability of his assumptions about the relationship between what one is and what one does."

As regards the mechanism of such reevaluation in producing a homosexual identity for individuals, Weinberg (1978:154–155) notes:

> If, within his reference world, the behavior that "goes with" being a certain sort of person changes in ways that are difficult to reconcile with these assumptions [about the meaning of their feelings and behaviors], he is led to reassess these assumptions and reconsider his conception of what he is.
>
> ...
>
> ... it would be difficult for a person to think of himself as a homosexual if none of the other males with whom he is having sexual relations perceive either

their behavior or themselves to be homosexual. If, however, one comes into contact with another male or group of males who consider themselves to be gay, one may develop a very different definition of the situation, with consequent implications for one's own sexual identity."

At risk of over-quoting him, I reproduce Weinberg's (1978:155–156) conclusion on this matter for it is directly relevant here:

> Upon examining the factors that caused many of the men to reevaluate their sexual behavior and themselves in terms of homosexuality, it was found that coming into some sort of sustained contact with gay people was very important in changing the meaning of their feelings, fantasies, and behaviors and in helping them to make the link between "doing" and "being." Other homosexuals enabled the men to develop less negatively evaluative definitions of homosexuality and to learn what the gay community would regard as more accurate ideas about homosexuals. This contact, however, usually came well after the onset of self-suspicion [of their homosexuality]. The men who felt that gay people had facilitated the development of their homosexual self-identities indicated that other homosexuals had done this by providing a setting within which they felt more comfortable, accepted for themselves, and happier than they had ever felt when they were among straight people, by serving as positive role models for them, by breaking down the sense of "difference" and isolation they had felt while they were growing up, by aiding some of them in the development of "gay pride," and, in general, by giving them supportive feedback.

II. THE EXTENT AND TYPES OF IDENTIFICATION

There are at least four related, behavioral elements of identification which relate to the extent or range of identification and distinguishing among them is critical to this discussion of homosexual identity. First, individuals identify themselves to themselves in terms of their group or category memberships (self-identification). Second, they identify themselves to others, who are not members of their own category (self-(re)presentation). Third, they identify other people as not belonging to the category of their membership (identification of others). Fourth, individuals identify others as fellow category members (identification of one another). In contemporary (polite) English slang, homosexuals are identified as "gay," that is, as belonging to the category of "gay people." The act of self-identification as homosexual in English gay slang is specially termed "coming out (of the closet)," probably a reference to the age-old quip that refers to a family's eccentric or immoral members as "skeletons in the closet." The term is also used, though, in each of the three other ways. In relation to my respondents' experiences with identification, I will employ each of these uses.

The language of inter-ethnic communication in the USSR was, by force and fiat, Russian. Although Soviet homosexuals of the same ethnicity and linguistic group almost certainly had at least some interaction in their native language, for Russians, for those who had been thoroughly "Russified," and for inter-ethnic homosexual (social and sexual) interaction, Russian was the *lingua franca* of the Soviet gay and lesbian population as well. The language of the Soviet gay subculture was borrowed, in part, from that of the world of prostitution and from the world of the prison labor camp. Козловский (1986) has made a good study of Russian gay slang, which I could not match here, but it is important to define a few key terms.

In Russian, the slang term for homosexuals is *"golubóy"* ("голубой"), which, literally, means "light blue." This may have come from the Bolshevik contention that homosexuality was "unproletarian," a bourgeois vice held over from tsarist times.[4] The Soviet gay slang term most often used to describe homosexuals as a category was not a simple application of the term for homosexuals, as in the West. Though one could say "gay people" in Russian ("голубые люди") and be clearly understood, Soviet homosexuals identified one another as "ours" or "one of us" ("наш", "наши.") Other terms were used occasionally, both for comic effect and for secrecy when speaking in public. One such moniker was "a member of our trade union" ("член нашего профсоюза"), or, in shortened form, "a trade-unionist" ("профсоюзный"). Thus, while individual gay people did exist in their infinite variety, they were basically undifferentiated, existing only in the general concept of "we."

Interestingly, there is no direct equivalent in Russian gay slang for "coming out," which immediately gives one pause when assessing the existence and strength of gay identity in the USSR. While there is a phrase that is sometimes regarded as a correlate: "to come out from under the floorboards" ("Выйти из подполя"), it is not widely used and has connotations of insanity by association with Fyódor Dostoyévsky's famous novel *Notes from the Underground* (actually, better translated as, "Notes from Under the Floorboards": из подполя).

A. "Coming Out" to Oneself

Self-categorization is one part of homosexual identification: the personal recognition of one's gay identity. This is signified by the realization: *"I am homosexual."* Nearly three- fourths (72.5%) of the men in my sample identified themselves as "gay" ("голубой"), and this should not be surprising, since involvement in gay-related activities and acquaintance with other homosexuals were among the criteria I used for screening respondents. I was concerned, however, not to exclude individuals from the study who lacked a homosexual identity, and I therefore made the appeal for "gay men, lesbians, and bisexuals" to participate in my research, and there was variation on this measure. (See Table 3.1)

Table 3.1: Sexuality Self-Identification of Respondents.*

	N of Respondents	% of Respondents
"Gay"	261	72.5%
"Gay" & "Bisexual"	4	1.1%
"Bisexual"	87	24.2%
"Straight"	1	.3%
Other**	7	1.9%

*N=360
** Of those who chose this option, three failed to note what "other" identity they might have, two indicated that they did not know how to identify themselves, one reported a "combined" [смешанный] identity, and one wrote-in that he was "homosexual."

The confusion among some respondents about the sexuality category to which they belong is interesting, but ambiguous. It may be that these individuals were as yet unsure of how to identify themselves in terms of their sexuality (or "uncommitted" to any particular "moral career" sexually), though they did understand the categories from which they were asked to choose. Alternatively, the categories "gay," "bisexual," and "straight" may not be sufficiently institutionalized in the Soviet homosexual subculture for respondents to define themselves satisfactorily with these terms.

B. "Coming Out" to (Non-Gay) Others

The second element of homosexual self-identification, representing oneself to others, means disclosing one's homosexuality. "Coming out" to others is an anxiety-producing event in any society which disvalues and denigrates homosexuals. It involves taking great risks: of rejection, harassment, physical violence, and even official punishment or "treatment" where homosexual sex is forbidden by law or diagnosed as unhealthy by medical practitioners. As all of these consequences were common in the Soviet Union (see Chapter Five), I expected only a small number of my subjects would be "out" to others who were not also homosexual; that is, I supposed it would not be common that someone else could identify them as having a homosexual identity.

Yet, among my respondents, a surprisingly large proportion (64.4%) was "out" to someone and of these who were known to be homosexual by others, most (68.1%) were "out" to a ("straight") friend. Relatives were less, but still often aware of respondents' homosexuality (41.7%), while coworkers and neighbors were least likely to be able to identify the respondent as homosexual. (See Table 3.2.)

Table 3.2: Category of Persons to whom Respondent's
Homosexual Identity is Known.*

Friend(s)	68.1%
Relative(s)	41.7%
Co-worker(s)	28.5%
Neighbor(s)	11.9%

* N=235

Significantly, the relative who could most often identify a respondent as homosexual was his mother (37.4%). Respondents were "out" to their fathers, sisters, and brothers in about equally unlikely proportions (15–16%). (See Table 3.3.)

Table 3.3: Type of Relative to whom Respondent's Homosexual
Identity is Known.*

Mother	37.4%
Father	15.3%
Sister(s)	16.6%
Brother(s)	15.3%

* N=235

Furthermore, it is somewhat surprising that most respondents who were "out" to someone (61.5%) said that those others learned of their homosexuality because they themselves disclosed it. It was far less common that others knew respondents were homosexual because they noticed it themselves or happened to find out about it in some way. (See Table 3.4.)

Table 3.4: Ways in which Respondent's Homosexual Identity
became Known to Others.*

Respondent Told Them	61.5%
They Noticed It Themselves	28.1%
They Found Out Accidentally	22.2%
Some Other Way	14.9%

* N=221

When Soviet homosexuals did come out to heterosexual others in this way, the language they used to describe this was that they "told (all) about themselves" ("рассказал (всё) про себе").

C. "Coming Out" to Each Other

Finding one another is an important task for gay men and lesbians in any culture, since the heterosexual majority of the population does not typically allow for open expression of homosexual interests. What is more, heterosexual oppression in society means that gay men and lesbians are usually punished in some way for such self-expressions and therefore must be careful to hide their interests and camouflage any and all homosexual contacts. This means that homosexuals need to be able to distinguish between homosexual and heterosexual others and they have had to develop a whole host of conventions of speech, dress, and behavior as a means of safely identifying each other and of making contact in ways that would not generally be obvious to the uninitiated (*id est*, heterosexuals). Although gay people often feel that they do not know how it is that they recognize one another in public or in situations that are not predefined as "gay events," there are both linguistic and gestural cues that they have been socialized to recognize as signals of others' homosexuality and, in certain instances, as indicators of sexual interest (Delph 1978). This was no less true in the USSR than in the West.

In Russian gay slang, those to beware of (heterosexuals) are called "naturals." The native Russian word for that, "*yestyéstvyenniy*" ("естественный"), is not used, however. Instead, Russian homosexuals use the borrowed, foreign word "*naturál*" ("натураль") or, in the plural, "*naturáli*" ("натурали") to identify "straight" people.

As I have been arguing, to self-identify as someone who belongs to a social group or category is to assert one's possession of the characteristics which define that social category. Thus, to identify someone else as (also) being homosexual and to reveal one's own gay identity to that other is to assert a commonality of social identity.

III. THE DEVELOPMENT OF HOMOSEXUAL IDENTITIES

Identifying oneself as homosexual is taking the risk of ostracism by others in society. As Goffman (1963:2–3) put it:

> While the stranger is present before us [whom we assumed, without knowing, has a certain "virtual" identity], evidence can arise of his possessing an attribute that makes him different from others in the category of persons available for him to be, and of a less desirable kind—in the extreme, a person who is quite thoroughly bad, or dangerous, or weak. He is thus reduced in our minds from a whole and usual person to a tainted, discounted one. Such an attribute is a stigma, especially when its discrediting effect is very extensive..... It constitutes a special discrepancy between virtual and actual social identity.'

In order to identify oneself with such a stigmatized group as homosexuals, barriers erected by socially-sanctioned discrimination against homosexuals and enforced through lavish social recrimination must be surmounted or breached. Without support and encouragement from others, doing so is unlikely. The pulls and pushes to engage (more fully) in homosexual behavior and in other social activities of the gay and lesbian subculture are many and varied, and even the terminology used to describe the process of "coming out" is inconsistent and problematic.

Over the last quarter century, several scholars have formulated models of homosexual identity "development" (Cain 1991; Cox & Gallois 1996), "formation" (Cass 1979; Minton & McDonald 1983–1984; Troiden 1988), "assumption," "acquisition" (Troiden 1979), "adoption" (Dank 1971; Weinberg & Williams 1974; Plummer 1975), or even "redocumentation" (Weinberg 1978). Most often, these terms are used interchangeably. In their connotations, however, these designations imply different things about the role of individual agency in self-identification. To discuss identity "development" implies that individuals are not at the helm of this process. It is as if first an identity is developed around some personal or social characteristic or behavior and then seen to apply to the individual, much as a girl going through the physiological changes of puberty "develops" breasts. She is not said to be "forming" them or "growing" them; they may be said to be "forming" or "growing" *of their own accord*. On the other hand, identity "formation" suggests that the individual does have the power to choose, or at least to control, self-identification. Identity "acquisition" goes further to imply that the individual actively seeks to take on an identity, as if s/he is aware that one can define and redefine oneself at will. Finally, to "assume" or "adopt" an identity implies that the identification is somehow illegitimate, or at least borrowed, that is, not innate or natural for the individual.

It is not my intention to argue that one or another of these terms better suits identification in general or homosexual identification specifically. It seems to me that each of these designations with its accompanying connotations is applicable to the description of identities and identification in some instances, and not in others.

I cannot say whether my respondents traverse a complicated path toward homosexual self-identification similar to that described by Cass (1979) because my survey data do not lend themselves to detailed, qualitative analysis of the psycho-emotional aspects of homosexual identity formation she possessed based on insights gained from her 20 years of clinical psychological practice. However, Weinberg's (1978) model of (male) homosexual identity formation can be tested in my sample, since it relies more on behavioral milestones than on psychodynamic issues to discern patterns of identity formation.

Weinberg (1978) employed three variables to delineate the path his study subjects took in reaching their present identity as homosexual: the age at which the individual first engaged in homosexual activity, the age at which he first suspected himself of being homosexual, and the age at which he labeled himself a homosexual. He discerned four patterns or sub-patterns among these variables and related these to alternative "types" of homosexual men.

The first pattern, of which he found three variant sub-patterns, consists of men who had engaged in homosexual behavior *before* labeling themselves homosexuals. Characteristic of the first variant of this pattern was childhood or early adolescent onset of homosexual activity (at a mean age of 11.4 years), suspicion of oneself as homosexual in the mid-teenage years (average age 15.2 years), and labeling of oneself as a homosexual in the late teenage years or in the early twenties (at 20.2 years old, on average). This was the most common order of the variables among his subjects and he termed these "ESL homosexuals" for the chronological sequence in which the three milestones were reached—"E" for engaging in homosexual behavior first, then "S" for suspecting themselves of being homosexuals, and "L" for labeling themselves as such last.

Those evincing the second variant of this pattern, in which he placed only two of his thirty subjects, had also had early homosexual activity (at ages 8 and 9) and had also labeled themselves homosexual at about the age of majority (18 and 19 years old). They did so, however, according to Weinberg (1978:148), "without passing through an intermediate self-suspicion stage. These men are EL-type homosexuals."

The third variant, or sub-pattern, which was the second-most common, consisted of men who had suspected themselves of being homosexual in their mid-teenage years but first engaged in homosexual activity and then labeled themselves homosexuals in their late teens or early twenties. This is the "SEL" pattern. Together, these three sub-patterns accounted for almost all of the study subjects (28 of 30).

Finally, the other pattern (without any variants) was made up of two men who had first engaged in homosexual behavior after labeling themselves homosexuals. They suspected themselves of being homosexual at a young age (13 years old) but labeled themselves as homosexuals and then engaged in homosexual activity for the first time only at the ages of 19 and 22. These two subjects with the "SLE" pattern were dubbed "homosexual virgins" (Weinberg 1978:149). (See Table 3.5.)

Table 3.5: Age at which Each Stage in Weinberg's (1978) Process of Homosexual Identity Formation was Reached, Mean Age [Age Range]*

	Engage in homosexual behavior before Labeling self homosexual (E<L)			Label self homosexual before Engaging in homosexual behavior (L<E)
	ESL N=17	EL N=2	SEL N=9	SLE N=2
Engage in homosexual behavior(E)	11.4 [**]	8.5 [8, 9]	18.9 [15-25]	21.5 [20, 23]
Suspect self to be homosexual(S)	15.2 [**]		16.6 [13-23]	13.0 [13]
Label self homosexual (L)	20.2 [**]	18.5 [18, 19]	19.7 [16-25]	20.5 [19, 22]

*Adapted from Weinberg (1978:149).
** Not reported.

Clearly, Weinberg (1978) considered the two general patterns described to be distinct because two of his three variables, age at first engaging in homosexual behavior (E) and age at which the men labeled themselves homosexuals (L), were in opposing sequence. To me, a different pattern in the data is more instructive.

Table 3.6: Age at which Each Stage in Weinberg's (1978) Process of Homosexual Identity Formation was Reached, Mean Age [Age Range], *Revised**

	Engage in homosexual behavior before Suspecting self homosexual (E<S)		Suspect self homosexual before Engaging in homosexual behavior (S<E)	
	ESL N=17	EL N=2	SEL N=9	SLE N=2
Engage in homosexual behavior(E)	11.4 [**]	8.5 [8, 9]	18.9 [15-25]	21.5 [20, 23]
Suspect self to be homosexual(S)	15.2 [**]		16.6 [13-23]	13.0 [13]
Label self homosexual (L)	20.2 [**]	18.5 [18, 19]	19.7 [16-25]	20.5 [19, 22]

*Adapted from Weinberg (1978:149).
** Not reported.

If one considers his third variable, age at which the men first suspected themselves of being homosexual, to be more important than age at self-labeling, Table 3.5 would look only slightly different, yet the conclusions one draws from the data would be quite discordant. Such a change would simply entail grouping the four patterns differently. "ESL homosexuals," together with those evincing the EL variant,[5] would be contrasted with the SEL variant and the SLE pattern as a second group. By so doing, between-group means for each of the variables would then be more aligned, chronologically, than they are in the original classification. (See Table 3.6.)

Those research subjects who had engaged in homosexual activity before suspecting themselves of being homosexual (those for whom E<S) had their first homosexual experience at quite a young age: when they were around 10 years old, on average. Conversely, those who suspected themselves of a tendency toward homosexuality prior to engaging in homosexual behavior (for whom S<E) had their first homosexual experience relatively late: at about 20 years of age. Yet, despite this difference, all subjects who recalled having suspected themselves of being homosexual did so at about the same age—in the early-to-middle teenage years—whether they had their first homosexual experience before or afterward. Similarly, all respondents also labeled themselves homosexual at about the same age—in their mid-to-late teens or early-to-middle twenties. The two groups are also more even in number (for E<S, N=19; for S<E, N=11), which is intriguing. In essence, these revised groupings better depict the patterns of stages traversed in the process of homosexual identity formation. They are more like each other than are the patterns of the two groups that Weinberg (1978) had constructed

It seems that the likely age at which people gain an understanding of sexuality (usually loosely correlated with age at puberty—mid-teens) is about the age at which all of Weinberg's (1978) subjects suspected themselves of being homosexual. The implication I draw from this is that self-suspicion of homosexuality is a more reliable indicator of subsequent self-labeling as homosexual than is actual homosexual behavior.[6]

A similar pattern is borne out in my survey data, though my variables differed slightly from Weinberg's (1978)[7] and not two but three categories emerge from the analysis. (See Table 3.7.) On average, four years lapsed between first engaging in homosexual behavior and later recognizing the tendency toward homosexuality among those of my respondents who had "played around" sexually (the "ESL homosexuals," in Weinberg's terminology). The same length of time—and indeed the same age range—separated the recognition of homosexual tendency (at an average age of 13.6 years) and the first homosexual behavior (at 17.9 years, on average) among those who recognized their homosexual tendencies before engaging in any homosexual activity.

The number of men falling into each of these three categories is roughly equal in my study, whereas for Weinberg (1978) the number of cases was much more uneven. This disparity between the two studies could be due to actual differences between gay men in the United States and the Soviet Union; it could be due to the difference in time frame between the two studies; or it could result from a plethora of other causes, including his very small sample size (N=30). Though I cannot claim representativeness in my sample, it seems likely given my much larger sample size (N=347 for this question), that the patterns of homosexual identity acquisition are much more evenly distributed among homosexual men than he found. Determining the validity of this assertion, however, would require access to Weinberg's (1978) data, which I did not have.

Table 3.7: Age at which Respondents First Engaged in Homosexual Activity and First Recognized their Homosexual Tendencies, Mean Age (standard deviation) [Age Range]

	Engage in homosexual behavior first (E<R) (Weinberg ESL/EL) N=117	Engage in homosexual behavior & recognize tendency at same age (E=R) N=108	Recognize homosexual tendency first (R<E) (Weinberg SEL/SLE) N=122
Engage in homosexual behavior* (E)	13.3 (s.d.=4.0 years) [5–25]	16.6 (s.d.=4.2 years) [5–26]	17.9 (s.d.=4.4 years) [8–33]
Recognize own homosexual tendency** (R)	17.4 (s.d.=3.5 years) [9–30]	16.6 (s.d.=4.2 years) [5–26]	13.6 (s.d.=4.2 years) [5–27]

* One-Way Analysis of Variance: F-ratio=38.2414, p=.0000; Mean age for E<R group significantly different (at p≤.05) than that for the other two groups by Scheffe Procedure, all three group means significantly different by Tukey HSD Test
** One-Way Analysis of Variance: F-ratio=30.9546, p=.0000; Mean age for R<E group significantly different (at p≤.05) than that for the other two groups, by both Scheffe Procedure and Tukey HSD Test

Though quite interesting, it is not very important for the purpose of this analysis, that the age at which my Soviet homosexual respondents ultimately identified or labeled themselves as homosexuals be determined. Rather, what is important is the demonstration that the process(es) elsewhere found to lead to such identification were, indeed, taking place among this population. This is so because possessing a homosexual identity will be required before Soviet gay men and lesbians can improve their situation and develop more and better opportunities for meeting one another. Yet, identification alone will not be enough for them to engineer a social environment in which homosexual community could be developed. Homosexual identity is either expressed or internally repressed within a broader context, and it is to this social and physical environment that I turn next in examining the gay and lesbian subculture of the Soviet Union. In the next chapter, I will show how the social-geography of the Soviet gay world ordered and controlled the forces with which Soviet gay men and lesbians had to struggle throughout the course of their lives.

NOTES

1. Kertbeny was an alias of Karoly Maria Benkert. (Dynes 1987:13)

2. I am not arguing here that a homosexual identity is always a concomitant of homosexuality. Indeed, it is well known that not all of those who engage in homosexual activity think of themselves as homosexuals (Humphreys 1970; Troiden & Goode 1975). It is also clear that not all individuals who have feelings of homosexual attraction or all those who identify themselves as homosexuals choose to act on that basis. I only mean to assert here that the construct "homosexual identity"—where it exists—is the cognitive element of homosexuality. (Same-sex erotic attraction and sexual activity, and same-sex romantic attraction and coupling behavior are, respectively, its behavioral and affective components.)

3. For this reason, it is not meaningful to say that one "identifies" with someone who has, say, tripped on a crack in a sidewalk and fallen down. While the situational comparison one wishes to make may well be apt, the experience is so nearly universal that there is no recognized social category of "sidewalk fallers"—unless one asserts that the person who has fallen is a "klutz" and is admitting to having the same frequent difficulty in any matter of bodily coordination.

4. What term was used in the tsarist Russian Empire is unclear. At least one prerevolutionary watcher of homosexuals (Розановъ 1913 [1990]) used the phrase "people of the moonlight" ("люди лунного света").

5. The decision whether to include the two men with an EL pattern of stages in the process of homosexual identity formation in a group with those with the ESL pattern or whether to consider them a group apart from all others hinges on whether one fully believes Weinberg's (1978) contention that these men passed through no stage of self-suspicion as homosexual, no matter how briefly. To believe that they constitute a truly separate category, one would have to agree that they must have simultaneously understood that they fit the category of homosexual men and accepted the label as such immediately upon first hearing of the concept. Though not impossible, such an occurrence must be exceedingly rare, as it requires a very decisive and unquestioning acceptance of a theretofore unknown personal categorization—an "instant identification," as it were. I am inclined to include the men with an EL pattern in the ESL group, interpreting their true response to learning of such a thing as homosexuality more likely to be something akin to: "Oh, so that's what I am! Now it all makes sense to me!" This would indicate at least some consideration of the self as different from others on these grounds prior to hearing that a homosexual identity exists, but that the category itself and its label were simply unknown.

6. As for men who had suspected themselves of being homosexual, or who had homosexual experiences, but did not (at a prior time or subsequently) label themselves homosexual (develop a homosexual identity), nothing can be said here. Such a "control group" was not used in Weinberg's (1978) research.

7. Rather than asking respondents about the age they suspected themselves of being homosexual, I solicited information about the age at which they recognized their own homosexual tendencies, which, I believe, is a very similar question. Unfortunately, I did not

ask my respondents about the age at which they first labeled themselves homosexual, so data on that point are unavailable.

> We play out our lives in space as well as time, and the places we inhabit become rich with social meanings. Locality itself is a proper element of social structure and plays an important part in shaping the content of human relationships.
>
> James C. McCann,
> "Human Ecology"
> in: *Society Today, Second Edition,* p. 419

Chapter Four
Ecological-Level Institutions as Soviet Gay Places

PAINTING A GOOD LIKENESS OF THE SOCIAL ENVIRONMENT AND GEOGRAPHIC "landscape" in which Soviet gay men and lesbians lived is as crucial to understanding them and their lives as is appreciating the nuances of their gay identities, since social-ecological factors formed the boundaries of the social space which Soviet homosexuals inhabited and shaped the contingencies with which they had to contend. The array and arrangement of these social-ecological institutions limited or allowed the formation of intimate relationships, friendship groups, and subcultural institutions among Soviet homosexuals. By influencing the nature and extent of such relations, the social ecology of the Soviet gay and lesbian world affected the level of institutional development that could be achieved in the gay and lesbian subculture as a whole.

No group in any society is ensconced only in unique ecological conditions, so discussion of social-environmental institutions in the Soviet gay and lesbian world will be accompanied by description of the "lay of the land" in Soviet society generally. The ecological institutions of the Soviet gay world had their precedents and patterns in the Soviet context, and in many ways the forms and features of the gay and lesbian social ecology mimicked those of the Soviet Union. On the other hand, as Soviet society did not afford gay men and lesbians the same openness as it did heterosexuals, in the Soviet Union (as in the West) gay places and mobility patterns differed somewhat from those of their heterosexual counterparts. The extent of this difference was determined, in part, by social and political constraints on where and when they would be able to express themselves in a manner consistent with their homosexual identities or where and when such expression was too dangerous.

Harsh anti-sodomy statutes and an especially oppressive social climate in the Soviet Union (as I will discuss in Chapter Five) made all expressions of homosexual interest illegal and/or acutely negatively sanctioned there. In addition, the generally difficult living conditions and restrictions on personal mobility imposed by the governing Communist Party often made gathering spontaneously problematic for gay men and lesbians in the USSR—as it was for everyone. Gathering publicly in an organized and planned fashion was almost always out of the question. Yet, despite the antagonistic socio-legal conditions under which they were constrained to live, Soviet homosexuals were able to carve out some special places for themselves. In fact, a relatively predictable set of physical locations served as havens in which they could clandestinely express their homosexual interests.

Two general categories of locale mark the endpoints on a spectrum of places that served as safe meeting spaces for Soviet gay men and lesbians and developed into geographical institutions for this population—at least during the last years of Soviet rule. On the one hand, **public places** were tentatively but regularly taken over for the special purpose of socializing, gay "cruising,"[1] or even as places for anonymous homosexual encounters. On the other hand, **private places** served as more constant and secure havens for homosexuals to get together with friends and lovers, where they could be alone and out of sight of others—and, therefore, generally safe from the repression of heterosexual society and Soviet law.

Gay meeting places that occupy intermediate positions on this spectrum combined some of the characteristics of public places with other features of private ones. Homosexuals were allowed to gather for both social and sexual interaction at **partly-public places** largely because managers or workers at an establishment tolerated their presence and activities. They also borrowed or rented **semi-private places** for specific gay-related events or homosexual liaisons.

The fact that these meeting places were located all across this public/private continuum might suggest that institutionalized opportunities for Soviet gays and lesbians to gather were not much different from those available to homosexuals in modern Western countries. However, the number and variety of such places amenable to homosexual encounters was not nearly so great in the Soviet Union as in the West, nor could the institutional basis of the Soviet gay world be so solidly established there as in Western countries for legal and social reasons. In stark contrast to the myriad safe and stable gay places created by and for Western homosexuals in gay recreational, cultural, social, economic, and political organizations, in the USSR the complete lack of any such organizations left individual gay and lesbian Soviets fending for themselves. They managed primarily by appropriating open, public spaces as places in which to make contact with one another, sometimes by fashioning workable private or semi-private places from whatever accommodations were available to them, and, more rarely, by subverting the official use of partly-public places to suit their special needs.

In this chapter, I will seek to illuminate the "social geography"[2] of gay life in the USSR first by drawing on information from my observational research. I will describe in some detail the layout and uses of those locations that were well-established enough to be considered geographic institutions, detailing the social arrangements each place fostered among Soviet gay men and lesbians and making historical references and cross-cultural comparisons where appropriate. After describing each place, I will present statistical data from my survey research to indicate the extent to which Soviet gay men and lesbians in my sample made use of each of these public, private, and semi-private or partly-public gay places for gathering and making one another's acquaintance. By providing this information, I hope to encourage readers to envision these places where Soviet gay men and lesbians gathered—the places they called "theirs" ("наши места"). To do so is, in effect, to "see" the "social space" they inhabited, the "landscape" of their separate and distinctive Soviet "gay world."

I. PUBLIC PLACES APPROPRIATED FOR GAY PURPOSES

Public places had to meet several criteria in order for them to be suitable to appropriation as gay meeting places. Most public places suitable for gay cruising in the USSR had to be centrally located and convenient to public transportation, since far fewer citizens of the Soviet Union had private means of transportation than is common in the West.[3] In the interest of safety, they also needed to provide a clear "cover" for homosexuals so that their presence at such places for a moderate length of time would not be suspect. Finally, to be suitable places for gay men and lesbians to gather, these public locales had to provide some measure of privacy for homosexual expression to take place there.

The open public places appropriated for gay purposes in the USSR included the well-established "cruising grounds" of certain public parks or city squares, public toilet facilities, transit stations, and secluded beaches. These kinds of open, public spaces are often among the most congested areas of a city by day, which fact allowed homosexuals, an "invisible minority," to "hide in plain sight." The transformation of these places into gay meeting places, though, usually occurred at times when they were not likely to be heavily utilized by heterosexuals, such as late in the evening and at night. This enhanced privacy there and diminished the chances of Soviet gays being observed by unsympathetic others.

A. The *"Pléshka"* ("Плешка") or Gay "Cruising Grounds"

The most common public place that gay men—and a few lesbians—congregated in the USSR was the *"pléshka."* Although literally this word means a "little bald spot," *pléshka* is the Russian gay slang term for an outdoor space known to homosexuals as a "cruisy" area. The *pléshka* was a place where Soviet gay men gathered in the evenings to meet friends or potential partners for sex, dating, or friendly comradeship. A "cruisy" area could be a large or a small public space, but it usually included a cruising "strip" (or *"panél"*: "панель")[4] on a busy city street for strolling, a nearby public park or city square with benches used as stopping points, and some hidden spaces useful for more private interaction. A description of the *pléshkas* in a few Soviet cities will give the reader a better idea of how the gay "cruising grounds" appeared to and were used by gay people there.

In Moscow, the *pléshka* was located in the very center of town, stretching along a main thoroughfare that carried motor traffic past some of the city's most important historical and government buildings, including the Kremlin. It was located in an area highly congested with pedestrians and motor traffic during the day as it contained the seat of government, the largest shopping district in the city (including Moscow's two largest department stores), three large hotels for foreigners, and the central telephone station, telegraph, and post office. Three subway lines converged at this location and it was a central transfer point for several bus and trolleybus routes. Millions of people passed through this part of town each day, and its centrality made it easily reachable by all who wished to go there.

The most active part of the Moscow "cruising grounds" was a small square with numerous park benches all sheltered by several large trees in front of the world-renowned Bolshóy Theater. This park was meant for "hanging out" in, and Soviet gays made good use of that fact. Most evenings one would encounter many gay men in this place (perhaps dozens over a period of several hours on warm summer nights) circling around, chatting, sitting for a time on the benches, getting acquainted with one another, and making their way home together for the night.

For years there was a vacant half-lot next to the square, thick with trees and bushes. Just around the corner was an alley with a few unlighted doorways, and there were many dimly-lit courtyard entrances to all of the buildings nearby. The overgrown lot and dark courtyards offered a certain amount of privacy, and from time to time served as places for more intimate interaction than was acceptable in the open, such as hugging and kissing. Men could sometimes even be seen skulking off there for a few minutes of "quickie" sex.

Extending down the avenue from the square was the gay "cruising strip," where gay men strolled alone or in groups to look each other over and get an idea of who was out for the evening. There were no obvious places to linger long there, though a bus stop did provide a place to stand for a while, and some denizens also made contact under the pretense of asking for directions. Frequently men would "bum a cigarette" (in Russian, "shoot for" a cigarette: "стрелять сигарету" or ask for a "light" (a "fire": "огонь") as a way of striking up conversation.

The *pléshka* in Leningrad (now again known by its original name: Saint Petersburg) was also located in the very center of the city, on the main avenue for commercial shopping. In the evenings and into the night, gay men could be found walking along the sidewalk pretending to do some window shopping at an arcade of shops and stalls that was the largest department store in town. There they would look one another over more intently than the merchandise displayed, make acquaintances, and perhaps arrange a sexual *rendezvous*.

Most of the cruising activity on the Leningrad *pléshka* took place along a less-traveled side-street that passed behind the department store and was less visible from the main thoroughfare. Conveniently, the building overhung the side-walk there, so that the "strip" was amenable for strolling in almost any weather. There were several recessed doorways and large pillars along the sidewalk into or behind which two men could step if they wished to share a brief kiss or some other expression of interest. Several phone booths also provided some, though very limited, privacy as well as a convenient excuse for tarrying there if a policeman should happen by. If men cruising on the Leningrad *pléshka* wanted the privacy to engage in even more unreserved erotic encounters, however, they had to cross the side street to another building that served as the warehouse and loading dock for the department store. There, in a long, dark courtyard, referred to by some local gay men as "the suck house" ("сосальня"), men sometimes had quick, casual sex among the idle trucks, empty packing crates, and garbage dumpsters.

In Sverdlóvsk, a large industrial city of about 1.5 million people in the Ural Mountains (also once again given its tsarist name, Yekaterinbúrg), a similar situation prevailed. A central city square with park benches served as the center of the *pléshka*, while a nearby busy shopping street was the gay cruising strip at night.

The layout of the *pléshka* in other cities of the Soviet Union was roughly similar to that described here. However, as one would expect, areas used for gay cruising in smaller cities were generally smaller in area, less well-established, and less well-known. Going cruising there was also likely to be more perilous, since residents of smaller cities and small towns were more likely to be recognized by passers-by who would question their presence in such public places for long periods of time or at late evening hours. The same behavior was not as suspect in large cities, where individuals could "cruise" more anonymously.

Sóchi, a small resort city on the Black Sea coast, was an exception to this rule. A very popular vacation destination, it sported an infamous gay cruising grounds stretching along a well-tended walkway which winds past some large beach hotels in the city and overlooks the sea. During the day, these paths were filled with tourists padding their way to or from the beach or eating at a few sidewalk *cafés*. This established pattern of foot traffic provided a ready excuse for Soviet gay men to be there in the evening and even through the night. Gay men from all parts of the Soviet Union could be found there at odd hours, sometimes blatantly cruising one another, hoping to "trick out" (or "be taken": "сниматься") for the night. The slope of the embankment which holds up this walkway is thick with trees and grasses, and as this afforded more privacy, it was sometimes used for erotic interludes, but usually only under the additional cover of darkness.

In my survey sample, fully 72.5% of respondents overall reported having a gay cruising grounds in their city, and it was by far the most likely place for respondents to cruise regularly for sex partners (33.8% said the *pléshka* was where they "usually" go). Yet, gay men who lived in large cities (those with 500,000 residents or more) were significantly more likely than those from smaller towns to report having such a gay place where they lived. (See Table 4.1.)

Table 4.1: Percentage of Gay Male Respondents Reporting the Existence of A Gay Cruising Grounds (*Pléshka*) Where They Lived, by City Size.*

Population	Percentage
< 50,000	35.7%
51,000 - 150,000	44.0%
151,000 - 500,000	54.5%
501,000 - 1,000,000	80.0%
> 1,000,000	88.9%

* χ^2=65.03904; df=4; p=.00000

The existence of a *pléshka* also varied by the region of the country in which respondents lived. About four-fifths of respondents from Russia and the Baltics indicated that they had a gay cruising grounds in their city (80.3% and 78.0%, respectively), whereas only about two-thirds of those from Byelorussia, Ukraine, or Maldavia and the Caucasus republics said they did (65.6% and 66.7%), and in the Central Asian republics only half said so (50.0%). Region of the country was less important than city size though, in determining whether respondents had access to a gay cruising grounds where they lived. These results indicate that the *pléshka* was a very widespread institutionalized meeting place for Soviet homosexuals—probably common in all republics, but one that generally owed its existence to a concentration of population in large cities.

B. Public Parks and Woods

Apart from central cruising grounds, other public parks and wooded areas (леса, лесопарки) in and near Soviet cities sometimes also served as meeting places for homosexuals. These may or may not have been close to a *pléshka* and they were much less-used as gay places, but the manner of their use by homosexuals was substantially the same. Benches provided places one could rest, as well as a good excuse for loitering and a comfortable vantage point for cruising. Strolling along pathways, alone or with friends, gay men could look one another over, signal interest with a glance or a gesture, and make contact by most any of the means they would use on the *pléshka*.

For example, not far from the *pléshka* in Moscow, a well-kept English-style garden with grassy knolls and manicured flower gardens along one wall of the Kremlin (which had been the promenade for tsars and nobles before the October,

1917, Revolution), served as one such gay meeting place. This public garden was less popular than the *pléshka* itself as a cruising area, however, since it was often much more crowded and access to it was more restricted.[5] There were at least two other areas of large Moscow parks that were used by Soviet gay men as cruising and meeting places. One was at a side entrance to a huge park and recreation area with bandstands and festival grounds located just outside the city center, the other at one side of another recreation area about half an hour in a different direction from the center of town.

Leningrad also had such a park used by gays as a meeting place: an English-style garden in the center of town several blocks up from the main cruising grounds. This grassy garden has wide dirt paths ringed by dozens of benches, and although it was less used as a cruising area than the *pléshka*, it was known as one of Leningrad's gay places. Down the avenue in the opposite direction from the main cruising grounds, a public park sits in front of an important city theater surrounding a large monument to Catherine the Great, Empress of Russia from 1762 to 1796. Leningrad gays referred to this as "Cathy's Garden" ("Катин сад"). Its shaded pathways lined with park benches were used for strolling, and one could sit and talk there with friends or with a prospective "trick."[6] Leningrad gays often arranged to meet one another in this park at the start of an evening of cruising with friends or as a *rendezvous* point for dalliances.

In smaller cities and towns, where there was unlikely to be a full-fledged cruising area, or *pléshka*, similar city parks and pathways in wooded areas must often have served the same purpose. This was certainly true of a small city in the North of Russia, which I visited on several occasions. There, a wooded area within the city limits, located just beyond a small public square, was known to local gays as the public place they could occasionally go to meet other homosexuals. Even in smaller city parks, sometimes enough privacy may have been available for gay expression to occur, if only in the form of conventional social distance from strangers, but acceptable close contact for "friends." In such places, and even in the largest Soviet cities, residents could no doubt furnish many more examples than I have given of city parks and wooded areas that they used as gay meeting places.

C. Public Toilets ("Tea-rooms")

Another very important set of public spaces used by Soviet gay men as places to make contact with one another was the network of public toilets maintained by municipal authorities for the use of visitors to the city and city dwellers while they are away from their homes. As in Western countries, these were perhaps the first public spaces subversively used by homosexuals for clandestine, sexual purposes.

Public toilets were suitable for such use for several reasons. Firstly, they are sex-segregated. Secondly, public toilets are used at one time or another by nearly everyone in a given city, and therefore the range of individuals one was likely to meet up with there was very broad. Thus, a taste for all manner of partners could usually be satisfied. In addition, in a public toilet the viewing of genitals and blatant signaling of intentions with them is easy. This was especially true of many Soviet public toilets where urination was often not done at individually isolated urinals, but along an open, tiled wall with a drain or drains in the floor below.[7]

What is perhaps even more significant for gay men though, is that public toilets are also usually intensely anonymous places. Individuals generally do not wish to be identified and engaged in conversation there. Therefore, it is customary for people to ignore who goes in and out of public toilets, when they do, at what intervals, and for what length of time they stay in them. This fact gives homosexuals considerable "leeway" in their use of public toilet facilities, and, especially if they are unaccompanied, most bystanders will not be aware of their comings and goings, the length of time they have spent "using" the facilities, or their early and repeated return visits there. This is true even if people around them do notice the odd intensity with which certain men are eyeing one other there. Cruising in public toilets throughout the Soviet Union, then, often could be indulged in with relative impunity.

In Moscow, several of the public toilets used as meeting places for Soviet gays were located within walking distance of the *pléshka*. Perhaps the most "active" and well-known was one located at the very corner of the Kremlin. Sometimes by day and always by night, men loitered and met there, and, if the opportunity presented itself, they may have performed quick sex acts with one another in the stalls. My observation was that this particular public toilet was more of a contact place than a place for actual sexual encounters, though. It is located near some very popular tourist attractions and Red Army soldiers were on constant guard nearby. A short stroll away, within the confines of the garden described in the previous section, are two more public toilets that were likewise "active," but not as popular. They are somewhat smaller, however, and laid out in such a way that they were more amenable to sexual activity. Nearby, in the basement of the country's largest department store is another public toilet used as a gay meeting place, though even less often. Probably because its entrance is directly across a large city square from an important national monument and can be accessed only from the outside of the building, this seemed to be the public toilet most often searched by police looking to flush out homosexuals (pun intended).

Leningrad also had its share of public toilet facilities serving as gay contact points, most notably the one located at the central department store that was the main part of the *pléshka* there. Other locations included public toilets at the city's train stations and at least one major tourist attraction. In addition to these, as in any other city, local gays would likely be able to identify more such "active" public toilets: probably at major universities, in or near large factories or other industrial workplaces, and in large government buildings.

In smaller cities and small towns there were also some public toilets known to the homosexual population as gay places. These were likely to be found in the same sorts of places as those in major cities, *id est*: in public spaces that are centrally located, and/or convenient to public transportation; places which had heavy foot traffic and provided some anonymity and an acceptable excuse for loitering.

Overall, two-thirds of respondents from my survey sample (67.6%) indicated that there were public toilets which gay men used as meeting places where they lived, and 17.8% said that they "usually" went there to find sex partners. However, it does appear that larger cities were more likely than smaller ones to have had public toilets where gay men went to meet one another. While a very significant percentage of respondents from towns of less than 50,000 population reported "active" public toilets (more than 4 of every 10), those from cities with over one million residents did so nearly twice as often (almost 8 in 10). (See Table 4.2.)

Table 4.2: Percentage of Gay Male Respondents Reporting the Existence of A Public Toilet Where They Lived That Was A Gay Meeting Place, by City Size.*

Population	Percentage
< 50,000	42.9%
51,000 - 150,000	52.0%
151,000 - 500,000	68.2%
501,000 - 1,000,000	73.3%
> 1,000,000	79.3%

* χ^2=22.35223; df=4; p=.00017

Regional differences in respondents' reports were also significant, with those from the Baltic republics and the Russian Federation being more likely to say that there was a public toilet that served as a gay meeting place in their town (up to 80%), while those from other areas were less likely to say so (as low as 50% in Central Asia). However, whereas the effects of city size remained statistically significant within each region, effects of region largely disappeared when analyzing cities of comparable size.

Additionally, it is notable that significantly more gay men over age 30 reported public toilets as a place they usually went to find homosexual partners (as many as 38.5% of those aged 35–39 years) than younger men did (12.1% for those 20–24 years old). This is likely because younger men, who had come of age during the period of *perestróyka*, were more able to find partly-public and even private places in which to meet one another, whereas older men were either unwelcome at such places or felt uncomfortable there or both (for reasons of fear or of being "out of their element" age-wise).

Also, Soviet gay men either with a higher education (27.4%) or with only an uncompleted secondary education (25.0%) used public toilets most as places to find sexual partners. This could be so for several reasons, but a simple, structural explanation seems to be most likely. Individuals with a university education and those still pursuing their high-school education may have meet one another in public toilets more often because it was convenient. Being in and around a university campus or high school grounds would have provided a much larger set of people nearby, who, there for a large part of the day, would have had greater need of public toilet facilities than those who would have been found at public toilets in other areas of the city—be they industrial, commercial, residential, or recreational areas.

An economic change of the late Gorbachóv era is worth noting here as well, as it directly affected this clandestine use of public toilets by Soviet homosexuals. Under *perestróyka*, public toilets were among the first "enterprises" allowed to be privatized,[8] and this drastically reduced the number and range of them that could be subverted for gays' purposes. Partly in exchange for providing what were considered extra niceties (toilet paper, soap, and hand towels) and for allegedly keeping the premises clean, private operators were allowed to install turnstiles in the toilets and to charge a fee for use of the facilities. These new entrepreneurs or their representatives sometimes actually lived in one corner of the toilet and kept a constant vigil there, thus making loitering—much less cruising and making sexual contact with other homosexuals—impossible. This happened especially often with public toilets situated in places where gay men would have been likely to make the greatest use of them: in or near busy central-city shopping districts; in and around city parks; and at train, bus, and subway stations. These were the facilities most heavily used by all people and therefore those where proprietors were most easily able to turn a profit.

D. Train, Bus, and Subway Stations

Since the vast majority of the population in the Soviet Union traveled from city to city by some form of mass transportation, it stands to reason that central locations on these systems would be likely places to be perverted for the gay purpose. Further, as rail travel was more widely used there than any other means of long-distance transportation, one should not be surprised to learn that large inter-city and commuter train stations in Soviet cities became known as gay meeting places. Such train stations offered the features critical to creating a gay place under the conditions of oppression and stigmatization of homosexuals that existed in Soviet society. They presented a clear justification for loitering: one was waiting for a train, of course. Anonymity was heightened at these places, since gay men were in the company of multitudes of travelers and this fact also provided great variation in the "types" of homosexual men available for cruising.

In Moscow, at least two of the city's central train stations, which are relatively near the center of town and connect with the Moscow subway system, were used regularly as gay meeting places. In Leningrad, gay men also met at three of that city's train stations. An additional reason to favor one of these stations was that it was close to one of the public bathhouses frequented by Soviet gay men. In Tashkent, capital of Uzbekistan, the main bus and train stations were rumored to be places gay men used to meet one another.

Most likely, gay men traveled to large cities from outlying areas or even from other parts of the country to take advantage of the possibilities for homosexual contact available at these gay places. Certainly, some gay men who lived in such cities found them quite amenable for the pursuit of sex partners. (Personal Interview, 1991) In fact, the use of inter-city bus and railroad stations as gay meeting places was so widespread that a nickname was conjured up for those gay men who preferred to meet potential partners there: "station queen" ("вокзальная девка").

Inter-city transportation hubs were not the only ones used as gay meeting places. Metropolitan transit systems were also sometimes appropriated by Soviet homosexuals for this purpose. One of the three subway stations which had lines crossing underneath the Moscow *pléshka* was regularly used by Soviet gays as a meeting place, especially by young gay men. At each end of the platform this station is equipped with benches on which passengers could wait for a train or for other passengers, thereby providing an excuse for loitering. In Leningrad, the subway station underneath the cruising grounds was similarly used by Soviet homosexuals as a place to gather.

These stops are not only among the most centrally located stops on the cities' underground train routes, but also ones very likely to be used by gay men traveling to the *pléshka*, to city parks that served as gay meeting places, and to the most active public toilets. At these locations, most of the typical means for signaling one's interest in and availability for homosexual encounters discussed above were utilized: posturing, extended eye contact, asking for directions, *et cetera*. (A major exception is that one could not ask for a light or "shoot for" a cigarette, as smoking is not permitted in the subway.)

In cities without subways, loci of other mass transit systems were sometimes used as gay meeting places in a similar way. In one city in the Russian Far North, for instance, the central bus station (автовокзал) was rumored among local gay men to be a place where homosexuals would sometimes congregate. In Sóchi, a bus stop adjacent to a "cruisy" public toilet and near the *pléshka* was also used as a gay contact point. This must also have been the case in many other medium-sized cities throughout the USSR.

As they are places of transit, however, such train, bus, and subway stations are usually constituted only of hallways, walkways, and ticket windows. They therefore offered very little in the way of privacy. In most inter-city train stations, moreover, there are often not even any seats for waiting passengers to sit on, so many people scattered themselves about on their luggage to wait for their train connections and had little else to do but watch the goings-on. For these reasons, public toilets in these stations were usually the only place any homosexual affection could be displayed or actual sexual congress could take place. Such stations were nonetheless vital links for communicating and making contact among Soviet gay men. Among my survey respondents, 12.2% indicated that train, bus, or subway stations are where they "usually" went to find sex partners.

E. Public Beaches

Another place that gay people gathered to meet and socialize in the Soviet Union, during the summer months, was at the beach. Taking advantage of the relatively undeveloped state of public beaches and generally wide expanses of riverfront and ocean-front lands set aside for unorganized public use, Soviet homosexuals—with caution and trepidation, to be sure—created gay places there. The formation of a "gay beach" ("голубой пляж") was quite unofficial, of course, and most such gay meeting places were well off the beaten path for privacy and safety reasons. Their locations could be made known only "by word of mouth." In addition, gay people often had to share these remote beaches with another group of people whose interests also were not condoned by the Soviet authorities: (heterosexual) nudists. By dint of this affiliation, many of the Soviet Union's "gay beaches" were also nudist ones. In my observation, this coexistence of Soviet homosexuals and nudists was quite an amicable one, perhaps because these two groups shared the clandestine pleasure of enjoying themselves freely in natural surroundings.

In Moscow, the most well-known and most heavily frequented "gay beach" was located within the city limits, but at a distance from the center of town in the middle of a huge preserve of pine and broad-leaf trees, tall grasses, and sandy dunes along the Moscow River. Accurate directions to the spot where gays (and nudists) congregated in this undeveloped area were vital as was an eagerness to get there. A long subway trip, a tram ride, a bridge crossing on foot, and then a half-hour walk through the woods and grassy areas were necessary to reach the place. Once there, however, gay Soviets were rewarded with a couple of small sandy beaches, a stretch of river clear of weeds and pollution, and the personal freedom provided by the remoteness of the site.[9] They were usually also rewarded by the presence of a dozen or more other gay men and lesbians, some of the former signaling their availability for casual sex while sauntering back and forth along a set of pathways which lead into a heavily-wooded grove with thick underbrush adjacent to the beach areas.

Danger was not completely absent even there, however, as on some days River Patrol boats passed by the beach at very close range and unnervingly irregular intervals, or even landed on shore, to investigate the situation. Whether they were scanning for nude sunbathers or for homosexuals to arrest was unclear on my visits to this beach, but both groups of people felt a need to cover themselves, hide, or leave altogether when the patrol boats approached.

In Leningrad, the most easily accessible beach where gay men gathered was a sandy spot on the largest part of the Nyevá River, on the delta islands of which this city was built. As the Nyevá is the main shipping route and tour-boat course in Russia's second-largest city, though, it was not secluded enough to provide any measure of privacy except, perhaps, in the stalls of the public toilets there. As neither the freedom of nudity nor open gay self-expression could be safely enjoyed at this beach, it was not the one most frequented by Leningrad homosexuals. Visible water pollution there doubtless kept many bathers away as well, both homosexual and heterosexual.

A more private beach could be found outside of Leningrad, about an hour's trip by subway and commuter train, where gay men gathered in greater numbers and with far greater freedom. At the distant (about a half-hour walk) end of a large public beach on the Baltic Sea near a small resort town, gay men met and sunned, generally free to carry on as they pleased and to cruise for sex in the nearby trees and shrubs.

In Sóchi, as might be expected of a resort city, Soviet homosexuals swam and sunbathed with the rest of the Soviet tourist crowd at the long, pebble beach that is the city's main attraction. Even so, they tended to cluster in a small section which was nearly the southernmost spot open to Soviet and Soviet-bloc citizens. (Further south was a fenced-off section of beach directly adjacent to the two major hotels reserved for Western tourists exclusively.) Again, although this was known as a "gay beach," the openness with which gay men could express themselves there was limited to their strength in numbers, since its location along the boardwalk meant that it was traversed by tourists and tourist-industry workers. This left them vulnerable to public scrutiny. The high concentration of (mostly) men at that location in and of itself probably was enough to make both passersby and city authorities suspicious.

A much more private beach was found among the rocks along a narrow stretch of coast a few kilometers from Sóchi. It served as an additional place for gay men to gather, much more freely and usually nude. Getting to this haven was, predictably, difficult. First, one took a 15–20-minute bus ride out of town.

Knowing where to get off the bus was key. Those who did not know where they were going, would get lost. After waiting until the bus drove away (a safety precaution), it was then necessary to scramble down the embankment that supports the two-lane highway to the railroad tracks below. Being careful to monitor train traffic, one walked along the railroad tracks about a kilometer before coming to a clearing that reveals the presence of the "gay beach" below. Finally, there is a cliff about 2-3 meters high at that spot which one had to climb down or jump off in order to get to the beach.

Of the gay beaches I was able to visit in the USSR, this was the most flagrantly gay, perhaps because it was the most remote. For one flamboyant young "queen" ("девушка": girl), parading around in a make-shift, seaweed robe and crown with a driftwood scepter was quite permissible behavior and, following that lead, his entourage decked themselves out accordingly. Accessible only at low tide, the beach lacked both the preferred cover of trees or bushes and the luxury of trails into the woods for even moderately private cruising. That had to be done in the open. On more than one occasion, I observed male couples engaging in oral and anal sex directly on the beach, though either modesty or a strong desire for privacy led one pair to build a small shelter of rocks around them to hide their activities somewhat. Neither was this lively locale ultimately safe from the Soviet authorities, however, as I myself found out. Sources told me that it was one of the gay men gathered at this beach who, working as an informant for the KGB, notified the authorities of my unapproved and illegal presence in the city and of my efforts to study the Soviet homosexual population.[10]

Aside from the places described in detail here, there were other well-known public beaches at which Soviet gay men congregated. At a small village near the Black Sea resort of Yalta, another very rocky "beach" was frequented by Soviet gay men. In the Baltic republics there were at least two beach areas well-known to local gays as meeting places: one several kilometers from Riga, Latvia; and one on the Lithuanian coast.

Although the suitability of public beaches as gay meeting places was only seasonal, because they were often in very secluded places, "gay beaches" allowed much more freedom of expression than was afforded by other public gay places. What is more, as large cities like Moscow and Leningrad and resort cities like Sóchi and Yalta attracted large numbers of tourists from throughout the country in warm weather, beaches brought together gay men from all over, thus tieing together various strands of the Soviet gay subculture. Anecdotal information from informal interviews indicates that it was not uncommon for Soviet gay men and lesbians to travel to these beaches specifically to take advantage of this fact and that groups of gay friends arranged to vacation there at the same time. Analysis of my survey data shows that neither city size nor region of residence was related to respondents' reporting of public beaches as gay places in the USSR, which supports the notion that public beaches were used by Soviet homosexuals as meeting places, wherever they lived.

II. SEMI-PRIVATE AND PARTLY-PUBLIC PLACES SUBVERTED FOR GAY USES

Every society has leisure organizations and enterprises devoted to serving the interests and needs of its population. Most Western societies have multitudes of such organizations and enterprises, some for the general population and some specifically targeted to sub-populations with various interests. In the generally sparse leisure and service economy of the Soviet Union, however, such places for the general population were not legion, and those created for special groups were even less available. Without a doubt, the most significant difference between the "gay worlds" of the Soviet Union and the West was the almost complete lack of enterprises that met the needs of the gay and lesbian population. Given homosexuals' illegal status, no one could openly cater to a "gay market."

Guides that publish lists of gay-owned, gay-operated, or even just "gay-friendly" establishments in the West boasted listings of over 12,000 gay places worldwide and 6,000 in North America in the same year that my data was collected.[11] These listings include descriptions, locations, hours of operation, and contact information for such organizations as: gay bars, discos, and restaurants; gay bathhouses, sex clubs, and sex shops; gay hotels, bed and breakfast establishments, and travel services; gay bookstores, clothing stores, florists, and stationers; gay activist organizations, sports organizations, social clubs, and community centers; et cetera. In the entire Soviet Union, there were no official gay-identified establishments and there were probably less than a few dozen places where Soviet homosexuals could meet unofficially—rarely more than one or two in any city.

Without such gay places, arranging informal, sexual or non-sexual interaction among Soviet homosexuals was exceedingly difficult, and building a sense of common welfare, mutual service, and "community spirit" was impossible. Perhaps the most important difference in this regard was the complete lack of gay bars in the USSR. As a social institution, the gay bar is considered to have been central to the development and continuation of the homosexual subculture in the West.[12] This is because it is a meeting place where all patrons share a common personal interest (homosexual orientation) and can depend on relative freedom from the antagonisms of the wider society in which they live since it is a privately owned establishment.

Most places that served as substitute social institutions in the Soviet Union were successful at meeting the needs of Soviet homosexuals in only a limited way. While they could sometimes supply the safety and freedom to homosexuals that privacy allowed, their ability to do so was always precarious. Because their continued functioning as safe places for gay people to gather and socialize was a result not of the owners' or operators' intention to create such a space, but of their willingness to overlook the presence and behaviors of gay people in their establishment, one could not always count on the freedom to "be oneself" there. What is more, these places tended to fulfill the role of meeting place and safe haven for only a small and usually select number of Soviet gay men and lesbians.

A. The Public Bathhouse, or "*Bánya*" (Баня)

The *bánya* is the Russian bathhouse, a social institution with a long history in Russian society, and one with both practical and cultural roots. In traditional Russian villages, an out-building containing the "summer kitchen" and the bathhouse was usually built near to each family's living quarters. Its most important feature was a wood stove for cooking food in summertime and for heating bathwater year-round. In a small cabin in which water is being heated, steam is a constant byproduct. The bathhouse was therefore also a steam room and was appreciated as such. Bathwater would be heated infrequently, and family members usually bathed together to cut down on the time and firewood it required. This made bathing also a family affair, and even a communal tradition, since neighbors and friends might be invited to join in the relaxation a steambath can provide.

This old Russian communal tradition has carried over in time and geography, because even in the late 1980s and early 1990s in the countryside houses often had no running water and because in modern Soviet cities using the *bánya* was sometimes still a pleasant necessity. Before the advent of indoor plumbing, most Russian houses in the cities also did not have built-in facilities for bathing and, even afterward, many pre-existing apartments could not accommodate them, especially in city centers. Bathing communally in public bathhouses was therefore a necessary aspect of city life as well as life in the countryside from the 17th Century on, and the *bánya* continued to serve as a place where men and women would gather—though separately, by gender—for steambaths, massage, and general relaxation (Рубинов 1991).[13]

In all Soviet cities of any size there is likely to be at least one public bathhouse operating from afternoon to late evening, most days of the week for the paid use of all residents. In large cities, there is such a bathhouse in most neighborhoods.[14] The layout and facilities of city bathhouses varies greatly, but the basic necessities are three: a dressing and sitting room (раздевальная, or "предбанник": "pre-*bánya*"), with benches for resting and hooks for hanging one's clothes; a tiled washing room (мыльная), with hand-held wash basins and hot and cold water spigots; and a steam room (парильня, or "горячая": "hot room"). Larger bathhouses may also have a swimming pool near the steam room, showers and massage tables in the washing room, and semi-private booths in the dressing room. In addition, attendants often sell beer and *kvás* (a traditional Russian drink of fermented bread) for consumption while resting. Attendance at the *bánya* is by scheduled sessions (сеансы), which usually last 1½ to 2 hours. Tickets can be purchased for more than one consecutive session at a time, however, and many people do so.

The Russian *bánya* shares several key characteristics with the public places appropriated for gay uses discussed above. As with public toilets, the sex-segregated nature of the Soviet public bathhouse made it quite amenable to homosexual interests. The general belief that taking a steam bath is "healthy" for you, and the tradition of spending a long time at the *bánya* (preferably a few hours) provided excellent "cover" for Soviet homosexuals: a ready and laudable reason to visit the bathhouse as often as they wished and a "built-in" excuse for lingering there as long as possible.[15] In addition, any dark corners, out-of-the-way nooks, and divided (but open) shower stalls in the washing room made covert sexual activity possible at public bathhouses, and, given the limited outlets for homosexuals in the USSR, these features made it likely to occur.

Though likewise only appropriated by Soviet homosexuals at certain times and under certain circumstances for their special purposes, public bathhouses also had some distinct advantages over the open, public spaces in the Soviet Union that became gay places. Because *bánya*s are facilities with finite space and requiring paid entry, they are more restricted than the *pléshka*, parks, public toilets, or subway, train, and bus stations, and this made them safer for homosexual activity, as the number of heterosexuals there was limited. It was common for gay friends and acquaintances to go to the bathhouse in groups and/or arrange to meet one another there so that they could be assured of comradeship, and because "there is safety in numbers." Moreover, the openness of social interaction expected among attenders at such communal gatherings, the existence of semi-private booths for patrons in the dressing room, and the expectation of nudity at the bathhouse heightened its suitability as a gay meeting place. That public bathhouses served as an important gay place is under scored by the fact that Russian gay slang provides a special term for gay men who regularly find sexual partners there: "bathhouse queen" ("банная девка").

The presence of the broader Soviet public at bathhouses did put some strict limits on the openness with which Soviet homosexuals could conduct themselves there, however. Not all *bánya*s were gay meeting places: only certain ones were used for sexual purposes. Typically only one bathhouse in cities of medium or smaller size in the Soviet Union was known as a gay meeting place—most often a centrally-located one convenient to public transportation. In the largest cities, there were usually a few public bathhouses where gay people gathered, also likely the ones located in the center of town and/or near major transit hubs. Additionally, the time during which a *bánya* became a gay place was limited to only a few hours. The most opportune bathhouse hours for gay Soviets to meet one another were from about 8:00 PM until closing (usually about midnight), especially on off-days.

In such bathhouses, at these times, one could see a gradual thinning of the ranks of heterosexuals—especially those with children—among bathgoers until a critical mass of gay people was reached, at which juncture signals of homosexual interest could be more-or-less-safely given. Typically, gay men were able to cruise around from one area to another in bathhouses searching for a homosexual encounter or to demonstrate their availability by posing provocatively at a shower stall or in a dark corner, silently inviting interested parties to join them. Sexual interests among gay men at bathhouses in the Soviet Union had to be pursued carefully and furtively though, since any homosexual activity was a potentially dangerous use of the bathhouse facility. Indiscretion in conversation or blatant display of sexual urges was not common, as one had to be certain to present oneself in such a light only to those who, one could be sure, shared the homosexual interest. In my observation, virtually all advances were made in extremely limited view of others, for to attract too much attention to oneself was to take a great risk.

Neither were all places in a public bathhouse safe for Soviet homosexuals to express themselves. Most homosexual activity in bathhouses of the Soviet Union occurred in isolated areas—often in the last row of showers or in an area of the washing room walled-off for massages. In one Moscow bathhouse, for instance, an unlit anteroom to the steam chamber regularly served as an "orgy room."[16] Though it may occur, I have never observed homosexual activity in a steam room, probably because there is no possibility of privacy there, though adverse health risks of having sex in the intense heat of a steam room may also have prevented it.

Opportunities for homosexuals to socialize were also easily created at the *bánya*. Socializing usually took place in the semi-privacy of a booth in the dressing room area with a sheet as an improvised barrier closing off the entrance.[17] Quiet conversation anywhere in the bathhouse was usually private enough to be safe, and the communal traditions of the *bánya* provided many opportunities for interaction. In the washing room it is quite common to see both homosexual and heterosexual men scrubbing each others' backs, heads, and legs with a scrubbing brush, loofah pad, or sponge. If there is space for stretching out, a full-body massage can be given. In the steam room patrons beat each other all over with specially-prepared birch branches in an effort to bring the blood closer to the surface enhancing the effect of the heat, and infusing the skin with a sensation and aroma thought to have medicinal qualities. All of these courtesies can be politely requested of or offered to a total stranger without hesitation, and they provide a perfect opportunity for gay men to introduce them selves to someone they have been cruising.

It should come as no surprise then, that the *bánya* was one of the most widely-recognized gay places in the Soviet Union. In my survey sample, 68.4% of respondents reported having a public bathhouse where they live that served as a place for homosexual interaction, and nearly one in five (19.8%) said they regularly find homosexual partners there. Predictably, Soviet gay men living in large cities were much more likely to have a "gay bathhouse" in their city than those who lived in smaller cities or in rural areas. While just over one-third of my respondents living in cities of 150,000 population or less reported having such a gathering place where they live, three-fourths and more of those who live in cities of over 500,000 residents did (Table 4.3).

Table 4.3: Percentage of Gay Male Respondents Reporting the Existence of A Public Bathhouse (*Bánya*) Where They Live That Is A Gay Meeting Place, by City Size.*

Population	Percentage
< 50,000	35.7%
51,000 - 150,000	36.0%
151,000 - 500,000	59.1%
501,000 - 1,000,000	75.0%
> 1,000,000	84.3%

* χ^2=52.64621, df=4, p=.00000

It is interesting to note that older gay men in my sample (those aged 30 and over) were more likely to go to *bányas* to find sex partners than are those under 30 years old. Those with a higher education also reported cruising there for sex partners more often than those without it.

The existence of a public bathhouse where gays meet in the Soviet Union also varied by region of the country in which respondents lived. Overall, respondents from the Russian Federation, from the Baltic republics, and from the Caucasus republics were most likely to report having a gay *bánya* where they live. When analyzing within each region of the country, city size remained a strong predictor of the reported availability to respondents of a "gay *bánya*." Generally, the larger the city respondents lived in, the more likely they were to have one. However, the regional differences remained strong when analyzing only comparable-sized cities (at least for respondents living in cities of more than 150,000 population) indicating that both are significant factors.

B. *Cafés* and Restaurants

Cafés and restaurants in the Soviet Union were another type of partly-public place sometimes used as gay meeting places, though they were much less common than any of the public places appropriated for use by homosexuals. Although they were ostensibly open to the entire Soviet public, as with the *bánya*, some restaurants could be subverted for gay purposes if staff members maintained a carefully "controlled environment." In addition, simply by force of their regular presence at particular places, some Soviet gays and lesbians forged "gay-tolerant" spaces in certain *cafés* that were anyway popular youth hangouts.

Moscow probably had the most "gay restaurants" of any Soviet city, with four sit-down restaurants within walking distance of the Moscow *pléshka* that were known for their "gay atmosphere." One of these places was the official restaurant of an arts-workers trade union, and though it may have seemed like it was restricted to union members and their guests, more often than not, gay staff seemed to be surreptitiously screening out most heterosexuals as well. A second restaurant that served as a gay meeting place is a "touristy" place popular with very young gay men, some of them homosexual prostitutes, as well as with government officials and mafia bosses. The third such restaurant was a fancy place frequented by famous literati and stars of the Soviet stage and screen. It catered to a considerably, though far from exclusively, gay clientele. Finally, for years one Moscow restaurant operated almost as private homosexual club, with a doorman whose duty seemed to be turning away any heterosexuals from among the patrons standing in line to gain entry.

In Riga, Latvia, a restaurant connected with the Latvian Writer's Union was also sometimes used unofficially as a gay place. One of the union leaders was a gay man active in nascent local gay groups and since he apparently had *carte blanche* to use the place, in the very last years of Soviet rule it was sometimes even rented out for gay gatherings. One *café* at a very busy intersection in the heart of Leningrad was heavily used as a meeting place by young gay men and lesbians, although this was not widely known. Famous as a "hippie" gathering place, for a time it was considered to be the most interesting "alternative hang-out" in Leningrad. In Sóchi, one of the outdoor *cafés* along the promenade that was a cruising strip for gay men was also known as a gay place. Another restaurant there was also used as a place for gay men to gather, though not without consequences.[18]

No doubt there were other *cafés* and restaurants used by Soviet gays as places to congregate, but I do doubt that there were many more. Data from my survey sample show just how much less available restaurants and *cafés* were to Soviet homosexuals for use as gay meeting places than were *bányas* or any of the public places discussed above. Overall, only 28.6% of respondents reported having such a gay place in their city. As one would expect, those living in large cities were much more likely to have a restaurant or *café* in the place where they live that is used as a meeting place by gay men than are those who live in smaller cities or in rural areas. Only about one-tenth (10.7%) of my gay male respondents living in towns or villages of less than 50,000 population reported having such a gathering place where they live, but nearly four in ten (39.4%) who live in cities with more than 1,000,000 residents did. (See Table 4.4)

Table 4.4: Percentage of Gay Male Respondents Reporting the Existence of A Gay Restaurant/*Café* Where They Live, by City Size.*

Population	Percentage
< 50,000	10.7%
51,000 - 150,000	4.0%
151,000 - 500,000	27.3%
501,000 - 1,000,000	20.0%
> 1,000,000	39.4%

* χ^2=24.24821, df=4, p=.00007

In fact, of those who indicated that they do have a restaurant or *café* where they live that is a gay meeting place, more than three-fourths (78.0%) live in cities of over a million residents. Fully 90.0% of them live in cities of more than 500,000 population. Thus most of these respondents are probably referring to the same few places.[19] The existence of a restaurant or *café* where gays met in the Soviet Union did not only depend on city size. It also varied by region of the country in which respondents lived.[20] Overall, respondents from the Russian Federation and from the Baltics were much more likely to report having a gay restaurant or *café* where they live (with 34.6% and 34.0% of respondents, respectively, reporting that they did) than were those from Byelorussia, Ukraine, or Maldavia (9.4%), the Caucasus Republics (6.7%), and Central Asia (where no respondents reported having such a place). Further analysis of the data indicates that city size and region are both important (separate) determinants of whether gay men will have a *café* or restaurant that is used as a gay place where they live.

C. Bars and Discos

Even less available to Soviet homosexuals were bars and *discothèques* serving as partly-public places subverted for gay uses. In fact, such places scarcely existed. I know of only one disco, in Leningrad, where a few venturesome young homosexuals sometimes made arrangements to meet each other. Even though only scheduled *rendezvous* were generally made there, I was told that they felt it was necessary to ensure that both gay men and lesbians would be there together so heterosexual pretense could be used as a "cover" if necessary. One valiant effort was also made at establishing an exclusively-gay *discothèque* in an abandoned building in Leningrad. While it lasted, this was a much-celebrated success for Soviet gays. Unfortunately, it was also well-known to police who raided it regularly. Only one person in my sample indicated that gay people in his town gather at a (beer) bar (пивной бар).

D. Hotel Rooms

Though it was difficult to arrange in the USSR, on some occasions Soviet homosexuals were able to rent hotel rooms for use as semi-private gay places. The obstacles were regulatory. Registration in a hotel, whether for foreigners or Soviet citizens, required presentation of official identification papers—an internal passport. The number of people staying in each room was strictly regulated and no unregistered people were allowed in. Moreover, since hotels are meant for guests, by law, residents of the city in which they are located were not permitted to stay in them.

As an additional "security" measure, aside from registration clerks and building security personnel, attendants (дежурные) were located on each floor of most hotels for Soviets and all hotels serving foreigners. Such posted guards might not be a formidable obstacle by themselves—and most often these positions were filled by middle-aged or elderly women—but other factors made them difficult to get around. Guests were never permitted to take room keys out of their hotels but were required instead to leave them with the attendant on their floor. Since these women were also given registration information and were charged with familiarizing themselves with each guest, sneaking friends or acquaintances past them was the only way to entertain in a hotel room. Unlike in the West then, probably only if one had gay "contacts" who worked at a hotel could hotel rooms be a regularly-subverted gay place in the Soviet Union.

III. PRIVATE PLACES FASHIONED TO ACCOMMODATE GAY NEEDS

Private accommodations in the Soviet Union were in very short supply compared with other highly-industrialized countries so that the accessibility and availability of private apartments or of private rooms in shared ("communal") apartments was thereby limited.[21] It was very common for Soviet citizens to remain living with their parents (or their spouse's parents) well into their adult years while they were on the government waiting list to get a housing allocation of their own. Many others spent much of their adult life living in a shared room at student or factory workers' dormitories. Needless to say, much creativity had to be used in order to create regular, safe gay meeting places in such shared spaces. Nonetheless, it was sometimes possible for gay men in the USSR to fashion gay places out of whatever private space they had available to them.

A. Private Apartments

The public spaces homosexuals appropriated for their special uses in the Soviet Union did not provide opportunities for gay people to spend large amounts of time together or to fully "be themselves." Since there were not many partly-public or semi-private places for Soviet homosexuals to use for their own purposes, peoples' private apartments served as gathering places for gay friends who could not get together publicly. They were also the chief private locale for personal homosexual activity between gay "tricks" and lovers. Aside from plain deviousness, two cultural features of Soviet life made this possible.

First, in a Soviet-era tradition of "kitchen culture" ("кухонная культура"), adult Soviets were accustomed to entertaining visitors to their homes in their eat-in kitchens. Unlike in North America, social gatherings in the Soviet Union (as in the rest of Europe) are commonly held around the dinner table. They tend to involve large meals and ritual drinking of liquor. As Soviet apartments were generally small, most families did not maintain a separate dining room reserved for eating, and if only a few people were invited (probably less than six) the gathering would take place in the kitchen. This was convenient because other household members not taking part could retreat or be banished to another room. The vodka and food for such occasions would also be handy in the kitchen. Moreover, most modern Soviet apartments came equipped with a standard radio receiver mounted on a kitchen wall which was often switched on during such occasions creating "background noise" to cover up any illicit conversation.[22] Soviet homosexuals took advantage of this "kitchen culture" to define a temporary safe space for gay get-togethers.

The second Soviet cultural tradition that facilitated gay use of private apartments was a kind of "code of silence" that generally held sway over peoples' urge to implicate or accuse one another of wrongdoing. Although it is common for Westerners to note that the Russian language lacks a word for privacy, this does not mean that Soviet citizens had none. Despite decades of communist propaganda and periodic government campaigns to increase citizen vigilance in the "self-policing" of social and legal affairs, Soviet citizens had apparently learned something important from the betrayals of Stalinism. The widely shared perils of life under an authoritarian regime seemed to foster an unspoken etiquette in Soviet society of willfully ignoring other peoples' personal activities, sometimes even making an obsession of respecting one another's personal privacy.

Under the right conditions, in the Soviet Union gay men did socialize with one another in their apartments. They did have "gay parties" and invited homosexual partners to their homes. Although it was illegal and extremely difficult to arrange, in some rare cases Soviet gays even arranged to live with homosexual lovers.[23] Most commonly, they would gather at the home of a single gay man, someone who lived alone, whether in his own apartment or in his own room in a communal apartment. This gay man—sometimes called an "auntie" ("тётушка") in Russian gay slang—usually became the center of a social circle and friends would frequently borrow his apartment for gay sexual liaisons.[24]

A very important drawback to the use of private apartments in the USSR as gay places, however, was that many gay people did not have them. Due to bureaucratic limitations imposed by the government to deal with the severe and widespread housing shortage, people often could not get their own apartments until their parents died and they could "inherit" the lease right to it. In addition, Soviet citizens could not change their residence freely or have much choice in where they lived. Though they may have liked to, Soviet homosexuals therefore could not choose to live near one another, clustering together to form a "gay ghetto" as is common in the West (Levine 1979), particularly in North America.

Sometimes a need for greater freedom led Soviet homosexuals to go to great lengths to ensure their personal privacy, even preparing years in advance. Aside from borrowing someone else's apartment, heterosexually married gay men might get divorced (in part) to get a separate apartment. Single gay men might marry lesbians, creating a mutually useful alliance that would provide both a "cover" and a safe space for homosexual interaction. It was not uncommon for gay men eligible to receive their own room in a communal apartment to seek out one with an elderly woman as the only other tenant. By plying them with practical favors (helping with shopping, bill paying, *et cetera*), Soviet gays could usually buy the tolerance of otherwise "snoopy old ladies" and, if they were very attentive and didn't take too much advantage, they might even hope to be "willed" lease rights on the entire apartment after the old woman died.

Thus, if they were lucky enough to have their own apartment or to have their own room in a communal apartment, Soviet homosexuals could generally do as they pleased behind closed doors since even "nosy" neighbors usually overlooked any odd but not seriously transgressive behavior. Though they could not own their apartments and were therefore were not legally guaranteed the "sanctity of private property" with the inalienable rights of use, sale, and destruction that property owners are accustomed to in the West, gay Soviet citizens could count on reasonable freedom from the intrusion of authorities into their personal living space, even if only because such raids were rare, though not unlawful.[25]

In my survey sample of Soviet homosexuals, 53.2% reported that they can and do invite gay sex partners to their homes. Similarly, 53.0% said that they go to the homes of others. More than one-fourth (26.8%) indicated that they regularly borrow a friend's place. Of those that do not invite "tricks" or lovers home, 18.8% said this was because they do not have their own housing and 46.3% said it was because they do not have the right conditions at home to do so.

B. *Dáchas*

In addition to their own or friends' apartments, another refuge from the judgment and punishment of heterosexual Soviet society was the private *dácha*, a small shack or cabin built by Soviet citizens on state-allocated garden plots near the city where they live. Meant to offer a way of increasing the supply of fresh fruits and vegetables for the population, *dáchas* were fairly common in the USSR, with around 20 million people there having access to one. (Госкомстат СССР 1990:207) They were usually not very convenient as gay meeting places, though, since they tend to be located an hour or so from the city center and are frequently used by all members of the family. Around 10 million people annually spend their summer vacations there.26 If they had access to one, however, and if they could arrange to have private use of it, Soviet gay men and lesbians sometimes did use *dáchas* for gay purposes.

IV. GAY PLACES IN THE SOVIET GAY WORLD

At first glance, it might appear that Soviet gays have a lot in common with their Western counterparts as far as meeting places are concerned. To be sure, in North America and Western Europe homosexuals also meet one another in "cruisy areas" of city streets and public parks (Delph 1978), in public restrooms (Humphreys 1970, Weinberg & Williams 1975), in train stations and bus depots, and at particular public beaches. Gay men in the West also get together in bathhouses, certain *cafés* and restaurants, and in bars and dance clubs. They frequently meet in private homes and apartments for sexual and social purposes. Indeed, the public places Soviet homosexuals have appropriated for their clandestine use, the partly-public and semi-private places they subvert for gay purposes, and the private spaces they fashion into gay places for themselves are similar to those used by homosexuals in the West in that all the places available to Soviet homosexuals are also available to gay men in the West. The reverse, however, is not true.

Though the development of these kinds of gay places in the West is nearly identical to that in the Soviet Union, there is much more "gay space" available to homosexuals in the West than that created by simply appropriating, subverting, or fashioning for themselves any gay place they can out of spaces meant for non-gay purposes. The need for careful secrecy and guarded anonymity in the affairs of homosexuals in most areas of the West has vastly diminished over the course of the twentieth century. The social and legal status of homosexuals in Western societies has improved dramatically and the development of social and political organizations whose express purpose it is to provide gay people with a safe place to meet one another has made it possible for Western homosexuals to lead a much richer "gay lifestyle" than that afforded Soviet homosexuals. The availability of gay community centers, gay discussion groups, gay hotlines, gay literature and pornography, gay sports organizations, gay business and professional associations, gay stores, and even whole gay neighborhoods are only a few of the expanded possibilities. If Western homosexuals so desire, they can live a very open (or "out") gay existence.

Being able to create at least some safe spaces for the expression of homosexual interests in the harsh socio-political environment of the USSR was nonetheless vital to the survival of Soviet gay men and lesbians. Achieving this required much ingenuity and persistence. Tracing and retracing their steps around public parks or city squares and up and down cruising strips, regularly and mindfully sitting "too near" another bather at a public bathhouse, posing provocatively at a "gay-tolerant" *café* every time one goes there, repeatedly and obviously fondling oneself at a public toilet, and frequently borrowing a friend's apartment for homosexual liaisons—these are the activities that made a place "gay." When such actions were repeated with enough frequency over a sustained period of time, and when visits by gay men and lesbians to these places were not only common but habitual, *pléshka*s, gay beaches, and gay *bánya*s became predictable and recognizable gay social institutions in the Soviet Union. Together they composed the social-geographic features in the "landscape" of the Soviet "gay world," the spatial and temporal boundaries of which were made especially clear when they were traversed.

NOTES

1. The (American) English gay slang term "cruising" refers to the act of explicitly seeking out others for the purpose of possible sexual involvement by travelling to and "hanging out" in certain places and attracting them by flirting and/or other erotic posturing. In Russian, *"mandítsa"* ("мандиться") is a more-or-less direct equivalent of this term, though many gays and lesbians in the former Soviet Union also use the euphemism *gulyát* ("гулять," "to stroll") in this sense.

2. I use the term "social geography" here to evoke a sense of individuals' and groups' surroundings as not merely physical spaces, as the ecological niche of animals is usually thought of, but as a physical reality which is overlaid with the social meanings that humans themselves give to their shared "habitat." (Perrow 1967; Hannan & Freeman 1977; Aldrich 1979; Scott & Meyer 1983)

3. According to figures from the USSR State Committee on Statistics, only 17% of all Soviet families had an automobile in 1988. This amounts to 53 of every 1,000 individuals. In all, 1,262,000 private cars were produced in the Soviet Union that year for a population of about 286 million. (Госкомстат СССР 1990:24, 28, 142-143 Note: the population figure quoted is for 1989.) In comparison, in the United States, 86.4% of households owned their own automobile in that year (HHES 1995).

4. The Russian gay slang term "panél" is taken from the lexicon of street prostitutes to whom it denotes the place where they stroll to present themselves as available to customers. The term is used similarly in the gay context as the place where one goes to present oneself as available for sex and/or to look for a prospective partner.

5. The garden contained one of the main entrances to the Kremlin and was a central meeting place for groups of tourists. Surrounded by gates, it closed at 10:00 P.M. Leading from the main "cruising strip" of the Moscow "*pléshka*" to this park was a long underground walkway, which also served as a "strip" for strolling and "cruising," but usually only in inclement weather.

6. Although the Russian gay slang term for "tricking" (literally, "taking" someone: "снимать" кого-то), was well-known as a reference to casual sex, I know of no Russian noun correlate for the American gay slang term "trick" meaning "casual sex partner." (The American slang term is, not coincidentally, also drawn from the twilight world of prostitution.)

7. Signaling availability for and interest in homosexual activity often was made easier also from and between toilet stalls in the Soviet Union for a similar, structural reason. Although toilet stalls were usually divided and closed off with doors as is common in the West, most Soviet public toilets did not have toilet seats on them, and —rather than sitting directly on the cold porcelain rim— people there were accustomed to standing on it, straddling the toilet bowl, and squatting to defecate as is the Asian custom. This elevation usually made their faces, if not also their arms and shoulders, visible above the toilet stall partitions, and if an individual was there to make contact for sexual purposes, this made signaling such intentions that much easier.

8. The form of private enterprise allowed in such instances was called "Individual Labor Activity" ("Индивидуальная трудовая деятельность" или "ИТД"), which authorized non-state management of single-person enterprises, though not private ownership of them.

9. Because of the popularity and relative safety of gathering at this beach, it was no coincidence that coordinators chose to take 70 American gay and lesbian activists there to celebrate the culmination of the highly successful International Gay and Lesbian Symposium and Film Festival held in Leningrad and Moscow in July and August 1991. (For more about this and other gay and lesbian activist events, see Chapter Five.)

10. Fortunately, my encounter with the KGB in June 1991 ended relatively quickly and with minimal consequences. As I was able to safeguard all of the completed survey questionnaires I had received from Soviet homosexuals, none fell into the hands of the authorities and, though a few of my acquaintances were called in for questioning by the KGB, no charges were pressed. The ill-ease with which the very idea of my research was received, however, was evident.

11. The "worldwide" guide (Ferrari 1992) contained place listings for only one country in Asia (Thailand), only some in Eastern Europe (Poland, Czechoslovakia, Yugoslavia, and Bulgaria) and none on the continent of Africa. To infer that this means there were no "gay places" elsewhere in these areas certainly would be inaccurate, but as a listing of well-known and openly gay places, it seems probably representative. The North American guide (Damron 1992) contained listings for the U.S., Canada, Mexico, the Virgin Islands, and Costa Rica.

12. For exposition of this widely accepted thesis, see: Hooker (1967), Achilles (1967), and Greenberg (1988), among others.

13. While many contemporary city residents do not use public bathhouses for much of the year since most apartments have modern bathrooms, many people in the largest cities do use them at least during the one month each summer when all hot water is shut off, neighborhood by neighborhood, for maintenance of water pipes.

14. In 1987, there were 34,800 bathhouses operating in the Soviet Union: 9,500 in cities and 25,300 in rural areas. This overall number had not changed much since 1975, although the rate of introduction of new bathhouses seems to have risen in each 5-year-plan period since then. Introduction of new bathhouses went from 2,607 (room for 64,000 more patrons) in 1976-1980 to 4,377 (room for 90,200 new bathers) in 1981-1985 to 6,296 (room for 110,700 new patrons) in 1986-1990 (Госкомстат СССР 1991:208).

15. While it was considered something of a luxury to be able to go to the *bánya* frequently due to the time it took away from other daily pursuits like shopping for food and other necessities, it was considered important to go there when one could, and people who were able to go often were usually admired.

16. It is a bittersweet tribute to both the ingenuity and the predicament of Moscow homosexuals that I had occasion to observe, over time, the battle between homosexuals and bathhouse attendants over this use of physical space. When bathhouse attendants attempted to preempt sexual activity from taking place in the anteroom by installing a lighting fixture, the bulb was soon vandalized by bathhouse patrons so that they could once again huddle there under the cover of darkness. Since light bulbs were a deficit commodity difficult to obtain, it was only replaced a couple of times before attendants gave up. On a subsequent visit, I observed that attendants had removed a door that had closed off the anteroom from the washing room. This left the area open to greater scrutiny. Its only lasting effect, however, was in pushing those men interested in having sex in the anteroom further into the corner —and therefore even closer together.

17. Rather than towels, Soviet bathhouses provide large bedsheets (at an extra price) for their patrons to dry off with and lounge in. An unintended consequence of this practice is that creative individuals can subvert their use for other purposes. Much smaller, a towel would not make a sufficient barrier to provide even this (unquestionably limited) privacy.

18. Information from several sources about one incident at this *café*, during which gay men gathered there were arrested and beaten, interrogated and then let go, is recounted in the first issue of a gay newsmagazine published semi-legally in Moscow (РИСК 1991).

19. The relatively high percentage of all respondents (10.7%) reporting the existence of a restaurant or *café* that served as a meeting place for homosexuals in towns of less than 50,000 people is almost certainly explained by the fact that all of the gay men in my sample living in cities with less than 150,000 residents who reported such gay places in their city lived in suburban areas of major Soviet cities (Leningrad, Moscow, and Riga, Latvia). Thus it seems very likely that their reports were based on the fact that there is a restaurant or *café* where gays meet "in the larger metropolitan area" where they live.

20. For example, the unexpectedly high percentage of respondents from cities of 151,000–500,000 residents who said that they have a "gay restaurant" or *café* where they live is explained largely by the fact that two-thirds of them are from Tallinn, the capital and largest city in Estonia, which happens to be much smaller (and much more liberal) than any other Soviet Republic capital.

21. As the Soviet construction industry could not keep up with demand for housing, even with the strict limits on individual allotments of living space, the list of Soviet citizens waiting to receive their own apartment was notoriously long. Even though eligible, often

people had to wait years, even decades, to be allocated their "appropriate" living space. In 1989, 32.9% had already waited 5-10 years (Госкомстат СССР 1990:202). Apartments in buildings built before the Russian Revolution, especially large ones, were typically rented out room by room as "communal" living space to several unrelated individuals or to separate families. In 1990, for the USSR as a whole, the average amount of living space per person was 16 square meters (Госкомстат СССР 1991:189). This is an area of about 9 feet by 7 feet —about the size of a tiny bedroom or a large walk-in-closet in the West.

22. Most Soviet citizens were aware that the government "secret service" could be eavesdropping anytime, anywhere and even if they had no reason to suspect that they were under surveillance, force of habit made taking the precaution of turning on the radio nearly universal.

23. In one case I know of, a gay male couple in Leningrad lived together in one room of a communal apartment where one of them was officially registered. The other stayed there illegally and, in order to discourage people questioning their arrangement, they kept a second bed in the room "just for show." In another such case, a male couple in Moscow lived separately most of the time —one man with his ex-wife and child— while maintaining a second apartment gained through the divorce for themselves. In a third instance, a truly exceptional one, the mother of a lesbian I knew was accepting enough of her daughter to allow a lover to move in with them in the one-bedroom Moscow apartment they shared.

24. The American gay slang term "queen" seems to have originated with just this same sort of character. A pattern of social organization very similar to that found in the former USSR was common in America before the burgeoning of the gay rights movement in the latter half of this century (Leznoff & Westley 1956; Reiss 1961). A male homosexual who had enough freedom from family and neighbors to entertain gay guests in his own home usually became the center of a closely-knit circle of gay friends with whom, as the "queen," he was said to "hold court."

25. It must be noted here that even in the United States such unwarranted intrusion into the supposedly sacrosanct privately-owned home of gay citizens by police with no previously obtained, court-approved search warrant is also not illegal, pursuant to an infamous 1986 Supreme Court decision known as "Bowers versus Hardwick." (Amnesty International USA 1994) This ominous verdict was given in consideration of a case in which a gay man was arrested in the state of Georgia for engaging in anal sex with another man in the privacy of the bedroom of his own house by police who had come to his home in regard to a traffic violation, but who, without a legal search warrant, could not enter the premises. Instead, they peered through the windows and, upon observing two men together in bed, they broke into the home and arrested their suspect on sodomy charges —a crime which is so threatening that Georgia law requires no search warrant for entering private accommodations to arrest a person suspected of committing it. While such intrusions are exceedingly rare, American gay men must be aware of the possibility of such events taking place, at least in the score of states which as of this writing retain anti-sodomy statutes in their criminal codes. In this sense, they share a somewhat precarious freedom in private places with Soviet homosexuals who had not even this, shaky "right to privacy."

26. These figures are for 1988.

... there is a sense in which particular groups have specific needs. Obvious examples are women, groups subject to racial oppression and people with disabilities. Members of each group are commonly subject to *additional* threats to their health and autonomy over and above those [which all members of our species have in common]. As a result they require *additional and specific satisfiers* and procedures to address and correct them.

Len Doyal and Ian Gough,
A Theory of Human Need
p74 (emphasis in the original).

Chapter Five
Group-Level Institutions and Soviet Gay Politics

AT LEAST TWO INSTITUTIONS OF THE POLITICAL-LEGAL ENVIRONMENT IN THE USSR conditioned gay life there in an extremely negative way. First, the legal restrictions on the social and sexual activities of homosexuals in all of the Soviet republics, as expressed in the penal codes outlawing "sodomy"—as well as the harsh sentence for breaking them—were substantial sources of anxiety oppression for gay and lesbian citizens of the USSR. Second, the social-political institution of condemnatory attitudes toward homosexuals ("homophobia") was evident in Soviet society and also contributed to the difficult life situation gay men and lesbians faced there. Of course, such conditions are hardly unique to the USSR. However, the history of the institutionalization of sodomy in Soviet society (and in the societies of Kievan Rus, Muscovite Russia, and the Russian Empire before it) was different in key ways from that which occurred elsewhere in Europe. Individual and group activist efforts on the part of Soviet gay men and lesbians directed at changing this situation were generally not met with much success for several reasons the elaboration of which will be the chief topic of this chapter.

I. LEGAL RESTRICTIONS ON HOMOSEXUAL ACTIVITY ("SODOMY")

While the long history of the codification of an official, negative attitude toward homosexuality is not identical in all places in the western world, the origin of this restriction is nearly universal in its adaptation from the Judeo-Christian religious tradition, whether in late medieval times (13th-14th centuries) or in the early modern period. (Greenberg 1988) The religious prohibition against homosexuality was based on the Biblical story of Sodom and Gomorrah, "You shall not lie with a male as one lies with a female; it is an abomination," in which the vices of the residents of these Canaanite cities led God to destroy them by heavenly firestorm—

but not before Lot, the only righteous citizen of Sodom, was made aware of God's plans and impelled to flee the city along with his family, not looking back.

Stemming from the Medieval belief that vice could be contagious, euphemisms were often used to describe sexual sins, lest explicitness tempt otherwise righteous people to take them up. The most common euphemism for homosexuality, among both clergy and laymen, was "the sin of Sodom," and where they were enacted, prohibitions against homosexuality or homosexual behavior in the legal codes of most countries were also institutionalized as statutes against "sodomy."[1] By the same thinking, at times it was thought better not to distinguish clearly the sexual sins when discussing them. As a result, there was significant variation in what came to be defined as "sodomy." In different places and at various times it has been defined as: (only) anal intercourse between men; as oral or anal intercourse between men; as oral or anal sex between any two people, heterosexual or homosexual; as any sexual relations between two men; as any sexual relations between two people of the same sex, men or women; or even as any sexual relations at all between two people that do not make procreation possible. However imprecise or shifting the definition, though, at the very least it always referred to male homosexual anal intercourse, which has usually been assumed to be synonymous with homosexuality.

Geographically distant from the major economic and political centers of Rome, Paris, Amsterdam, and London and socio-culturally isolated by adherence to the Eastern Orthodox Christian tradition rather than to the Roman Catholic Church, Russia's history in the Middle Ages was quite different from that of Western Europe,[2] and this fact had some important consequences for the institutionalization of the prohibition against homosexuality there.

The relationship between Church and state in the East was less problematic because rulers of Orthodox kingdoms were seen as carrying out the will of God (kings were inaugurated by the Church Patriarch), and much of Slavic Orthodox canon law was inherited directly from the Byzantine Church.[3] Having come under the influence of the (Greek) Orthodox Church since the first introduction of organized religion in 988, during the rule of Grand Prince Vladimir, the rulers of Kievan Rus,[4] like those of the Byzantine Empire, never needed to battle with the Orthodox Church over the issue of moral authority.

Russia was even further cut off from Western influence by the conquest of Rus from the East by Ghengis Khan's "Golden Horde" and its long domination by the "Mongol Yoke" (from 1240 to 1480). As a result of both Orthodoxy and Mongol domination, during the time when Western kingdoms and the Roman Church were battling to extend their power bases, the conflicts and contests between and among religious and secular authorities produced neither a religious Reformation movement nor an anti-religious scientific Enlightenment as happened in the West. Greenberg (1988:292) explains the situation in the Byzantine Empire:

because church and state were integrated, the dynamic of church reform seen in the West was not present. Though the Justinian prohibition [against homosexuality] remained in effect, it became little more than a dead letter. Though homosexuality was frowned upon, the ready availability of eunuchs at court, and of slaves until the twelfth century, facilitated the indulgence of homosexual tastes among men.

This does not mean that there was not a moral proscription against homosexuality and other forms of illicit sexual expression in the Byzantine and Slavic kingdoms as this passage may seem to indicate—only that the proscription did not become important for the state as a means of asserting moral primacy, and therefore was not used as a political weapon.

A. Enactment of Anti-Sodomy Statutes in Russia and the USSR

The first known secular restriction on homosexuality in Russia was introduced in the Russian Empire of the Romanov dynasty (18th to early 20th Centuries) as a provision of the Military Legal Code put in force by Peter I (Peter the Great) in 1706—a part of his Westernizing reforms. The code enacted was an adaptation from the Swedish military code of that time which called for transgressors to be burned at the stake. In 1716, Peter's Military Legal Code was amended, calling for corporal punishment for homosexual relations and the death penalty or hard labor for life only if it could be proved that force or other use of violence was involved. As a part of the Military Code, this proscription was applicable only to those in the ranks of military service and perhaps owing to Peter's own occasional homosexual dalliances, it was apparently not much used.[5] (Karlinsky 1989)

Since the prohibition against sodomy had not been enacted into civil law in Russia, it would seem that there was no need to borrow from Western debate among the *philosophes* on this issue. Nonetheless, through a legal edict in 1785, Empress Catherine II (Catherine the Great), who was in correspondence with Voltaire, is said to have instructed judges, through the Senate, to exercise "the utmost clemency and mercy" in sodomy cases, since "the victims must be considered to have been more temporarily out of their wits, than really criminal" (as quoted in Greenberg 1988:350).

The first secular and *civil* code proscribing homosexuality in the Russian Empire came in 1832 with the enactment of statute 995 of a new legal code promulgated under Tsar Nicholas I. The text of the prohibition, which stayed in effect through the rest of the Tsarist period, was as follows:

One proven guilty of [or "exposed at": изобличенный в] the unnatural vice of sodomy [мужеложства][6] is subject to the following:

>deprivation of all special rights and property, personal or conferred by status, and removal to the arrested's correctional division for a period of four to five years.

Above that, if he is a Christian, then he is transferred to the Church penitentiary [покаянию] at the disposal of its spiritual leadership. (My translation from Козловский 1986:147)

From the time of the Bolshevik Revolution (October 1917) until Stalin's revision of the Soviet legal code in 1934, there was no law against homosexuality enacted in the USSR, but the legal situation of gay men and lesbians in this period was not as straightforward as that simple fact might suggest. In the general chaos of the Civil War and Soviet state-building that followed the Revolution (1918–1921, the period of "War Communism"), there was no penal code enacted at all by the Bolsheviks, and therefore no law against homosexuality. This general state of lawlessness, however, should not be equated with legalization of homosexuality as some have implied (Lauritsen & Thorstad 1974), for while there was no legal code enacted, this does not mean that no legal action was taken. Officers were instructed that the Tsarist legal code should be followed in the interim, unless it referenced a law that was "contrary to the revolutionary ideals" (Karlinsky 1989, 1991).

When the Union of Soviet Socialist Republics was created in 1922, however, a new Penal Code was enacted which did not mention consensual homosexual sodomy, thus making homosexuality legal. There is some controversy over whether this decriminalization of consensual homosexuality was an integral part of the Bolshevik reform movement (Lauritsen & Thorstad 1974) or is more properly viewed as an aberration allowed by the early Communist government more as an oversight, which was corrected when Stalin came to power (Karlinsky 1976, 1977).

Further, Karlinsky (1989) argues, it should not be assumed that the existence of this legal loophole made everyday life for gay men and lesbians in Russia better than it had been under the tsars. He (Karlinsky 1989) and Kozlovsky (Козловский 1986a) have especially cautioned against taking this as a sign of great tolerance or a "blossoming" of gay culture in Soviet Russia,[7] arguing that the lack of legal restrictions on homosexual behavior was accompanied by a more restrictive social environment for gay men and lesbians under an ever-more-powerful medical view of homosexuality as a disease or psychological disorder. Indeed, although the Tsarist prohibition against homosexuality had been lifted, there appears to have been a gradual lessening of tolerance toward the open expression of homosexuality—at least in literary and artistic circles, and Aleksándra Kollontái's "free love" was once again silenced by officially sanctioned scorn and social opprobrium.

With the rise of Stalin to the leadership of the Communist Party and of the state, new, repressive social legislation as well as repressive political and economic policies were put into effect. As Williams (1995:131) put it: "Stalin made homosexuality illegal on the grounds that Russia had witnessed a period of moral decline in the decade and a half since October 1917 and therefore it was time to reimpose a new moral order [sic]." Now officially seen as a "bourgeois aberration," homosexuality, which would not produce new citizens for the Soviet state, was outlawed in 1934 (as was abortion, for the same reason). The relevant article (154) of the revised Penal Code for the Russian Federation reads as follows:

> Sexual relations between men (sodomy [мужеложство]) is punishable by deprivation of freedom for a term of from three to five years. Sodomy committed with the application of force or by taking [advantage of] the dependent situation of the victim is punishable by deprivation of freedom for a term of five to eight years. (Уголовный Кодекс РСФСР 1935:61)

At that time, nearly identical laws were enacted in all of the republics of the USSR that did not already have them and thereby sodomy was made illegal throughout the Soviet state.[8]

Homosexuality had come to be seen as "anti-proletarian," was equated with the old ruling order, and was therefore deemed counterrevolutionary. (Lauritsen & Thorstad 1974; Greenberg 1988; Karlinsky 1989) A quote from the speech given by the Russian Soviet Federated Socialist Republic's Commissar of Justice, Krylénko, in 1936 illustrates the new ideology, even as its author conflates the views of homosexuality as "sick" and "criminal" (dangerous to the state):

> It is for doctors to decide in each specific case whether the accused is a sick man or not. But if we have no reason to think he is sick, and he nonetheless commits these acts, then we say to him: "My good fellow, there's no place for you here. Among us workers, who believe in normal relations between the sexes and who are building up a society on healthy principles, there is no room for gentry of this sort." Who in fact are our chief customers in this line? Are they working men? Of course not—they are either the dregs of society, or remnants of the exploiting classes. (Applause.) They don't know what to do with themselves, so they take to pederasty. (Laughter.) And beside them, along with them, there is another kind of work that goes on in little filthy dens and hiding places, and that is the work of counter-revolution.
> That is why we take these disorganizers of our new social system, the system we are creating for men and women and working people—we put these gentlemen on trial and we give them sentences of up to five years. (As quoted in Chalidze 1977: 143–144)

In the heady days of the Khrushchóv "Thaw," reform of the legal system was undertaken as a part of the general policy of "de-Stalin-ization." Amendments were made to the Soviet Penal Codes, during which time the penalty for homosexual sex was lessened somewhat. The new article (121) of the revised Penal Code for the RSFSR states that:

> 121.1. Sexual relations between two men ("sodomy") are punishable by the deprivation of freedom for a term of up to five years. 121.2. Sodomy committed by

the application of physical force or threats or in relations with a minor or by taking advantage of the dependent situation of the victim is punishable by the deprivation of freedom for a term of up to eight years. (Уголовный Кодекс РСФСР 1960)

The difference here is that lighter sentences could now be given—under 3 years for consensual homosexual acts among adults, and under five years for "aggravated" sodomy (homosexual rape) or homosexual "statutory rape." One should also note the addition of threats as a condition defining homosexual rape.

Under Soviet leader Gorbachóv (1985–1991), efforts were underway once again to revise the Soviet Criminal Codes in conjunction with his fresh policy of "new thinking," his call for sweeping economic reforms (*perestróyka*), and for dramatic changes in the social life of the country (*glásnost*). During this time, in the Russian Federation and in several other Soviet republics there were attempts to repeal the anti-sodomy statutes. At least two social scientists, including Ígor S. Kón, who served as advisors to the RSFSR government commission reviewing the penal codes, lobbied for omitting article 121.1 from the revised law. Newly-formed gay and lesbian activist groups also called for the elimination of article 121.1 from the penal code, but as the reform process lagged and faltered, changes in the criminal code were put off repeatedly.

As the economic situation in the country came to the point of crisis, changes in economic legislation were seen as paramount while social and political legislative reforms were not high on the reformers' agenda. In the summer of 1991, Kón informed me that, after three years of discussion, he and his colleagues had had little success in convincing the reform commission of the importance of lifting the legal restrictions on homosexual behavior for the development of a "civilized," democratic political system. He predicted no greater than a 50/50 chance that the anti-sodomy statute would be absent from the new criminal code—whenever it was to be enacted. (Кон Interview 1991)

B. Enforcement of Anti-Sodomy Statutes in the Soviet Union

Data on the application of these anti-sodomy statutes is sketchy at best. According to legal experts, both court proceedings and data on sentencing were kept strictly secret throughout most of the Soviet period (de Jong 1982), and as a result it is not clear how frequently men were actually punished for sodomy under these statutes. However, the information that is available can be pieced together well enough to produce a rough sketch of the situation.

According to Williams (1995:131–132), at the time of the reimposition of the anti-sodomy statute in the Soviet Union, punishment for violations were swift and harsh:

In 1933, prompted by fears of a German-led 'homosexual conspiracy', a clampdown on known homosexuals began. This culminated in January 1934 in a wave of arrests for alleged homosexuality in Moscow, Leningrad, Kharkov, Odessa and other major cities. Victims included the prominent writer Mikhail Kuzmin and his partner Iu Iurkin, who disappeared without a trace in 1938. The justification for a reversal of policy was that homosexuals shared the same characteristics as 'fascists' who wished to undermine the moral fabric of Russian society and corrupt youngsters.[9]

De Jong (1982:346) estimates that 690 men were convicted of "pederasty"[10] under either paragraph of article 121 in the Soviet Union in 1966, which figure represents 0.1% of convictions for all crimes that year. IGLHRC, the international gay and lesbian activist organization, has documentation of the numbers of men imprisoned for sodomy in the Russian Federation, during its last five years (Gessen 1994). (See Table 5.1.)

Table 5.1: Number of Men Convicted under Article 121 in the RSFSR, 1987–1991.*

Year	Total
1987	831
1988	800
1989	538
1990	497
1991	462**

* Sources: Gessen (1994:11) and Kon (1995:246).
** Kon reports 482 convictions for 1991.

These figures suggest a reduction in the number of men prosecuted for acts of sodomy in the later years of the Gorbachóv regime. It may be reasonable to assume that the number of sodomy convictions was declining due to the general easing of restrictions and enforcement under *glásnost* and *perestróyka*, but without a study of police attention to this issue over the years, we cannot be sure that this is the case. Without earlier data we cannot know by how much these figures were down from previous levels. What is more, these data do not tell us anything about the number of other Soviet citizens who were prosecuted under this article but not convicted, who were charged with sodomy but not prosecuted, who were arrested but not charged with sodomy, who were detained for "suspicious behavior" or "hooliganism" but not officially arrested, or who were questioned about their behavior but not detained.

Only 13.8% of my respondents report having had a run-in with the police related to their participation in gay-related activities—up to and including a court appearance or a prison sentence. (83.4% reported no such trouble with the police and 2.4% declined to answer this question.)

II. SOCIETAL ATTITUDES TOWARD HOMOSEXUALITY

While it is not possible to characterize definitively the attitude of contemporary Soviet society toward homosexuality, since it is not a well-studied issue, there are several clues to the social situation of gay men and lesbians in the USSR which can be culled from reports in the news media on the topic, from a public opinion survey done on attitudes toward deviant social actors, including homosexuals, and from the incidence of violence against lesbians and gay men ("gay bashing") in Soviet society.

Extreme social opprobrium is starkly reflected in the only nation-wide research done on popular attitudes toward homosexuality in the USSR. The study, carried out by the All-Union Center for the Study of Public Opinion (VTsIOM) in December 1989, showed a sharply hostile attitude toward gay men and lesbians among an almost-two-thirds majority (64.4%) of those surveyed. When asked what, in their opinion, should be done with homosexuals (among other people "whose behavior deviates from the generally accepted norm"), fully one-third (33.7%) of respondents said to kill them—actually, to "liquidate" them ("ликвидировать"), using the Stalinist euphemism. Nearly another third (30.7%) indicated that they should be "isolated from society," the implication of which is that they should be either incarcerated in prisons or committed against their will in mental institutions. One in ten respondents (10.1%) said that homosexuals should be "left to themselves," and only 6.4% felt that it would be right to "provide them help." (Левада и Левинсон 1990; Левинсон 1991)

One of the study's authors (Левинсон 1991:7) summed up the situation this way:

> The problem of intimate contacts between people of one sex was under the same heavy taboo and began to "spill over" into this epoch of speaking out [*glásnost*]. To people who are inclined toward that form of contact, it is well known how few are those in society who, not sharing their leanings, will acknowledge their right to structure their own personal life. According to our researches, they are 10–15% [of the population]. Whereas, those proposing to "isolate them from society" are three to four times as many [in number].

Yet, even this 16.5% of respondents did not necessarily take kindly to gay men and lesbians. After all, to leave someone alone is hardly charitable; often it is negligent. What is more, given the way the question was worded, it not clear what proportion (if any) of the 6.4% preferring to offer help to homosexuals actually meant to indicate that they feel medical and/or psychiatric "help" is needed so that they can be "cured." Thus, to say that even 10–15% of the Soviet population acknowledged homosexuals' right to make what they will of their personal lives may well be an overstatement.

In fact, there is another response category to this question that the researchers did not sufficiently analyze. Respondents were allowed the option of choosing "it's hard to say" if they could not chose from the four positive or negative reactions. It is this response, I submit, that is the truly neutral position, since both isolating them from society and leaving them alone can be forms of ostracism—though certainly not ones of equal severity. Only by ordering these data in this bipolar fashion, I feel, does one accurately represent Soviet citizens' attitudes toward homosexuals. The result is a consistently increasing proportion of respondents endorsing increasingly negative positions. (See Table 5.2.)

Table 5.2: Public Opinion in the USSR about What Steps Should Be Taken With Homosexuals, 1989.*

Opinion	Percentage
"Liquidate" Them	33.7%
Isolate Them from Society	30.7%
Hard to Say	19.5%
Leave Them to Themselves	10.1%
Provide Help For Them	6.4%
Total:	100.4%**

* Data are from Левада и Левинсон (1990).
** Presumably, data do not add to 100.0% due to rounding error and/or weighting, but the source does not indicate a reason.

Of course, the most extreme options given—helping people and killing them—are also not directly opposite positions to take, considering their varying degrees of generosity and cruelty.

This data must not be taken as hyperbole. Kon (1995), for one, demonstrates the existence of a "wave of anti-homosexuality" as a backlash against Soviet gay men's and lesbians' increased visibility under the government's campaigns of *glásnost* and *perestróyka*, slight as it was. At the beginning of Gorbachóv's administration, for instance, representatives of the Western fashion industry (Bookbinder, Lichtenstein, & Denton 1985:115) reported encountering open expression of this desire to eliminate homosexuals: "One Leningrader developed an uncontrollable rage at the idea of men being homosexual. [He said:] 'I think they should all be lined up and shot. No, I mean it, I'd be happy to shoot them myself.'" This may be no idle threat.

To be stigmatized is misfortune enough, but these data indicate that nearly every third person they pass on the street wants homosexuals killed and that another of those three individuals think they should be imprisoned or committed just because of their sexuality identity.[11] With such a hostile attitude on the part of the population, it is no wonder that few, if any, well-organized, gay-oriented social institutions developed in the Soviet Union. It was not fertile ground for such marginal groups. It is also small wonder that those gay places that do exist are racked by violent crime against gays and lesbians and are perceived of as dangerous by residents.

Of the respondents in my survey sample, 31.4% had been the victim of gay bashing of some sort, 56.5% had not, and 12.1% would not divulge this information. Over 80 unspecified "gay bashing" incidents ("ремонт") were reported, including 49 beatings by an individual or a group (избиение, насилие, нападение). Respondents said they had suffered 33 muggings (грабёж) because, as homosexuals, they were seen as an "easy mark." Among the other "bashing"-type incidents reported, there were 6 robberies, 5 rapes or attempted rapes, 4 cases of surveillance, 4 public name-calling incidents, and 17 other hostile encounters of various sorts. It is beyond doubt that this is not a full accounting.

III. THE PROSPECTS FOR GAY POLITICAL ACTIVISM IN THE FORMER USSR

Explaining the development of political institutions among Soviet homosexuals involves some considerations that would be the same when analyzing gay and lesbian activism anywhere as well as some that are peculiar to the analysis of the Soviet political system. After some description of the new social movement groups and their publications, I will discuss what I feel to be their importance for the development of gay and lesbian community in the former Soviet Union. First, however, it will help to delve into recent developments in the sociological and political science literatures on social movements because, as movement organizations, that is the standpoint from which these groups should be evaluated in any country.

A. Identity Politics in Collective Action

Tilly, Tilly, & Tilly (1975:283) described the situation faced by oppressed groups when they are considering taking collective action as rather dire:

> the range of collective actions open to a relatively powerless group is normally very small. Its program, its form of action, its very existence is likely to be illegal, hence subject to violent repression. As a consequence, such a group chooses between taking actions which have a high probability of bringing on a violent response (but which have some chance of reaching the group's goals) and taking no action at all (thereby assuring the defeat of the group's goals).

An extraordinary amount of shared energy, coordination, and resolve must be marshalled in order for such a powerless group to overcome the natural paralysis of this seemingly lose-lose situation. Their concerted collective action must be perceived of by group members as "their only hope."

This dilemma of whether or not a movement group should act and thereby risk repression was complicated in this case, by several factors. Like its counterparts throughout the world, the emerging Soviet gay and lesbian movement was one that challenged not only the country's legal code, but also social norms of "decency" and "morality." In addition, as among homosexuals everywhere, the undertaking of collective action was of great personal significance to Soviet gay men and lesbians, since their own sense of self-worth depends on a successful challenge to the *status quo*. As Arato (1991) has pointed out, most of the new social movements in the former USSR are engaged not only in mobilizing resources and building social organizations to bolster their cause, but also are engaged in the fundamentally ideological task of promoting new social identities as they transform the political culture. Thus they are engaging in symbolic forms of self-expression.

B. Community Institutions and Organizational Success in Social Movements

Theorizing on the causes of success or failure in such social activism, McAdam (1982:40) argues that there are three key factors that affect the emergence of social movements among minority groups: 1) the degree of organizational "readiness" within the minority community, 2) the level of "insurgent consciousness" within the movement's mass base, and 3) the "structure of political opportunities" available to insurgent groups. Without these conditions, a group cannot sustain its efforts at a level sufficient for successful collective action.

1. The Structure of Political Opportunities

To begin with the last of these conditions, it is McAdam's (1982:41) contention that "*any event or broad social process that serves to undermine the calculations and assumptions on which the political establishment is structured occasions a shift in political opportunities*" (*emphasis in the original*). Among such precipitating events likely to disrupt the political *status quo*, he lists: wars, industrialization, international political realignments, prolonged unemployment, and widespread demographic changes. Skocpol (1979) has found that the challenges to a state's political order are often mounted right after recovery from times of social and economic turmoil begins, partly due to the disillusionment often felt among the populace when increased moral and material expectations out-pace new political and socioeconomic possibilities.

During most of the 73 years of the Soviet regime, the "structure of political opportunities" was quite unfavorable for the very development of non-state organizations in all spheres. Opportunities for dissident and disgruntled people to mount collective action plans against the Soviet system were exceedingly difficult to concoct and extremely dangerous to enact. To be sure, **individual protest** could be made and individual or small-scale insubordination was, generally, possible. A small, but significant number of Soviet citizens failed to vote in regular single-party, single-candidate "elections," for instance, despite strong social and political pressure to show up at the polls. The social institution of "kitchen culture" was another example of the expression of opposition to the Soviet regime. The Soviet "marriage market" was a complex web of individuals colluding in protest against the state housing system. (Fisher 1980) Bribes, or "*blát*" (блат) in Russian, and "connections," or "*znakómstvo*" (знакомство), goods speculation, and the organized criminality of the "black market" were also elaborate protests against the (mal)functions of the Soviet planned economy. Yet, independent collective actions could scarcely be taken in economic, social, or cultural life—much less opportunity was there for collective action on the part of insurgent groups that might wish to press their political aspirations.

It can hardly be doubted that all of Eastern Europe, and all of the countries of the former Soviet Union are currently undergoing such changes, and that these changes are indeed bringing about a major realignment of the political structures of these countries. That process has been underway at least since Gorbachóv announced his plan of *perestróyka* (literally, "reconstructing" or "restructuring") in 1985, if not since the waning years of the Brezhnev leadership. To be sure, the realignment taking place has led to the collapse of the entire communist political system in most of these countries. In such a situation, McAdam (1982:42) argues,

> Generalized political instability destroys any semblance of a political *status quo*, thus encouraging collective action by *all* groups sufficiently organized to contest the structuring of a new political order." (*emphasis in the original*)

This does not mean that in a situation of political instability all groups will be able to launch successful social movements and press their demands in the political arena, however, for the other two conditions have yet to be considered.

2. The Level of Insurgent Consciousness

The level of insurgent consciousness among the aggrieved group must be sufficient to motivate individuals to participate in the movement despite the risks associated with open political action. Members of the minority group must sense that their efforts **just might** "pay off." The group's insurgent consciousness must also be strong enough to overcome what Olsen (1965) has called "the free-rider problem":

the tendency for individual group members to eschew direct participation in collective action while waiting to observe and enjoy what progress others might make on behalf of all concerned.

While the Soviet gay identity was relatively well-developed and consistent across geographic regions, time periods, and age groupings of the USSR (as discussed in Chapter Three), the difficult and often repressive socio-political conditions of Soviet life generally quashed attempts at collective action made by Soviet gay men and lesbians.

3. The Degree of Organizational Readiness

Finally, there has to be a significant level of organizational development already existing within the minority community in order for challenge to be mounted. Any movement group needs members, a satisfying reward structure, a reliable means of communication, and respected leaders in order to operate. These must come from the aggrieved population mounting the challenge to the existing order. They cannot be developed "on the spot," at the beginning of a movement, because in such a case, the movement cannot develop fast enough to take advantage of the political opportunity offered by the disruption in the political *status quo*—and no disruption in a political system lasts indefinitely.

Soviet gay men and lesbians were not very successful at getting their voices heard and thereby contesting the restructuring of the old political order in ways that suited their interests. It is my contention that this was because the gay and lesbian world of the former Soviet Union did not have sufficiently-well developed community organizations to meet these demands. Although the shift was occurring to an increasing understanding of the need for such activism, this was just the beginning of the creation of gay and lesbian group-level institutions and the few organizations that did exist in the USSR were not very well-organized. (Schluter 1992b) A quick review of these groups and their activities will elucidate.

IV. GAY AND LESBIAN ORGANIZATIONS IN THE FORMER SOVIET UNION

The first Soviet-era gay and lesbian group that we now know of was begun in Leningrad by a migrant from Kiev named Alexándr Zarémba in May 1984, a year before Gorbachóv's ascent to the Soviet leadership. Having some knowledge of gay and lesbian groups in the West, Zarémba gathered about him several close friends and, calling themselves the "Gay Laboratory," they petitioned the International Lesbian and Gay Association (ILGA) for membership. Although their activities were soon discovered by the KGB, which had put a "tail" ("слежка") on them, the group did succeed in hosting a delegation of ILGA representatives to Leningrad in the summer of 1984. After that, the group kept up sporadic contact with ILGA through a liaison from its official sponsor, the Finnish organization SETA. In 1986 the group was infiltrated and, when they were denounced, several of its members were fired from their jobs, some were exiled from the country or to Siberia, and Zarémba was imprisoned. The group fell apart in August that year. (Щербаков 1991, Shcherbakóv Interview 1991)

In October of 1989, in a private Moscow apartment, a group that called itself the Moscow Association of Sexual Minorities was formed (Тема 1989). Led by Román Kalínin, a young gay college student, the group began to put out a newspaper, with the name "Tyéma," or "The Theme" in English, which is a Russian gay-slang term referring to homosexuality. Thus the paper would be "on the theme," meaning "about gays." The group soon made headlines in the now freer Soviet media, eager for a taste of sensationalist journalism, but by mid-1990 the group had already split in two with one wing leaving to form an alternative organization. The Association, radicalized by the departure of its more cautious members, renamed itself the Moscow Union of Homosexuals and Lesbians, and garnered a great deal of publicity both in the USSR and abroad, largely due to the rowdy exploits of Kalínin (such as his outlandish pretense to bid for the presidency of the Russian Republic) as well as those of co-founder Yevgéniya Debryánskaya, a 37-year-old Soviet lesbian with a history in the dissident movement, and by their travels in America. It didn't help matters that, along with espousing its platform for gay rights, the Union called for the legalization of prostitution, drug use, necrophilia, and sex with children (however facetiously).

The group that had split off from the Moscow Association formed its own organization in the fall of 1990, called "ARGO," the Russian acronym for: the Association for the Equal Rights of Homosexuals. This group took a more conciliatory stand in relation to the authorities and to Soviet society, disavowing the "shock therapy" tactics of Kalínin and Debryánskaya and started to put out their own publication, which looked a bit glossier and purported to be "of literary value."

In Leningrad another group was formed, called the Chaykóvskiy Fund for Cultural Initiatives and Aid to Sexual Minorities. Headed by a drug-addicted lesbian, Ólga Zhúk, it closely aligned itself with the Moscow Union, taking basically identical positions on gay and lesbian issues and supporting the drug-use habits of its members. Though the activities of this group were minimal, they did meet with some success. Their main effort seems to have been advocating for the rights of gay men imprisoned under the Soviet anti-sodomy statute (article 121 of the Soviet Penal Code). During the much-heralded International Gay and Lesbian Symposium and Film Festival staged in July-August 1991 by American gay activists of the International Gay and Lesbian Human Rights Commission (which itself was co-founded by Roman Kalínin in 1990), Zhúk even succeeded in getting Soviet prison officials to allow a delegation of American activists to visit men held in a Leningrad prison under this statute.

As in Moscow, another Leningrad group, calling itself "The Banks of the Nyevá (River)," formed in opposition to Zhúk's Chaykóvskiy Fund. Led by a fired university professor, who had served a sentence in prison under a provision of the anti-sodomy statute, this group's goal was to work within the system to resolve the problems of Soviet homosexuals. They stayed in close contact with the ARGO group in Moscow and made it their primary goal to be legally registered with the Soviet government as an official organization. Two court cases and a name change later (to the name "Nyevá Perspectives") they had failed completely. Since the group members had vowed not to begin their activist work until after they achieved official status, this group got essentially nothing accomplished in the first two years of its formation. After the failed *coup d'etat* of August 1991, this group was finally officially registered under the new name "Wings," a reference to a novel by the same name authored by a gay writer of the early 1900s, Mikhaíl Kuzmín. As far as I know, this group had no publication, and I heard of no activities undertaken before the breakup of the USSR.

In January of 1991, in the Altay region of South-Central Siberia, two young gay students, having heard of "Tyéma," but never having seen a copy of it, got together to form the Siberian Union of Homosexuals and Lesbians, and to put out a gay newspaper of their own, called "SV." The name of the newspaper was intended to be a code for both the first names of its two founders as well as the phrase "Siberian Variant." Only one issue ever came out, since the two founders soon quarreled and one denounced the other to the authorities. Their split was along quite the same lines as the breakup of the Moscow Association, and as in the former case, two different movement groups were eventually formed. One group continued the publication of a newspaper, now fully titled "Siberian Variant" and the other group teamed up with some young lesbians in a nearby town to form the Siberian Association of Sexual Minorities. After their press appearance at the International Symposium in August of 1991, several members of this latter association were kicked out of their parents' homes and expelled from their universities. After that time, the activities of both groups were minimal.

In other areas of the USSR things went even slower, but are worth a brief mention. In Riga, Latvia, a group with a profile similar to that of the ARGO group was formed. In Tallinn, Estonia there was a Lesbian Social Union, which had been operating since 1990, and in Vilnius a Lithuanian Gay and Lesbian Information Bureau was organized to publicize the imprisonment of gay Lithuanians under the Soviet anti-sodomy Statute there. Although there were individuals working to establish gay and lesbian groups in Minsk, Byelorussia, and in Kiev, Ukraine, I am not aware of the successful establishment of any such groups. Soviet Central Asia remains a "backwater."

Despite the fact that all of these organizations had similar complaints about the socio-political *status quo* and purported to represent the same constituents in their drive for change, they diverged on the issues of goals and tactics. As in many social movements, the internal conflict here can be equated with that age-old rivalry between "reformers" and "revolutionaries."

A. Reformist/Assimilationist Groups

Among these nascent movement groups were some that espoused a reformist agenda of promoting social tolerance of homosexuality: acceptance of gay men and lesbians as being "just like everybody else, **except for this one thing**." Such groups called for the open assimilation of gays and lesbians into the mainstream of social life in their country, without being subjected to the oppressive social stigma, physical harassment, and discrimination they would normally face.

In Russia, ARGO and the St. Petersburg group "Wings" were groups of the former, reform/assimilationist type. Evidence of this was ARGO's credo, which called for:

> the attainment of a civilized, spiritual way of sexual life for minorities, the cultural and medical enlightenment of homosexuals, the conditions for the normal family life of same-sex couples; and from society, help so that these efforts will not run up against indifference, hatred, or contempt (РИСК 1991).

Supporting this interpretation was the very name chosen for the newspaper put out by the group. It sought to encourage people to join in risking collective action for the gay and lesbian cause, but in a way that would be non-threatening to "the powers that be." It was: "RISK," the Russian acronym for Equal Rights (Равноправие), Sincerity (Искренность), Freedom (Свобода), and Compromise (Компромисс); and the acronym means the same thing in Russian as it does in English. Like the American "homophile" organizations of the 1950s and early 60s (after experiencing the horror of McCarthyism), this group and its counterparts in St. Petersburg, Riga, Latvia, and South-Central Siberia promoted the strategy of educating heterosexuals about the nature of homosexuality (not a vice, not an illness, not a choice) and of demonstrating by their example that gays are civil, law-abiding members of society (not pederasts, not criminals, not lechers). (Ortánov Interview 1991, Interview with "Andréy" 1991, Volnóv Interview 1991)

B. Revolutionary/Separatist Groups

Then there were those that took a "radical" or revolutionary stance, seeking to overthrow the Soviet system as constituted. They demand nothing less than the repeal of all anti-gay legislation, the right to live and love openly and as they please, and the replacement of the Soviet system of patriarchal control over the lives of the state's subjects with a system in which individual liberties and the rule of (much less restrictive) law are respected.

The radical, revolutionary type organization was represented most vociferously by Kalínin's and Debryánskaya's Moscow Union, and by Zhúk's Chaykóvskiy Fund. Among the Moscow Union's goals were:

> •the fight against discrimination against citizens on the basis of sexual criteria. •stopping criminal persecution of homosexuals in situations of non-forcible contact. •the social rehabilitation of AIDS patients. . . . •breaking the information blockade of homosexuality. (Тема 1989)

Fundamentally, their aim was "supporting the primacy of personal interests over the interests of the state as a condition for the establishment of a free society" (Пономарёв 1991:1). Kalínin had, on more than one occasion, called for the violent overthrow of "those damned communists" ("проклятие коммунисты," Kalínin Interview 1991) and his group did, in fact, take part in the defense of Borís Yéltsin and the Russian Parliament at the "White House" during the failed *coup* attempt.

C. Strength of the Movement

Although these groups had amiable goals—and the individuals who formed them must be admired for their courage—their importance for the creation of a gay and lesbian civil rights movement was likely to be negligible. This was because they had not been able to build much of a membership and because either their risky tactics or their compromised goals made large numbers of Soviet gay men and lesbians either hostile or indifferent to their existence.[12]

Although it's founding "Committee of 9" ("K-9") was formed in the fall of 1990, ARGO failed to get together the ten sufficiently courageous people that were then required to petition for recognition from the local government as an "informal organization" ("неформалька")—and it soon lost to other enterprises several of the nine it had. Similarly, the Moscow Union, which began with only a handful of dyed-in-the-wool radicals whose histories as political dissidents and drug addicts left them little to lose, was soon down to two permanent members and by mid-1991 all of its activities seemed to be initiated by the one carefree and charismatic Kalínin. The Chaykóvskiy Fund in Leningrad had precisely the same problems as Kalínin's Moscow Union, without the advantage of a charismatic leader.

In fact, in the heavily bureaucratic and legalistic Soviet Union, it took the utter political breakdown that followed the attempted *coup d'etat* of August 19-21, 1991, for any gay organizations to achieve official recognition (and thereby to obtain permission to operate legally).[13]

D. Shaky Success and an Uncertain Future

Thus, while the structure of opportunities (the chaotic socio-political environment) was there for the development of a gay and lesbian movement in the USSR, the level of social consciousness among Soviet gays and lesbians and the degree of their organizational potential were far too low to permit the realization of a politically oriented, sustainable social movement for liberation.

This lack of readiness was underscored by the fact that the historic Gay and Lesbian Symposium and Film Festival held in Leningrad and Moscow in 1991 had to be organized almost entirely by its American participants. Most of what was not organized by them and "imported" to the USSR, was arranged by non-gay sympathizers in the "host cities." In fact, there was no doubt that neither this conference nor any like it would have ever come off without the leadership of Western gay activists, who are familiar with grass-roots organizing.

Furthermore, it seems that the gay and lesbian population of the Soviet Union was not much interested in politics. Even in the heady days of 1991, when Soviet republics were fighting for independence from Moscow, national politicians were jockeying for power, and the USSR Supreme Soviet was challenging Gorbachóv's rule, the vast majority (80.8%) of gay men and lesbians in my sample said that politics played "an insignificant (незначительная) role," "a minimal role," or "no role at all" in their lives. Close to one-half (43.9%) indicated no role for politics in their lives. (See Table 5.3.)

Table 5.3: Percentage of Respondents Reporting the Role Politics Plays in Their Lives.

Role:	Percentage
the main role	1.3%
a substantial role	7.1%
a significant role	10.9%
an insignificant role	18.4%
a minimal role	18.4%
no role at all	43.9%
Total:	100.0%

It is important to remember that, as McAdam (1982:43) put it: "A conducive political environment only affords the aggrieved population the *opportunity* for successful insurgent action. It is the resources of the minority *community* that enable insurgent groups to exploit those opportunities." (*emphasis added*)

Thus, after a more sober assessment, I can only conclude that there really was not a viable "gay and lesbian movement" in the Soviet Union. Moreover, there really cannot be one until such time as the socio-cultural institutions of gay community development have advanced to the point at which they can provide enough members to sustain such a movement, provide sufficient incentives for participation in the movement (overcoming the barriers of internalized repression and the "free-rider problem"), provide a reliable network of communication for the information needed to launch such a movement, and provide the competent and respected leaders who will command a sufficient following to support a sustained movement.

NOTES

1. Likewise, masturbation and "withdrawal" (of the penis from the vagina before ejaculation in heterosexual intercourse), were referred to euphemistically as "Onanism" after the Biblical tale of the sinner Onan, who was said to practice these "vices." These "sexual sins" however, were generally not institutionalized by codification in secular (civil or criminal) law.

2. Roughly concurrent with the Medieval period in the West, Levin (1989:ix) defines a "Middle Ages" among the Orthodox Slavs not by the struggle between Church and emerging nation-states for moral and legal authority, but by the strength of the Holy/Royal alliance. "Throughout the medieval period, Orthodox Christianity reinforced and preserved the underlying cultural unity. The first conversions in the ninth century mark the beginning of the Middle Ages in the East; the rapid influx of Western and secular influences under Peter the Great [1682–1725] marks the end."

3. For this time period, the designation "Slavic Orthodox" refers to Serbs, Bulgarians, and Russians. (Levin 1989)

4. Kievan Rus was the main Eastern Slavic principality from the 10th to the 13th Centuries. It consisted of a large territory centered around the city of Kiev (now the capital of the independent, post-Soviet Ukraine) and was the predecessor to the later Russian Empire.

5. As Greenberg (1988:303) tells it: "In Russia, homosexuality had long been under church jurisdiction, but at the start of the eighteenth century Peter the Great, who often slept with his soldiers, hypocritically made the prohibition secular. While the initial legislation applied only to men, as in Spain, it was sometimes extended by interpretation to include women as well." This statement is a bit misleading, taken at face value. Peter made the prohibition secular in that it became applicable to some men outside of the church—to those in military service—but it was not universally so. It was not applicable to the civilian population (see Karlinsky 1989). Greenberg is right though, in pointing out that this imposition was hypocritical and that because of the use of the "principle of analogy," some behaviors that were not illegal, such as sex between women, were nonetheless punished under statutes against crimes that were judged to be "similar." (Chalidze 1977)

6. While most Western states followed the Roman Catholic Church in using the term "sodomy" as the general category of sin which encompassed (either consisted of or included) homosexual relations, the legal provisions of the Russian Empire referenced the term *muzhelózhstvo* (мужеложство), which was more narrowly defined by the Eastern Orthodox Church, rather than using the more parallel term *sodomíya* (содомія), also in use at the time. I translate *muzhelózhstvo* (which means, literally, "man-lying") as "sodomy" here, in part because there is no direct English equivalent to the narrow Orthodox definition of *muzhelózhstvo* (short of referring to "male homosexual anal intercourse"), and in part

because even this latter designation is disputed as the "real meaning" of the term. Similarly, in the West—especially in America—there is much dispute as to whether anti-"sodomy" statutes outlaw "homosexuality" or "(usually male homosexual) anal (and sometimes oral) intercourse." This makes *muzhelózhstvo* parallel to sodomy in ambiguous legal terms if not in highly specific religious ones.

7. Throughout the period discussed, laws against sodomy remained on the books in some other parts of the former Russian Empire: two republics of the Caucasus Region (Georgia and Azerbaijan) and two in Central Asia (Uzbekistan and Turkmenistan). In the Baltic states of Estonia and Latvia, which gained independence after the Revolution, anti-sodomy statutes were not enacted.

8. For the most part, the codes differed only by number. When the Baltic States were annexed by the USSR during World War II, anti-sodomy statutes were enacted there as well, *exempli gratia*: paragraph 126 in Latvia, paragraph 122 in Lithuania.

9. This irrational fear that there was some direct and sinister connection between German Nazism and homosexuality was not at all unique to the Soviet scene. At least in England and America, such accusations were also made: that the Nazis were led by a network of homosexuals bent on destroying good, Christian, Western society. Of course, it bears mentioning that only a decade later, during the "McCarthy Era" in the United States, the equation shifted to that of "Commie-pinko-spy."

10. De Jong (1982) translates *muzhelózhstvo* as "pederasty." Although the words are used virtually synonymously in everyday speech, as noted above, I prefer to render *muzhelózhstvo* as "sodomy," since this is the English-language term used in most legal codes. This practice also avoids the common confusion when using the more accurate meaning of the term pederasty (in Russian: "педерастия") which properly refers to sex between an adult and a minor, whether heterosexual or homosexual.

11. See Chapter Three for explanation of this term and discussion of identity in general.

12. There are two exceptions to this rule, though: the Leningrad group Banks of the *Nyevá*, which had a somewhat larger membership following the almost-motherly leadership of its middle-aged patriarch; and the Riga-based Latvian Association for Sexual Equality (LASR) whose activities seemed to be more recreational than political, and therefore more attractive to the young membership.

13. The Moscow Union's newspaper *Tyéma*, which had been officially registered since the early spring of 1991 was not registered as the official organ of a social group, as was customary for such publications in the Soviet Union, but as the sole property and business of its "owner," Román Kalínin. This was the only way he could find for operating (semi)legally, and it opened him up to significant personal and political danger.

As is the case with any other social minority that cannot detach itself and form a separate independent state, the emancipation of gay men and lesbians and their social and cultural integration are two sides of the same process. They are faced, in our view, with three basic tasks.

The first is to decriminalise homosexuality as part of the overall process of democratising the country. No people can be free if it oppresses its own social minorities—and gay men and lesbians are the most numerous minority, even if they are the least visible. . . .

Second, the general public needs to be systematically educated. Homophobia is the result of more than reactionary policy. A public for which all sex customarily appears shameful and sordid, and which experiences a sense of alarm even over heterosexuality is bound to regard homosexuality, about which it has heard nothing but monstrosities, with the utmost intolerance. . . .

Thirdly, a gay and lesbian subculture must be established. Homosexuals must turn their ghetto into a normal community of gay men and lesbians with its own publications, clubs, consultation and advice bureaux and suchlike, much as has happened in the West.

All these objectives are interconnected and have to be implemented simultaneously and in parallel, without shelving any of them or leaving them to someone else. This can only be done through cooperation and dialogue.

Igor Kon,
"Sexual Minorities" in: *Sex and Russian Society*,
Igor Kon and James Riordan, eds.
p.112.

Conclusion
Fraternity Without Community in the Soviet Gay World

IN THE INTRODUCTION TO THIS BOOK, I ADDRESSED MYSELF TO THREE ACADEMIC audiences that should find my study of social institutions among the gay and lesbian population of the Soviet Union relevant to their respective disciplines for the perpetual work of scholarship. That is, they should find this work useful for expanding the issues in their collective discourse and the scope of their independent empirical research.

First, I noted that, although many aspects of gay life among the homosexual populations of Western Europe and North America have been continually researched and much debated in the new academic field of Gay Studies, there has been a lack of attention paid to the study of homosexuality outside of modern, Western "First World" societies. This is especially true of the gay and lesbian populations in the "Second World" of Communist Eastern Europe, the Soviet Union, China, and Southeast Asia; whereas the social and political situation of homosexuals in the "Third World" of less-developed, pre- or proto- modern, and generally impoverished countries has received increasing attention by academics.

Second, I pointed out that Soviet/Russian Studies, in its efforts to understand the workings of the Communist regime in its political, economic, and historical aspects, has also neglected academic study of this population. This omission has left the field ignorant of some key elements of the Soviet system that accounted for the intense frustrations many Soviet citizens felt when pursuing personal fulfillment in matters sexual, whether homosexual or heterosexual. Citizens' personal needs related to sexuality (including their behavioral, erotic, and romantic interests) were scarcely considered by the Soviet state. As Geiges & Suvorova (Гейгес и Суворова 1990) so aptly put it: sex was outside the Five-Year Plan. Ignoring the study of Soviet homosexuals also led scholars of the USSR to overlook the significant role Soviet homosexuals sought to play in the development of "civil society" in the USSR during the years of *glásnost*, "new thinking," and *perestróyka*. (*Conferre:* Gessen 1990c; Chua-Eoan 1991; Dorf & Gessen 1991; Gessen 1991a-b.)

Third, as a sociologist, I made clear my dissatisfaction over the poorly defined, undifferentiated, and imprecise use of the concept "**community**"—both in common practice and in the sociological literature—to describe the aggregation of individuals into nearly any category. I resolved this problem by formulating a definition of community as a **social group**, the members of which engage in direct or indirect, predictable, regular, and sustained social interaction. Such interaction, of course, implies some form of communication among group members and some practical reason, historical legacy, or synergistic **complementarity** that acts as a catalyst for their visceral bond. Through this interaction they come to share a common group-identity and a sense that they have an important commonality in their shared interest or condition. In cooperation, they fashion innumerable social institutions out of their joint conduct (often without perceiving to) and, by the habitual use and replication of these institutions, they order "their" world.

Further, I labored to differentiate this concept of community from "**fraternity**," which I defined as a **distinctive category** of people who share some common interest or condition, and do identify themselves as individuals belonging to that category, but do not interact as a group often or consistently enough to develop (or "construct" or "invent") group-level social institutions specifically designed to satisfy the needs of category members. Individuals belong to such categories because of their **similarity** to one another, but only in regard to that specific aspect of their personality, appearance, behavior, life-circumstance, or other attribute by which they are categorized. They typically do not interact with one another because their similarity makes this less necessary, or less possible, given the danger. In fact, sometimes another individual like themselves would be in competition with them for the resources or attention they seek. This, I argued, was the condition of gay men and lesbians in the Soviet Union.

Some tourist accounts and journalistic reports on the state of existence and life conditions of homosexuals in the last years of the USSR had appeared in mainstream Western media (D.J.P. 1990; Friedman 1992), although most such information could be found only in specifically gay- and lesbian-themed

Conclusion: Fraternity without Community in the Soviet Gay World

newspapers and magazines (Gessen 1990a-c; Indiana 1990; ADVOCATE 1991a-c; Gessen 1991c; Karlinsky 1991; Tuller 1991; ADVOCATE 1992a-h; Dorf & Gessen 1992; *et cetera*). None of these articles were analytical explorations of social institutions extant in the Soviet gay world; yet, many of them seemed to indicate that gay men and lesbians in the former Soviet Union were making big strides in their efforts to create more, stronger, and more-positive conditions under which to live. These reports also labeled the condition of homosexuals in the Soviet Union "gay community"—wrongly so, if my sociological explication of the concept is taken.

This is no petty issue. Indeed, it is no coincidence that the study of and reverence for community as a fundamental form of social organization were the bases for the development of both the academic discipline of Sociology and the revolutionary political ideology and activism that later became Socialist and Communist systems of governance. The idea of community is at the heart of both endeavors. Moreover, a community is also a grouping of people, the very designation of which is usually so imbued with the positive connotations of an important, substantial, even a hallowed social institution that any collection of people who can lay claim to it thereby becomes "a force to be reckoned with." Social movements involving and on behalf of homosexuals, gay and lesbian civil rights activist groups, homosexual voluntary associations, sociocultural organizations, and economic enterprises, as well as political and social representatives of gay men and lesbians in the West have long fought for this designation and are well aware of its power. Nothing of the kind was experienced in the USSR, certainly not by Soviet homosexuals. In fact, "ideological work" was a boring and bureaucratic profession and the very word "activist" (активист) was anathema to most Soviet citizens, and it reeked with the connotations of overly zealous, blindly arrogant, and condescending attitudes.

I. DISTINGUISHING FRATERNAL INSTITUTIONS FROM COMMUNAL ONES

In Chapter One, by combining several approaches to studying the phenomenon of community, I put forth a theoretical framework for this analysis that addresses the problems with previous studies of the subject and establishes a basis for evaluating the development of community in any population or among any category of people. As a reminder, I will reiterate my position here.

In the history of the discipline, many scholars have criticized the confused thinking about, researches on, and analyses of community found in the sociological literature. I cited a few of them (Gillette 1926; Hillery 1955; Effrat 1973). Some students of community have sought to clarify what is meant by the term through analysis of its components (Nisbet 1952; Park 1952; Craven & Wellman 1973; *et alia*). Others defined and delineated the various forms community can take (Janowitz 1952; Henry 1958; Neuwirth 1969; Sagarin 1971; Effrat 1973; *et cetera*).

I drew two inferences from these works. On one hand, I agreed with the assertion sometimes made that, in order to clarify "the community concept" and make it more useful for empirical research, "communityness" must be problematized (Effrat 1973). On the other hand, I argued that the most fruitful way to accomplish this is not to labor at distinguishing different types of community one from another, but to focus on differentiating community from other forms of social organization that are often confused, or assumed to be synonymous, with it. It was with these things in mind that I stated and elaborated on my conviction that group-level social institutions are the essential components of community (Park 1952), whether the basis for interaction among community members is common residential locality, ethnicity, religious affiliation, specialized group interests, or some similar life situation. Each of these things (and many others) can inspire identification with some social group.

I then embraced the idea that the degree of "institutional completeness" (Breton 1964) can be a good gauge by which to evaluate the existence of community as opposed to "fraternity" (Webber 1964) in the population I set out to study. Doing so required specification of just what is meant by the term "social institution," which is another widely used and poorly defined sociological concept. For a clear and concise definition of this phenomenon, I turned to the social-constructionist school of thought, which most succinctly describes social institutions as repeated and well-recognized patterns of social (inter)action imbued with a shared social meaning (Berger & Luckmann 1966). In this scheme, a pattern of behavior is considered to be "institutionalized" when it becomes repeated often enough and becomes so habitual in its performance that people refer to it as a "thing" (often a process) unto itself.

The logic here is not difficult to understand. People perform actions in relation to others and interact with one another in consistent ways because they have some recurring need that they wish to satisfy or some opportunity they wish to take. Behaviors that prove helpful in satisfying those needs and wants will be repeated, while those that are not useful are likely to be abandoned—if not banned outright for being harmful. All manner of problems and opportunities present themselves to individuals and groups of people and, over time, their patterned responses to those situations become reified as recommended or required "ways of doing things." In this way, socially motivated actors can be seen as "inventing" social institutions associated with a given need or desire in response to the specific conditions of their lives (Abbott 1987). These innovations, whether technical or social (in intent or in effect), are not created simply to solve the **personal problems** of individuals, however. They are intended as general solutions to the class of similar needs felt by

Conclusion: Fraternity without Community in the Soviet Gay World

other individuals, that is, as ways of resolving the social issues of importance to all those who are likely to find themselves in analogous situations because of the type of person they are. (Mills 1959) Thus, the social institution of "community" and its likewise institutionalized components were the "inventions" of interest for this analysis.

In the rest of the book, I detailed the particular features of the individual-level and social-ecological circumstances that made such institutional development on the group level far too risky for gay men and lesbians in the Soviet Union to undertake. Indeed, the very idea of a solidary gay community was too unfamiliar for them to comprehend fully. Here I will summarize these points only briefly.

II. SECRET INDIVIDUAL-LEVEL INTERACTION ALLOWS FOR SOVIET GAY FRATERNITY

As I explained in Chapter Three, individual identity stems from interaction with others—or at least from knowledge about such possible interaction. Thus, identifying oneself with a particular social category or group is an indication of interaction or desired interaction with them. Under the Soviet Communist regime, though, any deviation from state-approved social interaction was seen as antiproletarian and anti-Communist—and therefore, a direct threat to the state. Homosexual behavior was against the law in the Soviet Union for precisely this reason and therefore, in the Soviet legal system, identifying oneself as homosexual was equivalent to engaging in illegal activity. It made being homosexual an abnormal, a stigmatized, and an outlawed identity.

All three types of homosexual identification were fraught with danger and uncertainty for gay and lesbian people in the USSR. First, they had difficulty identifying themselves as being homosexual, since discussing the existence of such a category of people was taboo. There was virtually no information about homosexuality available to the public that individuals could easily find to read—even surreptitiously—and what little could be found was quite negative.[1] Second, they found it extremely difficult to identify themselves to non-homosexual others as being members of this highly stigmatized category not least because sodomy (мужеложство) was punishable by up to five years imprisonment with hard labor. Third, they had difficulty identifying each other as proper candidates for homosexual interaction, because there were few clear cues that they could use as an indicator of another's homosexuality, mostly crude ones (obvious fondling, a bold approach on the street, or very specific innuendo).

Interaction between Soviet gay men and lesbians, therefore, had to be secretive and often anonymous in character. The safest contact could be made usually only on an individual-to-individual basis and the resulting ties they had to each other were very tenuous—easily broken and easily misunderstood. Identifying themselves as homosexuals made Soviet gay men and lesbians vulnerable—whether that identification was in the form of self-discovery or self-actualization, as acknowledgment or admission of their homosexuality to possibly hostile others, or in mutual affirmation and celebration of their homosexuality. They might face, among other things, KGB pressures to inform on their fellows and violent attack by individuals or groups who disliked them—in addition to being subject to legal prosecution and imprisonment. Thus to be a gay man or lesbian in the USSR was to be in a very precarious position.

The ties of fraternity between homosexuals in the former Soviet Union were simply not strong enough to support—or even to inspire—the development of social institutions around their common category membership. Socio-political conditions there would allow only self-definition and friendship-group formation on the basis of individual-to-individual interaction. In other words, categorization of people as "one of us" or "that way" ("наш" или "такой") does not, of itself, provide a bond strong enough to engender in individuals full solidarity with all who also can be characterized as homosexual. Soviet gay men and lesbians did experience a sense of fraternity with one another when they met or crossed paths, but the social-legal environment in which they lived prevented them from forming stronger and broader group-level bonds.

III. THWARTING GROUP-LEVEL INTERACTION PREVENTS SOVIET GAY COMMUNITY

For almost the entire existence of the USSR, as a rule, restrictions placed on individuals in Soviet society by the Communist Party and the state apparatus severely impeded the development of non-state social institutions that are necessary for the establishment and maintenance of subcultural community. Because the Soviet state considered it necessary to manipulate or "micro-manage" all social relationships, lest they emerge spontaneously as threats to the Soviet system, individuals were heavily discouraged from forming their own socio-cultural associations. If they did so anyway, all activities of the group were subject to Party and state scrutiny. Further, any group with three or more members was required to have a Party representative among their membership who would be present at all meetings. In effect, any category of people that was not previously recognized by the state as a valid social grouping was prevented from defining themselves in terms of their common characteristics, condition, behavior, or interests unless they could somehow argue for and obtain such a bestowal of that legitimacy from the Communist Party.

Due to this limitation in interaction, the types of places that gay men and lesbians in the USSR could go to meet, in which they could feel safe, and where they could express themselves freely as gay people were very few. They could not create any formal organizations, associations, or enterprises that would be recognizable as homosexually oriented. They could not seek the approval or the authority they needed to conduct their affairs in ways consistent with their own interests. They could not marshall social, political, or economic resources to mobilize a constituency and fight for the right to fulfill their own unique and self-defined needs. Instead, bureaucratized and regime-directed social definitions of the proper groups, associations, organizations, and social identities around which cohesion could develop were rigidly imposed. Individuals were compelled to perform behaviors, avow ideals, and show enthusiasm for state-created social institutions. It was mandatory, for example, that all children be members of the childhood "social-recreational" organizations operated by a wing of the Communist Party: the Octobrists (Октябрята, a reference to the Russian Revolution of October 1917 and to the Bolshevik revolutionaries who carried it out) and the Young Pioneers (an organization that had been modeled after the Boy Scouts of America, but with a much more blatant ideological program). In addition, it was encouraged strongly and was highly advantageous socio-politically for teenagers to join the Communist Youth League, or *Komsomól*.

Only the practical impossibility of controlling all the activities of all individuals in any society allowed people enough "self-determination" to develop their own self-identities that might include elements not consistent with the ideology of the ruling regime and enough "freedom" to sometimes interact with each other—to fraternize—in ways and in places which were officially forbidden. As a consequence, they could not completely act out the roles and rituals implied or expected from their fellows and they could not make a political claim for their right to existence. Group-level institutions of gay community that could have safeguarded the existence and identity of homosexuals as a group, promoted activities germane to category membership, and defended the rights of gay men and lesbians to self-determination, freedom of association, freedom of movement, and freedom from harassment, therefore, could not be created or their development could not be sustained in the former Soviet Union.

In the late 1980s and early 1990s, a handful of Soviet homosexuals were inspired to become active in developing ways to meet their own peculiar needs that had been repressed by the state. The impetus for this action came largely from the help and support of Western gay men and lesbians (chiefly Americans) who, under somewhat relaxed visa regulations, could travel to the USSR much more freely than ever before. These new Soviet "gay activists" attempted to form officially registered gay activist organizations and to found some specifically gay-themed publications to serve as promotional vehicles for their organizations. Some of them also tried to get their voices heard in the political arena. With little experience in political discourse and no skills at negotiating a compromise position, however, gay and lesbian activists in the Soviet Union could not develop political institutions capable of challenging the Soviet regime, even in just this one "personal" area.

This conception that gay and lesbian activists held of the problematic situation of homosexuals in the USSR as being only a personal problem between individuals also revealed their *naïveté* on sociocultural issues and confirmed my sense that they did not perceive of themselves as members of a social group, but as individuals with a particular condition in common—that is, as individuals who are related by fraternity rather than community. Moreover, since they did not exhibit a palpable group solidarity, they lacked even the incentive to form community institutions. Without fundamental changes to the Soviet political, economic, and social systems that would gradually help to change not only the viciousness of the (il)legal status, penal (mis)treatment and the public (mis)perception of homosexuals, but also to raise their own group-level social consciousness, furthering the cause of Soviet gay men and lesbians as a group was impossible. Lulled into a stupor by Communist ideology, that "narcotic of the proletariat," they were, like most of their compatriots unable to make change.

The halting and stilted activities of gay and lesbian activist groups in the Soviet Union that espoused reform/assimilationist type strategies for change showed that they were so vulnerable to doubt and dissolution, given the strictures of the regime, that their efforts never bore ripened fruit. Other groups, which took a revolutionary/separatist position, rebelled so outrageously against the Soviet "rules of the game" that they could not be taken seriously either in the political arena or by the vast majority of Soviet homosexuals whom they purported to represent. Because of this, I predicted, Soviet gay men and lesbians were apt to miss this "window of opportunity" for forming effective activist groups that could engender a gay-rights movement. (Favorable conditions do not last forever.) I also suggested that the new political order evolving in the former Soviet Union and in the whole Soviet "sphere of influence" would likely take form in ways that will continue to preclude the equal participation of gay men and lesbians in the social and political life of their country.

Such a "democratic" or pluralist socio-political system as may develop on the territory of the USSR will likely continue to outlaw homosexual activity and to tolerate or even authorize discrimination against homosexuals in such areas as employment, health care, and housing. Although obtaining these necessities was not really of concern under the Communist system, where housing, health care, and employment were guaranteed to all citizens (whatever the quality), each of these areas will become increasingly capitalized and therefore increasingly controlled by socio-economic elites under a market-oriented regime. Thus, whether or not they maintain anti-sodomy statutes, such "newly democratic" regimes are almost certain to disallow all secondary gay and lesbian movement goals such as guaranteed equal access to the resources, products, and wealth of their countries;

Conclusion: Fraternity without Community in the Soviet Gay World

an end to discrimination against them based only on their homosexuality; and social and legal recognition of same-sex relationships (whether as marriages, domestic partnerships, or in any other form). Even the right to challenge, in court, the unfairness of such discrimination or the implementation of anti-sodomy statutes may not be granted.

To demonstrate this, it may be sufficient to note that only a handful of the world's well-established "democracies" have so far undertaken any of these steps, and those that did so made these changes only quite recently, in the late 1980s and 1990s—that is, after 20–30 years of group-level institutional development (or "community building") and vociferous and unrelenting gay-rights activism. It therefore seems doubtful that the Soviet successor states will acknowledge or champion homosexuals' right to equal civil liberties protection any time soon. According to Breton (1964), however, the first steps toward community organization are the most significant ones since they spark the interest of others to try to do more. The fledgling gay and lesbian organizations in the USSR, then—such as they were—have given life to the idea that such a community actually could exist, with time.

In my estimation, the most significant contribution by these groups of gay and lesbian "activists" in the Soviet Union is probably the creation of what one can only hope will become institutionalized as a "gay press." I laud this achievement neither because the gay-themed publications circulated in Moscow and elsewhere were fine pieces of professional journalism much appreciated by their readers, nor because they succeeded in reaching a wide audience and maintaining a regular publication schedule. Actually, *The Theme* ["Тема"], *RISK* ["РИСК"], *SV* ["СВ"], and *Thou* ["Ты"] were rather amateurish broadsheets and circulars—in all honesty, one can hardly call them full-fledged newspapers or magazines—and they appeared very sporadically (about 3–4 times a year), usually with a circulation of under 1,000 copies. Instead, I find them to be important steps because they will be the standard for measuring improvements made by future attempts at producing substantial and stable gay periodicals that will meet the requirements of a professional, well-received, and sustainable gay press. They will become legendary as "the first Russian gay publications" and "the only Soviet gay newspapers ever." Indeed, these newspapers' availability to gay readers takes on even more importance in the light of Breton's (1964) finding that reading the one community-oriented publication, if that is all that is available, significantly increases an individual's integration into the community.[2] It brings one's reference group into focus.

In this way, these publications will likely be institutionalized in the post–Soviet homosexual subculture as pioneering efforts of the first promoters of the normalization of homosexuality and advocates of gay rights. They did, in fact create the idea that there could be—and **should** be—such a thing as an institutionalized gay press in their land which can give them reliable information about each other and connect them to one another in what may eventually be a full-fledged gay community.

However, the passage of legislation promulgating freedom of the press by the Russian Supreme Soviet in 1991 did not equate with widespread availability of these publications. The Soviet publishing organization (Союзпечать), which was responsible for the distribution of all publications, was still granted monopoly rights on retail distribution of periodicals, and its "rules" dictated that they would not distribute publications that do not have regular dates of publication. This meant that the gay "newspapers" and "magazines" were excluded from the newsstands. (Gessen 1994) Although there have been informal efforts by gay and other organizations to distribute their materials from card tables in a few major intersections and thoroughfares such as the sidewalk in front of the Bolshóy Theater, just as they did in the last years of the Soviet regime, even this poor means of distribution has been the victim of police harassment and the Moscow City Council itself has passed laws prohibiting such independent vendors from operating.

IV. CONSTRICTED DEVELOPMENT AND THE LACK OF SOVIET GAY COMMUNITY

Constricted development of non-state institutions in the USSR came about because the Soviet state took it upon itself to determine the needs of the population—in its own Marxist-Leninist terms. For this reason, both individuals and social groups were hindered in soliciting the satisfaction of their actual personal and group needs. This life-condition was seen not only among sexual minorities, but in all categories of people not recognized as legitimate, proletarian, or otherwise important to the state—whether or not such people would ever seek to develop group-level ties of community. In effect, only those in positions of power were able to articulate and advocate for their personal or group need satisfaction. This "fact of (Soviet) life" was most in evidence during the regime of the infamously dictatorial Communist Party General Secretary Iósef Stálin.

The additional fact that homosexuality was a criminal offense according to Soviet law (despite the religious origin of that proscription) meant that Soviet homosexuals were not only restricted to unofficial association, like most other minority groups in the USSR. Because of the illegal status of their very identity, *ipso facto,* they could interact one with another and form social bonds with each other solely on a criminal basis. These circumstances were livable, but hardly favorable. Interacting as homosexuals was manage able only secretly and only on the individual level—person to person. For the most part, formalized and recognizable group-level association was far too dangerous to be undertaken.

Conclusion: Fraternity without Community in the Soviet Gay World

Out of all this, the distinction to be made between community and fraternity should be clear. Fraternity is the condition of identifying with a particular set of people, being motivated to interact with them on the basis of that commonality—but only on an individual-to-individual basis. Nonetheless, actually doing so does indicate a sympathy born of what has been called "consciousness of kind." Community, in contrast, is a state of existence that includes these aspects of fraternity but also goes further to embrace the group and group-identity to such an extent that individual members are motivated to create group-level institutions for organizing their interactions and to purposefully create social roles and guidelines for their joint behavior. As is shown by my analysis of the data I collected and information I gathered for this analysis, such coordinated construction of identities, places, and projects for homosexuals as a social group was nonexistent in the Soviet gay world.

V. DIRECTIONS FOR FUTURE RESEARCH

Clearly, much is not known about the levels and processes of "institution-building" that took place in the "interstitial spaces" left by official, Communist-Party-dictated and Soviet-state-directed institutions in the Soviet social system. Somewhat more is known about those institutions being created in post-Soviet societies. This is one avenue for further research. I have used tenets, traditions, and methods of at least three academic fields to improve our understanding of the (im)possibility of gay community existing in the former Soviet Union as well as to explain why the idea of, energy for, and organizations necessary to make real such a possibility could not be sparked, sustained, or realized. I believe that this kind of analysis can be applied to the investigation of issues related to other "communities," identities, and minorities in Gay Studies, Soviet/Russian Studies, and Sociology. In fact, it is my hope that this integrated, institutional approach will be encouraged in all of the social sciences for the study of whatever other forms of (human or animal) social organization that students and scholars seek to understand.

For further research specifically on the topic of this book, there are several areas of investigation that would be fruitful.

One project that could provide information critical to "filling in the gaps" in our knowledge about the lives that homosexuals have led in the former USSR is an in-depth interview study of aging and elderly gay men and lesbians there. Despite their sometimes hazy accuracy as personal and social "reconstructions," retrospective recollections by individuals about their personal lives and modes of adaptation to their condition in Soviet society—from the time that they realized their homosexuality to the present day—could provide us with a much better sense of the lives of gay and lesbian Soviets in earlier periods which are not available for study directly or even indirectly through archives and memoirs.

Historical analysis of the life-conditions for and institutions created by homosexuals in two important periods of Soviet history could prove important and surprising. In the early part of the Twentieth Century, from about the time of the Revolution of 1905 through (and especially during) the 1920s, much discussion and experimentation was carried out by a very socially liberal group in the Communist revolutionary movement. Another period during which some gay people likely were organizing events and perhaps even creating activist organizations is the period of "The Thaw" in relations with the West and the relaxation of restrictions on and monitoring of Soviet citizens. This was the period from 1958 to 1964 under the regime of Nikíta S. Khrushchóv.

Another useful study would be research into the "intergenerational" differences among gay men and lesbians in the former Soviet Union. By comparing young gay men and lesbians now (say, those aged 15-29), who may have lived all of their gay life after the break-up of the USSR, with those who would have engaged in homosexual activity for a longer period of time under the Soviet regime (those aged 30-44, for instance). These could also be compared with homosexuals who must have lived most of their gay lives under Soviet socialism (those from ages 45-59) and even with those who are yet another generation older (aged 60+). Such a study might go a long way toward understanding the trajectory of homosexuality not just across the lifespan of the individuals themselves, but also across the lifespan of the Soviet Union itself.

NOTES

1. The most-readily available source of such information was the Big Soviet Encyclopedia (Большая Советская Энциклопедия, usually translated as the "Great" Soviet Encyclopedia). The entry for homosexuality (*gomoseksualízm*—гомосексуализм) in the third edition (Прохоров 1972:7:56) described it as "a sexual perversion" (половое извращение) and "an unnatural attraction" (противоестественное влечение).

2. If there are many community-oriented publications, as is usually the case in a highly developed community, then whether one actually reads the publications is not related to an individual's integration into that community (Breton 1964).

> The Soviet Union is dead, but the shock waves from its spectacular collapse still rip across the social landscape. In the realm of gay and lesbian life, some developments offer reason for hope: the [anti-]sodomy law was repealed in 1993, gay bars and discos have tentatively emerged on the scene, and the media routinely cover gay and lesbian issues. But a nightclub or two in Moscow and St. Petersburg is little balm for the injuries of a lifetime. Attitudes and patterns of behavior inculcated through decades of ideological bludgeoning do not simply dissipate with a change in government or leadership.
>
> David Tuller,
> *Cracks in the Iron Closet: Travels in Gay & Lesbian Russia*
> p.6.

Afterword
On the Development of Fraternity and Community in the Former Soviet Union

FOR THIS ANALYSIS, I CULLED THROUGH THE ACADEMIC LITERATURES OF Sociology, Anthropology, Philosophy, and Urban Studies for theoretical approaches to the study of community, on the basis of which I could construct an analytic framework for understanding the condition of and prospects for what others were calling "the gay community" in the Soviet Union. Among other things, this required redefining the traditional conceptualization of community as a territorially-based form of social organization in which people engage in substantial and sustained social interaction with one another and have numerous ties to the group—which, in turn, serves many functions for its members. A more comprehensive and more specific definition was necessary to account for newer, more "modern" types of communities that still depend upon significant social interaction and many, varied ties to the social group around which their common identity relates them, but which does not have any certain area of residence that is the basis for membership and community organization. This is the type of community that is widely understood to exist among gay men and lesbians in the West (especially in North America) and it is therefore the one by which the situation for homosexuals in the USSR must be evaluated. In addition, clarifying what is meant by this also necessitated differentiating this concept of community from other forms of social organization with which it is often confused or conflated.

Employing my reformulation of the community concept, I then undertook analysis of the degree and the forms of social organization that existed among the homosexual population of the Soviet Union. The goal was to explicate how this newer conceptualization could be used fruitfully to investigate the verity of conditions of social life that were being referred to rather blithely as "community" by Western gay and lesbian activists who had been to the USSR for other reasons, by Western media that had acquired an interest in this topic, and by some Western academics who are themselves gay and have made efforts of their own to describe the life-situation of this population.

Based on empirical evidence from my research in the USSR, I argued that homosexual **community**, conceived of in this way, had not developed in the Soviet Union as it did in Western Europe and North America—despite these simplistic assertions to the contrary—and I illustrated how and why it had not. Stable and cohesive group-level social institutions organized around individuals' identities as gay men and lesbians were unable to develop under the harsh legal and social conditions in the USSR, I concluded, even under the more permissive administration of Soviet President Mikhaíl S. Gorbachóv (1985–1991). Individual-level interactions in both public and private places did occur in habitual and predictable ways, however, and I indicated that the level of institutionalization that did exist among Soviet gay men and lesbians as a category of people could be designated best as "**fraternity.**" Further, I argued, because the specific legal-political and social conditions of life for Soviet gay men and lesbians at that time did not seem likely to change any time soon, a full-fledged "gay community" would fail to develop there in the near future, despite considerable political, economic, and social upheaval occurring in Soviet society generally.[1]

That was several years ago.

Taken as a whole, events in the ensuing period have supported both my conclusion and my prediction. Gay community still has not developed in what is now the former USSR.

In this follow-up report, I will first examine the larger socioeconomic and legal-political changes that have taken place since I concluded my study of Soviet homosexuals and that have affected the development of group-level institutions among them. With this, I will include discussion of changes that have not occurred and that, therefore, have perpetuated the lack of development of such institutions there. This will show that the social ecology of oppression continues to dampen the consciousness, aspirations, courage, and audacity of gay men and lesbians in the former Soviet Union, thereby inhibiting their widespread involvement in group-level social organizations. It will also demonstrate how some of the sharpest changes also have reinforced this consequence. Then, I will assess the legitimacy, stability, and likely longevity of the group-level institutions that have come into existence among former-Soviet homosexuals. I will explain how and why careful consideration of these issues indicates that the overall life-situation of most gay men and lesbians in the former Soviet Union has not changed substantially during the years since the disintegration of the Communist state edifice.

I. SOME ECOLOGICAL-LEVEL INSTITUTIONS IMPROVE, OTHERS CHANGE FORM

As the whole world knows, much has changed during the time since I conducted my research for this project. Most dramatically, the Soviet Union itself no longer exists as a political entity. Fifteen new, independent, ethnically based nation-states automatically came into being with the dissolution of the Soviet government in December 1991 on the unprecedented "vote" of the leaders of the USSR's constituent parts.[2] In its place, they established a Commonwealth of Independent States (CIS) that would maintain a loose confederation among most of the former-Soviet republics. Free-market reformers in the "new Russia," the Russian Federated Republic, and their colleagues in many of the other former Soviet republics, quickly abandoned all pretense of creating a "socialist market" economy in their country—a "Third Way" between Communist and Capitalist systems—which had been a hallmark of Gorbachóv's plan for economic restructuring, perestróyka. The availability of food, clothing, and other consumer goods has improved substantially in Russia, although the housing stock, transportation infrastructure, and industrial productivity either have not increased or actually have declined further. In addition, a system of multi-party and multiple-candidate elections was instituted in most of the countries of the former Soviet Union, and when elections were held most results were judged "(reasonably) free and fair."

Many of these changes were sudden and shocking, if not unpredicted. The attempted coup d'état against President Gorbachóv led by conservative Communist Party leaders calling themselves the Governmental Committee on the State of Emergency, or GKChP in the Russian acronym (Государственный Комитет Чрезвычайного Положения, ГКЧП), shook the nation and the world in mid-August 1991 and astonishingly quickly led to the almost cursory break-up of the Soviet Union.[3] Borís Yéltsin, president of the RSFSR, was hailed as a hero and moral authority when he held off army tanks and trucks sent by the GKChP to take over the Russian Federation's government building (the Russian "White House") and inspired tens of thousands of Soviet citizens to go out into the streets of Moscow to hold public demonstrations.

When the *coup* attempt failed, it was widely believed that Yéltsin had thwarted the conservative Communists, practically by himself, and, in so doing, had proved his leadership abilities courageously. Many felt that only he could make it possible for a "civilized" (цивилизованная) political-economic system to develop in "Mother Russia." Yéltsin was proclaimed president of the new Russian Federated Republic and a new era of post-Soviet Russia was born. A market economy was declared to exist and encouraged to grow in most of these new countries by their post-Soviet and often popularly-elected leaders—even by those who had been government officials and Communist Party stalwarts only a few months earlier.

While these events and the legal-political, economic, and social system changes they brought about certainly have affected heterosexuals in post-Soviet states as much as they did homosexuals, as citizens, these and other forces of change also have affected the life-situation and living conditions of gay men and lesbians profoundly as a separate category of people—that is, as homosexuals. Such areas of change (or a lack thereof) most germane to this work are those that establish the habitat and form the landscape within which homosexuals in the former Soviet republics have to live.

A. "Market Economy" Meets Gay Needs No Better Than State Planning Did

The economic reforms instituted during perestróyka had not gone far enough, Yéltsin felt, partly because Gorbachóv refused to abandon the Communist Party and its foolish allegiance to socialistic principles, while he himself had given up his own Party membership card some months earlier and embraced the laissez-faire market ideal. With haste, his government embarked upon an economic program of "shock therapy" recommended by Western economists and business interests to defibrillate the convulsing Soviet planned economy, which was near death. The jolts of "treatment" prescribed included a much wider legalization of some forms of private enterprise than the Soviet government had allowed as well as the re-institution of some types of private property which had been nationalized under the Communist regime. The privatization of many state enterprises seemed to be the logical next step, and price liberalization, currency devaluation, and banknote changes followed soon behind. These monetary reforms were intended to create a Capitalist industrial base and banking system, complete with a central bank and stock market.

Among the negative results of these reforms was a three-year bout with hyper-inflation that followed the nearly-complete price liberalization decreed at the beginning of 1993. Though prices were later stabilized by the creation of a "currency band"—a zone of acceptable value for the Russian ruble, pegged to the US dollar—the value of any savings individuals had before these reforms was wiped out. Homelessness has risen dramatically in Russia since that time (especially among the elderly) and the gap between the income of those at the top of the Russian "heap" and those at the bottom increased several-fold.

Another negative consequence is the formation of a new "market system" poorly regulated, if at all, by government agencies and not based on principles of free enterprise and the rule of law. Instead, the urge to amass wealth is promoted and money, as it accumulates, generates power. This situation has occurred partly because the edicts issued by President Yéltsin regarding economic issues often contradicted Russian parliamentary legislation in this area. This resulted in uncertainty about the commercial and tax laws by which entrepreneurs and foreign investors are to abide. The problem has been further compounded by disputes over the jurisdiction of corresponding, but often conflicting, laws passed by regional legislative bodies and decreed by chief executives of provincial governments.

Devoid of clear processes and procedures for production, distribution, and retailing, then, such economic activity as can be contracted yields, by default, to regulation by whatever means are at the disposal of the strongest power that operates locally, *id est*, the power that can cause the most immediate harm if not obeyed. In Russia, at least, this is almost never the police force, whether or not it is backed by the authority of juridical prosecutors. In effect, the power needed to control corporate excesses and to regulate the economy is abdicated to the businesses themselves, but with no effective police to enforce the "rules" of the economic "game," entrepreneurs often hire the power of thugs. The most powerful source of such control—the "mafia," or "racket" (рэкет)—is, of course, eager to offer protection to businesses and to threaten them with extortion, with the complicity of corrupt accomplices working in government agencies, of course. The privatization of industry has been neither well-managed nor fair, as many of the heads of production facilities, distribution systems, retail outlets, and even service enterprises simply have taken ownership of facilities they had previously managed. After all, they must have rationalized, control of the enterprise had been their allotment—plus perquisites—in return for faithful Party service.[4]

The net result of these unfair and draconian measures to reform the economy has been that the people who had controlled the distribution of power and therefore the allocation of wealth under the Communist regime are, for the most part, the same people who now have seized control of the distribution of wealth in the new Russia and thereby hold the reins of power. This situation is no better for homosexuals than the Soviet five-year plan was. They still have tremendous difficulties getting their particular needs met so they can "fully participate in their form of life" (Doyal & Gough 1991), that is, as gay men and lesbians.

The problem with the Soviet planned economy, as I discussed in the Conclusion, was that government planners did not consider issues of sexuality when making production, distribution, and sales plan directives. They were also not charged with forecasting and fulfilling the Soviet populations' demand for products and services of a sexual nature, which would include such personal items as contraceptives, sexual lubricants, and artificial stimulators. They might also include even "escort" or "massage" services, and prostitutes. Even indirectly— perhaps especially indirectly—the availability and condition of many other "normal" products and services that did fall under the bailiwick of planning officials also had considerable impact on the sexual life of citizens. These include, but are not limited to: housing availability, particularly the provision of adequate space for the privacy that is suitable to sexual interaction; provision of entertainment establishments appropriate for meeting others of potential sexual interest, dating, romance, and courtship; and facilities for avoiding and treating sexually transmitted diseases, unwanted pregnancy, and abortion procedures; *et cetera*.

That these things also are not well provided for in the new Russian economy means that the conditions of sexual life have not changed much, especially for post-Soviet homosexuals, since the break-up of the USSR. Instead, the reasons for such oversights and deficiencies simply have changed. Now, the "underground nature" of oppressed homosexuality keeps supposedly-free gay men and lesbians from expressing their needs and interests in a way that would inspire the enterprising energy and ingenuity of new business(wo)men to compete for the opportunity to satisfy those consumer demands. Gay or "gay-friendly" establishments, products suitable for use by gay men and lesbians, and services required by homosexuals have not sprung up to meet these challenges. This is not to say there has been no improvement over the complete lack of accommodation homosexuals were shown by the Communist government—not to say the incarceration it subjected them to. I do mean to insist, however, that the limited availability of products specifically meant for use by homosexuals is one important part of the reason that gay men and lesbians in the former Soviet Union continue to suffer from the lack of possibilities for fulfilling their special human needs.

The frustration of "ordinary people" in post-Soviet Russia with the lack of change in their individual circumstances is expressed in the following quote from a "human interest" newspaper article published some four years after the break-up of the USSR. (Specter 1995:A-4) That general sentiment is also supplemented and sharpened by the extra hardships homosexuals experience living under the same conditions as heterosexual people in the newly independent states:

> Long waits for housing and strict rules about who can live where make the idea of a gay enclaves [sic], like those in Greenwich Village or the Castro, highly unlikely. And if problems are large for [gay and lesbian] advocates and the rich [gays], they are mammoth for the many gay people who live in the provinces and cannot even dream of life in the fast lane.
> "I work in a factory, and I live with my mother," said a short, balding young man who agreed to be identified only by his nickname, Misha. "There is no space, no money, no choice." (Specter 1995:A-4)

B. Political-Legal Advances Are Made, but Human Rights Issues Remain

It did not take much time for the newly independent countries to realize that they were instantly subject to innumerable and sometimes colossal predicaments that accompanied their new-found political freedom. If they are truly free from subjugation by the former USSR, what laws should citizens of these new nations obey? Could they and should they enforce Soviet codes of law in no-longer-Soviet countries? There is, of course, no simple answer to such questions. Each of the fledgling nations of the former USSR is taking its own path toward building a future free from Russian colonial domination, as is natural for any independent country. For most of the former Soviet republics, though, the desire to be distinct from Russia meant expressing their independence in unique ways that would reflect their distinct sociocultural identities, and this common trend toward **nationalism** is often a major influence on how they act regarding all matters of state—including decisions that influence the many minority populations within their borders.

For several of the former Soviet republics, the social groups most obviously affected by this renewed or newly-created nationalism are minority ethnic groups or, in Soviet terms, "nationalities." The most serious consequence of this need among ethnic minorities to distinguish themselves from Russians is the eruption of inter-ethnic warfare, which has broken out in several places: Chechnyá, a tiny area that had been a part of the Russian Empire for centuries; in Abkházia, an independence-minded Muslim region of Georgia; and in Nagórno-Karabákh, an Armenian enclave in Azerbaijan, among others. Various ethnic "autonomous republics" within Russia—among them Kalmýkia, Tatarstán, Yakútia, and Buryátia—were able to compromise outright independence for some real economic autonomy. Long-dormant border disputes are also resurfacing. These include: conflicts between each of the three Baltic countries and the new Russian Federation over lands that were Estonian, Latvian, and Lithuanian before they were seized by the USSR and appended to the RSFSR; friction between Russia and Ukraine over the Crimean Peninsula, which had been Russian territory until it was ceded to Ukraine "as a gesture of friendship" under CPSU General Secretary Nikíta S. Khrushchóv; and clashes between Moldova, Ukraine, and Russia over the so-called Transdnyéstr region (Приднестровье). Some of several such disputes have been resolved through the use of threats, bravado, and, ultimately, negotiation. Others continue to fester.

Homosexuals are another minority population affected, though not so obviously, by the political course chosen by the governments of their new countries. For their freedom, members of this social minority also mean to fight, but it is not geopolitical warfare they must wage to win their emancipation. Theirs is a legal and social struggle. Gay men and lesbians in the former Soviet Union need to wage battle not for national sovereignty but for **personal autonomy**—that is, not to distinguish themselves from others, but to liken themselves to all people in their society. The main goal of gay and lesbian civil rights activists has been the repeal of Soviet anti-sodomy statutes. This is because they believed that legalization of the one factor that distinguishes them from the rest of society—and on the basis of which they are faced with discrimination, ostracism, and physical violence—would endow them with the legitimacy they need in order to assert their claim to equal human rights. Exercising the right to be themselves, they hoped, and to arrange their lives in whatever fashion they like (so long as it does not harm others), would help tremendously in improving their lives. However, the decriminalization of homosexual relations in the new countries was not made in reaction to any social movement led by homosexual activists from gay and lesbians organizations.

Indeed, it could be argued that some of these groups inhibited the progress of gay rights in Russia, given the radical positions espoused by the most outspoken gay activists there. In the first years of independence, the new Russia, like many of the other new nations of the former Soviet Union, continued to use the penal codes of its precursor Soviet republic. Although the legal prohibition of sodomy had been considered in the USSR under Gorbachóv, as part of the general overhaul of the Soviet criminal and civil codes, the changes to these laws were never formally agreed upon, much less actually implemented. Ultimately, the final decision to rescind the law in the new Russia, in May 1993, was due to the testimony and lobbying of Russian academics.

In the case of the Baltic states, this is most clear. The parliaments of Estonia and Latvia repealed the anti-sodomy statutes in their penal codes with no special forethought. Articles 126 in Estonia and 124 in Latvia were scrapped in 1992 as a part of the complete renunciation of all Soviet-era legal, economic and political institutions. Their goal was to turn back the clock on their annexation by the Soviet Union in 1939, during World-War-II. All three of the Baltic states had been independent between the wars, and when the Soviet Union collapsed, they quickly invalidated the constitutions handed to them by the government in Moscow and reinstated the constitutions they had created for themselves in 1920 and had lived under for twenty years. In Estonia and Latvia, those laws had not criminalized homosexual relations.

In Catholic Lithuania, the pre-Soviet legal code did proscribe homosexuality, but, eager to become a member of the European Union (EU), the Organization for Security and Cooperation in Europe (OSCE), and the Western NATO military alliance, the new Lithuanian government dropped the statute against consensual homosexual behavior (article 122.1) in June 1993. However, religious zeal and anti-homosexual sentiment were still in evidence after Lithuanian independence and arrests have been made under article 122.2, which continues to outlaw homosexual relations carried out using violence, by taking advantage of the dependence or helplessness of one individual vis à vis the other, and homosexual activity between an adult and a minor ("statutory rape"). Moreover, it has been alleged that fraudulent application of this second article of the anti-sodomy statute has been used against homosexuals engaging in consensual sex by prosecutors and judicial officials not happy with the repeal of article 122.1 (IGLHRC 1993).

The repeal of the anti-sodomy statute in Ukraine, in May 1992, seems above all to have been motivated by a larger desire to be seen as a "modern" nation, and the Ukrainian government immediately began modeling itself on the examples of Western Europe. Especially in far-western Ukraine, this sentiment was coupled with, perhaps caused by, an adamant insistence on distancing itself from Russia—the bully of the Soviet "Union." Russia was fond of calling itself, with outspoken condescension, the "Elder Brother" of the Soviet "brotherhood of nations" and had always felt that Ukrainians were not really a separate people, just southerners who speak Russian in a funny way. It came as quite a surprise to many when the government in Kiev moved to repeal the anti-sodomy statute from its criminal code—most of all to Ukrainian gay men and lesbians themselves. (MacDonald 1992)

In most of the former Soviet republics of Central Asia and the Caucasus, legal codes continue to outlaw homosexuality. There has been a resurgence in Islamic religious identification in Central Asia, which is in keeping with the trend toward nationalism in the former USSR. Only very recently have two of those five newly independent countries repealed their Soviet-era anti-sodomy statutes. In October 1997, Amnesty International reported that Kazakstan had omitted consensual homosexual behavior from its new criminal code. (Skolander 1997) In addition:

> Kyrgyzstan became the ninth former Soviet republic to legalize gay sex [on] January 1 [1998], said Amnesty International....
> Tajikistan is still using the old Soviet criminal code. Uzbekistan instituted a new penal code and kept the Soviet ban. Observers have been unable to determine the legal status of homosexuality under Turkmenistan's new penal code."
> (Wockner 1998:4)

In the former Soviet republics of the Caucasus, such reforms are still being considered. "In Armenia, Azerbaijan and Georgia, penal-code reform is underway that may lead to legalization of gay sex." (Wockner 1998)

There is, of course, no guarantee that the anti-sodomy statutes will not be reinstated where repealed or that backlash from decriminalization may take some other, even uglier form. Kon (1995:264) is almost certainly overly alarmist about this prospect:

> Gays and lesbians are now finally coming out in Russia as a social and cultural minority, but they still lack a clear self-image. And [sic] it is very dangerous to come out into a ruined and chaotic world, where everything is disconnected and everyone is looking not for friends but enemies. If the country takes a radical turn to communism or fascism, gays and lesbians and their "sympathizers," along with Jewish intellectuals, will be the first candidates for murder and the concentration camps.

However, the voices of newly ascendant religious groups appalled by the outspokenness of the more radical gay and lesbian activists and the hysteria of many healthcare workers poorly educated about AIDS have halted their repeal in some places ("1/10" 1992). A call for recriminalization is conceivable.

C. Societal View of Gays Improves; yet Discrimination, Hostility Worsen

Decriminalization of homosexual relations, *per se*, has not brought post-Soviet gay men and lesbians emancipation from official and unofficial discrimination in everyday life, freedom from police harassment and brutality, or deliverance from violent attacks perpetrated against them by intolerant fellow citizens. This is a lesson Western gay men and lesbians learned long ago. These traumas are caused by societal problems, not political or juridical ones, and although such legal changes can effect change in people's attitudes and behaviors toward homosexuals—over time—they cannot change public opinion or private hostility in and of themselves. In fact, often a change for the better in the legal status of stigmatized groups can heighten outward expression of animosity toward them, increase outright discrimination against them, and make them even more vulnerable to the emotional abuse and physical violence they faced before because of their behavior (and by extension their very being in the world). This is so simply because the subject of their existence is more likely to be presented by broadcast and print media and is thereby more likely to come up in day-to-day conversation.

Table A: Public Opinion in the USSR and in Post-Soviet Russia about What Steps Should Be Taken with Homosexuals, 1989, 1994.*

Opinion:	1989	1994	% Change
"Liquidate" Them	27%	18%	-9%
Isolate Them from Society	32%	23%	-9%
Hard to Say	23%	22%**	-1%**
Leave Them to Themselves	12%	29%	+17%
Provide Help For Them	6%	8%	+2%
Totals:	100%	100%	

* Data for 1989 are from ВЦИОМ (Левада и Левинсон 1990); those for 1994 are as reported in Kon (1995:264).
** Though not listed as such in the source, this was the only other response category provided in the survey question (Левада и Левинсон 1990). These percentages are my calculations.

In Russia, public opinion about homosexuality has become somewhat less hostile since the break-up of the Soviet Union as social condemnation of gay men and lesbians has lessened. In a partial replication of its 1989 survey, the renamed

Russian Center for the Study of Public Opinion (RTsIOM [РЦИОМ], formerly VTsIOM [ВЦИОМ]) found a nearly 10% decline in respondents who felt that homosexuals should be liquidated (-9%) or isolated from society (-9%). (Kon 1995:264) Conversely, there had been an even larger increase in those who said that homosexuals should be left to themselves (+17%). (See Table A.)

This does not necessarily mean that people have become more positively disposed toward homosexuals over that five-year time period, however. They may be simply less condemnatory, for to leave someone alone is to take a rather neutral stance. The idea that one should help homosexuals—to treat them, essentially, as inappropriately stigmatized minorities—is truly a positive attitude, but one that only increased among respondents by 2%. Unfortunately, it is still a view expressed by less than 10% of Russian citizens. So, while it is indeed heartening to see that some polls indicate "a growing tolerance" toward homosexuality in the Russian population (Kon 1995), the fact that over 40% of their fellow citizens still feel that Russian gay men and lesbians either should be killed or locked-up is still very unsettling.

It is worth noting here that about the same amount of those questioned in each year—more than one in five—found the question difficult to answer. This suggests that more public dialogue on this topic or more direct, personal experience with persons known to be homosexual (id est: more public visibility, more "coming out") must take place before many can truly express their opinion about "what should be done" with homosexuals. This prospect is not without its own dangers and is therefore an option that is still considered with much trepidation by gay men and lesbians in the former Soviet Union—as well as by those in many other countries around the globe, including the USA. Thus, becoming more visible in overall heterosexual society may actually incur more direct harassment of homosexuals than they had had to face previously. At the very least, it will make them more vulnerable to non-state oppression and discrimination.

Indeed, as a category of people declaring their "spoiled" identity (Goffman 1963), gay men and lesbians in the former Soviet Union will now come face-to-face with discrimination in several new areas: housing availability; employment prospects; access to the resources, recognition, and rewards customary for efforts in business or public service; and in opportunities for self-improvement and self-presentation offered in many kinds of social situations. As I predicted earlier in this work, these secondary goals of gay men and lesbians in the former USSR have not been achieved and are not even "on the table" for consideration by "the powers that be" (власти). Nicholls (1998: pages not numbered) quotes another report on the legal and societal conditions for homosexuals in the former Soviet Union about precisely this sort of grievances:

An American gay rights activist, Kevin Gardner, who has spent several years in Moscow, says the repeal of the anti-gay law did not change attitudes. In a report titled Gay and Lesbian Human Rights in the "New'[sic:"] Russia, Gardner concludes: "State law-enforcement agencies continue to treat gay-affiliated organisations as centres of criminal activity, and government structures refuse to register openly identified community groups. Gays and lesbians remain vulnerable to blackmail and intimidation, government-sanctioned and social violence, and have nowhere to turn in instances of job and housing discrimination."

On the subject of physical violence, his account (Nicholls 1998: pages not numbered) is much more chilling:

The prospect of being beaten up or even killed is a reality for gay Moscovites [sic: Muscovites]. Everyone seems to know someone who has been found dead. Clubgoers talk of a gay serial killer [sic: a serial killer of gays] being on the loose in 1996.

Gardner tells of the murder of a gay man in November 1996. His body was found lying on the floor of his apartment in his underwear with 22 stab wounds. "The murder was apparently one of many that occurred in Moscow throughout 1996, causing great fear in the local gay community," he says.

II. GROUP-LEVEL INSTITUTIONS OF COMMUNITY GENERALLY FAIL TO THRIVE

Western press accounts of the changes in the sociopolitical conditions of life for homosexuals in the former USSR have tended to laud the accomplishments of gay and lesbian activists there. This is properly so, since there is much to commend. While these reports generally seem to support the notion that gay community institutions are forming, read closely and objectively, actually they show a very mixed record of results from the attempts to organize homosexuals into activist groups, social-recreational associations, and other subcultural organizations for homosexuals. Though they now do have the legal right to develop these social institutions, homosexuals in the post-Soviet states still lack the financial capital and material resources necessary for the development of a gay market, the organizational skills required to achieve an integrated gay lifestyle, and the "cultural capital" important for maintaining the social patterns of a gay subculture.

This overly enthusiastic focus has resulted, in part, from the fact that Western media must report progress in order for a news item to be print-worthy. There really is no "story" if nothing has changed, right? The myopic focus of this sensationalist bias is further distorted by the blurry indications from gay and lesbian activists (both American and Russian) who are involved in efforts to change the circumstances of gay life there and exaggerate their successes to promote their cause. This is understandable; it makes strategic sense. In order to make progress, gay and lesbian activists and entrepreneurs in the former Soviet Union have often depended on Western capital to carry out their projects. Because this help is more likely to come from charitable contributions by Western gay and lesbian well-wishers than from venture capitalists, they are likely to raise more money if their efforts are seen as producing more rather than less change for homosexuals in Russia.

The level of intolerance of homosexuality still evident in post-Soviet Russian society, coupled with a general breakdown in the country's law enforcement system and the concentration of power and resources in the hands of a very small elite, has had an unfortunate effect on the ability of gay men and lesbians to develop and strengthen habits and routine patterns of social interaction. Still without the resources for establishing regular and reliable group-level social institutions, gay men and lesbians in the former USSR often have to bow to the "mafia's" (usually monetary) demands to get the assurance of their safety and the procurement of opportunities for success and survival. Otherwise, they would have to forego those assets usually needed for successful organizational development. By default, only "mafia" groups will help gay men and lesbians by making available to them the resources and connections necessary to create and sustain active organizations. Unhampered by the police and basically free to take for themselves what they want through extortion, organized criminals have little to fear from the negative impression they will contract by associating with such deviants. In exchange, they extract an ample return on their investment—with force, if necessary. This unhealthy and "unholy" alliance has not lessened the precariousness of homosexuals' position in post-Soviet society, since these racketeers can be just as capricious as the old Soviet bureaucrats were.[5]

A. Gay and Lesbian Activists and Organizations Are Still Stymied

There can be no doubt that much energy and effort, much courage and creativity, and much hope and expectation have been put into projects aimed at improving the lives of gay men and lesbians in the former Soviet republics since the break-up of the USSR. Many people—both in Russia and from abroad—have stepped forward to do what they can for themselves and for their gay "brothers and sisters."

Gay activist groups have been started in several cities across the vast territory of the former Soviet Union. In addition to those examined in Chapter Five, ILGA reports a gay group forming in Saratov, in the south of Russia, and Williams (1995:137–138) presents the following summary of information on gay and lesbian groups forming in several of the other newly independent nations:

162   Gay Life in the Former USSR

This trend is no longer purely confined to Russia. It has quickly spread to other post-Communist states. . . . The strengths and characteristics of individual [gay and lesbian] groups throughout the former Soviet Union vary reflecting different political contexts. Despite the difficulties, Belarus has set up [sic!] a gay group and paper Vstrecha (Encounter). Likewise, the Ukraine has Ganymede and Two Colours; Moldova, HOPE; Kazakhstan, Sluzhba znakomstv "kontrast" (Help for acquaintances of a different orientation)[;] and Uzbekistan, the Tashkent Gay Men's Collective. The gay and lesbian movement is also thriving in the Baltic States. Estonia has a Lesbian Union, led by Lillian Kotter, as well as a Gay Union, headed by Alexander Romenskii, which publishes Voimalus. Latvia set up [sic!] an Association for Sexual Equality in November 1990, which has published LOKS (The Window) since March 1993 under the guidance of Juris Lavrikos and, finally, Lithuania also has its own Gay and Lesbian Association which brings out a gay magazine entitled *Amsterdamas*.

While this is an impressive accounting, Williams is midleading on several counts. It is true that the diffusion of this social innovation did spread primarily from Moscow to the provinces and republics **within the former USSR**, the Soviet Union was far behind some of the Eastern European post-Communist countries in this regard. Gay bars and groups were allowed to operate (though not freely, of course) in East Germany and Poland during the Communist period and in Czechoslovakia and Hungary maverick gay groups, newspapers, and magazines appeared in the 1980s before those in Moscow and Leningrad did—and long before the organizations and publications that came into being in Russia after 1991. In fact, on the broader international level, one might say that the diffusion of such institutional innovations spread from the "periphery" of the "Eurasian" Communist "world-system" to the center in Moscow. Furthermore, at least one of the "groups" mentioned here is a matchmaking business, which a proper translation of the group's name clearly indicates: it is the "Contrast" Dating Service. Most importantly, this must not be read to mean that the governments of Belarus, Ukraine, Moldova, Kazakstan, Uzbekistan, Estonia, Latvia, and Lithuania have played any part in the development or "setting up" of gay- and lesbian-oriented groups and publications; they only have allowed such groups and magazines to exist. I trust that the author simply chose poor wording here.

Williams (1995:142) also reports on a conference of the leaders of these organizations held to motivate the wellspring of rage against oppression that is needed in order to create activist groups and to coordinate activist efforts in Russia:

150 gay men and lesbians met in Moscow between 13th and 15th August 1993. This culminated in the creation of Treugolnik (Triangle). The chairperson of this Russian Gay and Lesbian Association is Volya [sic: Valya] Ivanova. It has the following goals: to collect information related to the development of the gay and lesbian movement in Russia (the formation of regional groups, public events,

documents, demonstrations and so on); to expose and publicise all types of discrimination against gays, lesbians and bisexuals; to provide an emergency psychological support hotline; to collect information about the release of persons imprisoned under Article 121; to produce a bulletin 121+ with the help of the IGLHRC (monthly in 1993; twice monthly in 1994 at a subscription charge of US$10); to assess the role of the gay community in AIDS prevention; to promote a gay culture in Russia; to provide notification of new gay publications; and finally to encourage international co-operation.

This is all well and good, but simply enumerating the efforts to establish gay and lesbian social institutions without indicating how successful or unsuccessful they have been, how stable and regular they are, and by what interests they are supported presents a construction of reality that is at odds with what typical gay men and lesbians experience daily. However impressive, these rosy characterizations only tell half of the story.

Many similar accounts have exaggerated the development of gay activist groups in the former Soviet Union, both in the extent of their organization and in the success of their achievements. The understandable desire to revel in the idea that a gay community could come into bloom in Russia and that a gay-rights movement is "flourishing" there is clearly evident in headlines like these: "The Boys in the Baltic: Gay 'Liberation' Comes to the Soviet Union" (Indiana 1990), "Moscow/Leningrad Events Called 'Soviet Stonewall'" (Wockner 1991), "Coming Out of the Cold" (Jackson 1992), and "Gay Political Movement Takes Place in Russia" (Rubin 1993). In general though, the contents of these reports tell a different story and, ironically, that contradiction in these reports is what is most accurate about them. The positive headlines reflect real positive change, but much of the news, considered carefully, divulges the fact that most aspects of gay life in the former Soviet Union continue to be harrowing.

This confusion has come about, in part, because the authors of such press reports have not examined the institutional structures that undergird these organizations and publications. They have not understood that the presence or absence of habitualized relationships among people of a particular sort (*id est*, members of a recognizable social group) is precisely what makes the difference between social movements and individual acts of protest—between community and fraternity. They are not social scientists; they do not have training in and passion for investigating not only the occurrence of a newsworthy event, but also the underlying social processes acting in concert to allow such social phenom ena to take place.

Some of the groups mentioned above have disintegrated, others have been started to replace them, only to fold their operations also and for basically the same reasons as their predecessors had. Many groups joined the "umbrella organization" mentioned above, Triangle, but since it does not really operate as an entity unto itself, groups resign membership in frustration: they thought that they were going to get help for their own efforts, but the Triangle association asked for things from them instead. Specter (1995:A-4) reports the result of such good intentions getting mixed together with unfortunate misunderstandings:

> Tension has not always brought homosexuals together. Unwilling to be public, unsure of how to stay private, gay groups now fight bitterly among themselves, so much so that in Kiev, Ukraine, in May [1995], representatives of most major gay organizations from former Soviet republics voted at the end of a conference to agree that the conference never took place. It was the only motion on which they could agree.

As time wore on, many erstwhile gay activists in the new Russia feel that they have been naïvely taken in—especially by Western gay and lesbian civil rights advocates:

> "Of course there is a lot of anger and disappointment," Mr Yureyev [president of the St. Petersburg P. I. Tchaikovsky Fund for Cultural Initiatives and the Defense of Sexual Minorities] said. "Maybe like every other group in this country we expected too much from the West and too much from ourselves. We had no models of how to be a community. Nobody knew how to do it. So we put on leather and opened bars like they have in San Francisco and in New York. It was foolish. It will take decades before we can be that open. Maybe it will never happen here." (Specter 1995:A-4)

Essig (1996) has made a detailed accounting of the machinations and manipulations that transpired among gay and lesbian activist groups in the first few years after the break-up of the USSR. Given this situation, one must cautiously wonder how far in the future it will be when individual gay men and lesbians in the new Russia might act, not just in their own personal interests but in the interests of all people of their kind.

B. More Gay Publications Appear, Yet Content and Constancy Are Wanting

The number and variety of publications they have produced is another, much touted achievement of the new homosexual activist organizations. Williams (1995:137–138) provides a compact inventory of the valiant efforts that were put into producing newspapers and magazines specifically intended to address the unmet informational and entertainment needs of homosexuals in their countries:

> Alongside Kalinin's *TEMA* (*The Theme*), created in 1990, came trial issues of *RISK* from late December 1990, . . . edited by Ortanov, Anatonii [sic: Anatolii] Panov and Sergei Grekov. This was closely followed by Nikolai Sivolobov's *Impuls* (*Impulse*), tied to the Union of Sexual Minorities, and Lytchev's *One in Ten* in

December 1991. These are all Moscow based. *Gei Slaviyanie* (*Gay Slavs*), edited by Zhuk, Oleg Ul'ba and Sergei Shcherbakov, as well as the gay writer Gennady Trifonov, came into being in St Petersburg in 1992. Other regions also have their own gay newspapers, such as Valery Klimov's *Gei Dialog* (*Gay Dialogue*) produced from Svedlovsk [sic: Sverdlovsk, now Yekaterinburg]; *Shans* (*Chance*) in Rostov-on-Don; *Our News* in Kazan and *Siberskii Variant*, edited by Alexander Khoroshev, in Altaiskii krai.

Publications by themselves do not make a community, though, as I have argued earlier.

In his excitement, Williams (1995:138) goes so far as to declare that:

> Despite these difficulties [limits in avenues for distribution and KGB raids on gay press offices], many gay newspapers, magazines and journals are now no longer mimeographed or xeroxed but of a high quality. *Ty* (*You*) and *One in Ten* [*1/10*] are virtually on a par with [the longstanding British magazine] *Gay Times*, [*The*] *Advocate* or *Outlook* [which are among the most prized gay publications in the USA] in quality, but not content.

The characterization may well be accurate, but it is not very meaningful. What matters more than the style or production value of gay- and lesbian-themed publications is the amount and the sort of information they present for the personal nourishment and public vigor of their readership. It is the content and nature of the material that counts.

Most of the articles that appear in these gay-themed publications are not directly related to the lives that homosexuals lead in the newly independent countries. A large number of them are translations of stories that have appeared in Western gay and lesbian publications. While this may be "hardly surprising, as there is tremendous ground to be made up," as Williams (1995:138) suggests, reprinting Western gay and lesbian news items does not address the needs of homosexuals in the former Soviet Union. In fact, it probably just recommends to them what their needs "should be." More importantly, even those articles that do appear to relate matters of vital interest to post-Soviet gay men and lesbians do not substantiate the existence of gay community. Rather, they show how circumstances serve to keep it from forming by relating the stark realities of gay bashings, police brutality, and the lack of a solid base of readers to support the "indigenous" gay "press" in the former USSR.

The problems plaguing such publications in post-Soviet Russia that Williams (1995:138–139) spells out are precisely the same as those I described in Chapter Five, namely: "first, poor circulation due to a lack of a clearly definable audience . . . second, restricted access to printing equipment; and third, a lack of office space." The circumstances are the same; only the reasons are different. In the new Russia of "free-market" economics, the fact that most of these gay publications lose much more money than they make, does, eventually catch up with them. When Western financing ceases to pay for them, these papers have folded almost as quickly as they appeared. Tyéma, for instance, went out of business in 1993. Community is not something that can be presented to a people full-blown, as a matter of historical fact. Nor can it be taught. Community must develop among them out of interacting in such a way as to construct group-level social institutions.

C. Gay Places Are Not Much Different Than They Were Before

There have been some much-celebrated steps forward for the establishment of bars and *discothèques* in the new Russia that cater to a homosexual clientele. Mention of them is made in almost every Western news article about gay life in Russia. Williams (1995:139) seems scarcely able to contain his enthusiasm over the progress being made:

> In addition to gay and lesbian groups, papers and magazines, clubs and cafes are also emerging such as 'Underground' (including a bookshop), 'Dancing Club Palace', 'Mir Discotheque' and 'Bistro', as well as a women's cafe run by Alla Suchova, and Roman Kalinin's 'Olympic Concert Hall' able to accommodate 1,500.

What gets much less mention is that there are many problems that such places confront in trying to operate and there are a number of shortcomings that must be taken into account when evaluating the success and sustainability of these new "gay places."

The gay dance clubs established in Moscow and St. Petersburg have been inaccessible to most ordinary Russian gay men and lesbians. Many of these places were created on the American model, and, in fact, some were the inventions of American "event promoters" who wanted to bring their kind of dance party to their Russian brothers (these were mostly the endeavors of gay men)—and, of course, to make a lot of money in the process. Like their American progenitors, these *discothèques* serve mainly Westerners traveling to Russia's two largest cities or members of the (homosexual or heterosexual) "mafia" in Russia since the price of admission is charged in US dollars at a rate comparable to those charged for admission to the most popular "circuit parties" in New York, Los Angeles, or Miami: $20–$30. At the time they opened, that sum in Russian currency equaled 120,000 to 180,000 rubles. According to information from the Russian State Statistics Committee (Barringer 1994:4:5), this amount was nearly equivalent to the average monthly wage in 1994: 184,483 rubles. To fathom this point fully, take note that the currency exchange rate in effect at that time was 3,000 rubles to the dollar. By 1997, the rate had decreased by 100%—to 6,000 rubles equaling $1.

Not even considering the cost of drinks during the evening or a cab ride home afterward for the sake of safety, then, one night's adventure at one of these nightclubs requires spending around one month's pay. Few individuals can afford to spend that much money even once per year and probably no "average" Soviet homosexuals can afford to be regular patrons.

What is more, as Williams (1995:139) notes, "All these are located in Moscow. In the provinces, however, gay men and lesbians have problems finding places to meet." For example, one gay man living in central Siberia reports this about the situation there:

> Even though Novosibirsk is the third-largest city in Russia there is no official gay organization and no discotheque, bar or other gathering place for the gay community. The park in front of the City's Opera and Ballet Theater has long served as an informal gathering place for gays. . . .
> . . . gays in Novosibirsk responded with great enthusiasm when two years ago the city's first gay discotheque opened for a brief time. Twice a week the disco opened its doors to a grateful flood of customers, both gay men and lesbians, who took specially chartered buses to the site just outside the city. To their dismay, however, the disco closed after only a month, supposedly because the owner had a sudden string of bad financial luck and couldn't support the venture. ("Grisha" 1995)

The number of such places, even in the largest cities, has fallen off in the last few years, largely because these gay clubs and discos were unable to sustain themselves on what clientele they had. Gay discos also fell prey to harassment on the part of both the racketeers who supposedly supported them and from police.

> Many of the bars and clubs are shuttered now. Others, almost always owned by people who are not gay, charge far more for tickets than normal nightclubs. In some parts of town—here and in Moscow, the only other city with an obvious gay subculture—private clubs are like American speakeasies of the Prohibition era. You need a password to get in. To get out without being beaten by thugs, many patrons stay all night. (Specter 1995:A-4)

Frequent bar raids also plague these establishments in Russia and elsewhere in the former Soviet Union (IGLHRC 1995). Nicholls (1998: no page numbers) describes one recent, and particularly graphic example:

> With their balaclavas and camouflage, and armed with machine guns and batons, the Russian anti-narcotics squad knows how to crash a party. In a recent dawn raid on Chance, a gay dance club in Moscow, 14 officers pushed their way past the bouncer to where about 100 people were gyrating in front of a large video screen.
> Terence, a 20-year-old American, had arrived in Moscow the night before with a 12-month working visa. He was to get an introduction to the city he would never forget.

"They came in and started kicking people. People were screaming," he said. "The guy closest to me was kicked a few times and fell, then he was kicked again in the nose - his nose was bleeding all over the seat."

"There was one kid who was so scared, because the guy put a pistol to his head. He was told to put his arms behind his head, but he didn't because he was just frozen."

This is gay life, Moscow style.

A life where—even beyond communism and the arrival of "democracy"—you experience discrimination on a grand scale. Many say homophobia has increased rather than decreased in the new Russia....

Chance's owner, Pavel Chaplin, says the raids were an attempt to shut the club down.

"These kind of raids are normal in Russia," he said. "We'll keep fighting for this club because it's a rare place in Moscow where gays can get together in a safe space.

"You can talk about a democratic revolution, but this kind of incident shows a reversion to the situation there was in the 1930s. In front of everyone, they were planting evidence, they were beating people up. It was fascist aggression."

It would seem, then, that Chance actually is not "a place where gays can get together in a safe space" after all—at least not always. If attacks like this one are truly "normal in Russia," this disco and other gay places that are struggling to survive must be very rare indeed.

Partly because of these continuing personal dangers in the social-environmental situation in which gay men and lesbians in the new Russia find themselves, the main places used as homosexual meeting spaces are still the public places they have appropriated from the physical and social geography that surrounds them. This is perhaps even more perilous than it had been under Communism, where, if invisible, at least they could be overlooked more often. In the penultimate section of his article, Williams (1995:139) also points this out:

> Government clampdowns on gay clubs are also a problem.... As a result, most Russian gays still rely on their narrow circle of friends or cruise in front of the Bolshoi Theatre of Alexander Gardens in Moscow, Gostinyi Dvor in St Petersburg, or similar meeting places in other towns and countries of the former Soviet Union.

Much of the following description (Nicholls 1998: no page numbers) of the gay places available for homosexuals to meet in Moscow correspond directly to my discussion of cruising areas in Chapter Four:

> Many gays prefer to meet partners in parks or squares rather than go to gay clubs. Few would feel confident enough to come out at work.
>
> One of the most popular outdoor meeting areas is the square outside the Bolshoi Theatre, near the Kremlin. By night it's a hive of activity, with dozens of

On the Development of Fraternity and Community

men sitting or walking round as they talk. For some it's a pick-up, for others a social occasion. BMWs and Mercedes drive slowly past and youths go up to greet them.

"Mostly prostitutes," said Oleg, who works at the Three Monkeys, another gay club, where he estimates half the clients are prostitutes and the rest their customers.

For many it's a matter of survival. The prostitutes include government staff and soldiers, many of whom have not been paid for a year because there is no public money to cover their wages.

There are dozens of places around Moscow where men meet for sex late at night. Once they would have been jailed if caught. Now they are rounded up, driven to the other side of town and dumped.

Aside from the BMWs and Mercedes driving by the *pléshka* to solicit homosexual prostitutes, and except for the specific identification of the nightclub The Three Monkeys as a gay place, this is precisely the situation I described in Chapter Four when analyzing the institutionalization of gay places under the Communist regime.

Finally, the appearance of "new media" for communicating and publishing information in a faster, more targeted way has also opened up another kind of "gay place" just as it has created a new realm of interaction and interest for heterosexual people. The Internet and the World Wide Web, together with topic-oriented "bulletin board" services and "chat rooms" are the chief domains that make up this new land dubbed "Cyberspace." These new "virtual" geographies are being explored and charted by gay men and lesbians in the former Soviet Union, as they are in many, many countries around the world. This should be no surprise, since computer equipment and knowledge of its use are among the most dynamic and fastest-growing enterprises in what is being called the "new," "global economy."

Western gay men and lesbians have already established a substantial presence in the "on-line world" with the creation of vast numbers and types of "sites," "web-pages," etc. Among them are those put together by and/or for gay rights groups and community centers, gay bars and discos, gay roommate services, gay bulletin boards with specialized "gay chat rooms" and even "back rooms" where "visitors" can even engage in computer-mediated "cyber sex," gay dating and introduction services, gay pornographic sites, personal websites of individual gay men and lesbians, gay-oriented AIDS organizations, gay and lesbian elder and youth outreach programs, gay-owned and/or operated businesses with "floorspace" for selling their products, gay advertising, et cetera. In brief, gay men and lesbians in the West are interacting in cyberspace, in its full magnificence and expansiveness.

That people in the former Soviet republics are less able to afford the large costs of computer equipment and the extra expenses for training, maintenance, and connection services that are needed for interaction in this new social territory means that they are not making as many forays into cyberspace as Westerners (particularly Americans) are. Nonetheless, they are there staking their claim. Gay men and lesbians in these newly independent nations are also among those making such adventurous expeditions into virtual space. As they do so, they too are mapping the territory, scouting for hostile "natives," prospecting for gold or hunting for game, as they eke out whatever existence they can by founding their own gay-related websites, by connecting to each others' sites with the same kind of "hyper-text links" used by all "Netizens," and by making contacts, spreading the word about gay-related events and opportunities to interact with one another. The Russian-language world-wide-web site *www.gay.ru* has been in operation since late 1997.

III. INDIVIDUAL-LEVEL INSTITUTIONS OF FRATERNITY STILL CENTRAL TO GAY LIFE

It is important to keep in mind that the economic, political-legal, and societal issues I have examined here, though they are social both in nature and in designation, are manifested most forcefully on the individual level. Negative public opinion toward homosexuals, for example, is not just some abstract belief held by a certain percent of the population. It is reflected and inflicted much more palpably. It is experienced in the attitudes and expectations that individual gay men and lesbians encounter in everyday life—together with the hostile words and actions that they inspire and that inspire them. Generally, an **individual** homosexual has a "run-in" with the police or the KGB and usually **individual** gay men and lesbians are beaten and killed in gay-bashing incidents. Only **individual** gay men and lesbians face being shunned by their families and only **individual** homosexuals are confronted with intolerance and unfair discrimination **face-to-face**. It is **individual** people, in the end, who make personal life-choices and embark upon all moral or immoral paths of behavior. This singular statement says a great deal about the way the many momentous events that have taken place in the former Soviet Union over the last decade have been experienced: "'An incredible amount has changed for the better,' said Yelena Zabadikena, a lesbian who works at [the] Center for Gender Issues here [in Moscow]. 'But it takes a long time to create a cohesive movement.'" (Specter 1995:A-4)

Certainly gay men and lesbians are as courageous and enthusiastic about their future in the newly independent countries that were created upon the break-up of the USSR as they can be—and for a few years it seemed like there would be nothing ahead but progress. After several years without much practical, day-to-day improvement, however, they are also frustrated and demoralized:

On the Development of Fraternity and Community 171

> In a way that is eerily reflective of the rest of Russian society today, gay activists are confused, finding it hard to figure out what they want from their new world and increasingly afraid that their brief burst of freedoms is starting to end.
> Like reformers in other fields, they have become bitter about the American models they once eagerly embraced. Today, most want nothing to do with the West. They find the idea of coming out of the closet—crucial to the gay movement in the United States—naïve. (Specter 1995:A-4)

Although they were more "out in the open" a few years ago, managers of gay clubs apparently have felt the sting of society's disapproval at the appearance of "flagrant" signs of homosexuality in their midst. According to Nicholls (1998: no page numbers), "Until five years ago, there were no gay clubs in Moscow. The three or four which exist now are in back streets, and most hide the fact they have a gay clientele. Unless you're a regular, you may not get in." Individual gay men and lesbians in the former Soviet Union also seem to have learned that going about their private affairs in public places is ill-advised:

> "I know we are supposed to be free now," he [a young gay man being interviewed] said glumly. . . .
> "I mean we *are* free now," he said speaking in English. "At least it seemed that way for a while. They can't lock us up anymore. But that's about it. We are still considered scum here. I think we always will be." (Specter 1995:A-1, *emphasis added*)

Tuller, it would seem, picks up right where Specter left off:

> Like most people in Russia today, gay or not, Misha has little interest in politics. He laughed at the suggestion that if all homosexuals just announced who, and what, they were the need for secrecy would diminish.
> ". . . I know about how in America they all admit they are gay and tell on others. You people have different standards. Privacy is important here."
> Although Westerners often point out that the Russian language has no word for privacy, it can in fact be one of the world's most secretive cultures. Homosexuals have long known how to live secretly. Until recently a gay man or a lesbian would never even mention the fact to the closest of friends.
> "What everyone here knows—gay or straight—is how to have a private life that is different from their public life," said David Tuller, an American journalist who is writing a book about gay life here.
> "In the West we would call that living a lie," he said. "Here they don't think that way. . . . They just want to be able to have their lives and not be bothered. For people here that would be a big step." (Specter 1995:A-4)

The distinction implicit here between privacy and secrecy deserves more careful consideration than either Specter (1995) or Tuller—as quoted here, and in his recent book (Tuller 1996)—seems to have given it. For homosexuals to be secretive about their stigmatized status and illegal behavior is one thing, but achieving and maintaining a private life in whatever "style" they wish is something different.

Yes, in the Soviet Union, most people did know how to have a secret life, but not because they desired for it to be that way. Rather, they were forced, by the Soviet system, to break the law routinely and often in order to get the things they needed to live fully as human beings. They had to offer gifts and pay some bribes in order to get their children into the good schools and programs or to get a good lawyer for a relative in trouble, or to get that promotion on the job that they know they deserve. They had to keep many of their personal affairs to themselves because anyone who knew about their intimate dealings—with relatives, say, to concoct a plan for obtaining a larger apartment—might be persuaded to inform on them. They had to keep quiet about their unofficial involvements, in celebrations of religious holidays, for instance. They had to make deals with everyone to get food, drink, hotel rooms, train tickets, hospital care, a new dress. Withought this bribery and corruption, this maneuvering around and manipulating government bureaucrats, they would be unable to perform important personal tasks, and to perform professional ones as well. The Soviet system was so poorly planned and so easily thwarted that it actually compelled enterprise managers to engage in this kind of deal making and bribery in order to procure the tools and materials needed for production.

Homosexuals, it should be clear, had to be careful about these things, and more. As people who bear a social stigma, their private life had to remain secret or their job, their home, their family, their freedom, and even their life might have been endangered. In the new Russia, as long as similar or analogous conditions of existence are actualities (and I have detailed in this report that, for the most part, they are), homosexuals still cannot live an openly gay private life. Extreme socioeconomic inequality and corruption in the struggling "market economy," an unstable polity of haltingly developing democracy, and declining valuation of both traditional and oppositional culture in a chaotic and dis-integrated society are the things that now hinder group-level institutional development in the social life of post-Soviet homosexuals. Unfortunately, to be sure, this confirms my prediction that, while opportunities for the development of specifically gay and lesbian social institutions are now more favorable, the personal and material resources, organizational and leadership abilities, mutual concern for the welfare of their fellows, and open expression of shared values, concerns—and, yes, even interests—are all still insufficient to generate institutionalized gay community among the homosexual population of the former Soviet Union.

As I noted in the Introduction regarding gay and lesbian sociopolitical activism in the USSR, the degree of institutional development of gay and lesbian subculture in the new Russia seems very much like that which existed in the United States in the 1940s and 1950s. It is nothing like the homosexual activism of the late 1960s (contrary to Western champions of this cause) when the Stonewall uprising occurred in New York and a gay rights movement began to seem possible, and necessary. Nor is it like that of the 1970s during which the American gay community came into being and the gay rights movement was taking off and underway. Similarly, the availability and stability of organized and institutionalized openly-gay meeting places in the new Russia bespeaks a life-situation which is actually more akin to that of North America in the 1930s and early 1940s—before World War II.6 Except for the fact that homosexual relations in the USA at that time were still criminalized in most states, the hardships and harassment that gay barkeepers and their patrons suffered, the limited options among available gay places in which homosexuals could make acquaintance with other gay men and lesbians, and the difficulties experienced in creating and maintaining all group-level social institutions of homosexual subculture were quite analogous. (*Conferre*: Scagliotti 1986; Faderman 1991; Chauncey 1994; Kaiser 1997)

Observing this similarity, those of us who have a personal or professional interest in such social conditions and in those people whom it affects most directly, we, like Kon (1995:264), may well worry: ."... f there is no gay community, who will defend gays' and lesbians' human rights, which are by no means guaranteed in Russia? And who will give them professional social and psychological advice and help them deal with stressful situations?" Of course this is a question that can be answered only by the gay men and lesbians living in the former Soviet Union and then only in the light of the actions of those who would stand in the way of their creation of a more comfortable, more enriching, more fulfilling, and more fortunate future. It is also a question for the answer to which we can only anxiously wait. Perhaps we have hoped for, or even expected, more than is realistic in such a short time. We would do well to note that these people have only begun their new journey toward freedom. I believe that we will be able to help them better and to share information and strategies if we are unflinchingly honest with ourselves and each other.

While the idea of gay community has gained currency among homosexuals in post-Soviet society, there is a long way yet to go before there will be enough momentum generated to launch a successful movement or to create solid gay and lesbian community institutions.

NOTES

1. Here one must recall the argument I made in Chapter Five, which follows McAdam's (1982) contention that successful social movements among minority groups can arise from the efforts of determined and coordinated advocates for social change only when three key factors are in place. First, the degree of "organizational readiness" within the minority group must be high enough to give activists a legitimate backing for their struggle and to provide the resources required for action. Second, the level of "insurgent consciousness" within the movement's constituency—that is, among those people who constitute the social category or group for which activists claim to fight—must be stimulated thoroughly enough to incite individuals to follow their leaders by aligning themselves with the cause, by joining activists groups, or otherwise supporting the movement with volunteer time or money donations. Third, the "structure of political opportunities" available to insurgent groups must be conducive. Such opportunities appear when there is substantial discontent, dispute, and disorganization in a country's political, economic, and/or social systems. Without these three conditions, a social group cannot sustain its efforts at a level sufficient for successful collective action. As my research showed, while there certainly was ample disorganization and strife in the USSR during the years of *glásnost* and *perestróyka* to allow the political opportunities for social action, neither substantial organizational readiness nor an adequate level of insurgent consciousness was available among Soviet homosexuals for gay and lesbian activists to launch a social movement on their behalf.

2. These were the 14 Soviet Socialist Republics and the Russian Soviet Federated Socialist Republic, the status of which had been altered in the previous few years to be (at least nominally) equal to the other "union republics." None of the smaller, so-called "autonomous" republics, provinces, territories, or districts embedded within the boundaries of the RSFSR and the other SSRs were allowed their self-determination, however—whether they were based on ethnic, historical, industrial, or administrative divisions.

3. As much as six months earlier, Soviet Foreign Relations Minister, Eduárd Shevardnádze, had earnestly warned of a *coup* plot in preparation by "hard-line" Communist conservatives and he even resigned his cabinet position in protest of their plan (Keller 1990). Conservative politicians were so embattled and "on the defensive" at that time, however, that they seemed too weak to mount such a rebellion, so Shevardnádze's dire warning was poorly understood and largely ignored.

4. A popular pun has circulated in reference to this situation. In Russian, the term most often used for "privatization," *"privatizátsiya"* (приватизация), is clearly borrowed from the West and may therefore feel alien and even invasive to Russian speakers. It can be modified easily to express contempt for the concept of privatizing economic enterprises as an unnatural, foreign idea and/or anger at the greed and corruption exhibited in this part of the economic reform program. Simply by adding the letter "kh" (x) before the "v" (в) produces a hybrid of borrowed and native words: prikhvátizatsiya (прихватизация), which plays on the Russian verb *"khvat"* (хвать), meaning "to grab" or "to steal." This insinuates that privatization is really some kind of "just-grab-it-ization," in which those people who have the longest and widest "reach" by dint of their power and influence under the Soviet regime use the opportunity to take for themselves as many as they can of the spoils of the Soviet system.

5. This condition is in many ways parallel to that with which gay and lesbian "homophile" organizations in the United States were presented during the 1950s and 1960s. (Adam 1987; D'Emilio 1983b, 1984)

On the Development of Fraternity and Community

6. During World War II, women were drafted into the workforce almost *en masse* to replace the men who went off to battle. This put them in much closer and more frequent contact with one another, gave them spending power of their own, and made it possible to wear pants and to behave in a more gender-neutral or even masculine (or "butch") way. Men sent off to war, of course, had also been experiencing more frequent and prolonged, very stressful and closer contact with one another, which can also breed intimacy. At the conclusion of the war, many sailors and soldiers returned from the fighting were interested in settling in the large cities, especially port cities. As a result, much greater numbers of "single" gay men and "gay girls" were in contact with one another than had been previously. (D'Emilio 1983b, 1984; Bérubé 1990) Many men and women discovered their homosexuality at that time and among them what I would call gay fraternity expanded greatly.

References

ENGLISH-LANGUAGE SOURCES

Abbott, Philip. 1987. *Seeking Many Inventions: the Idea of Community in America*. Knoxville: The University of Tennessee Press.

Achilles, Nancy. 1967. "The Development of the Homosexual Bar as an Institution." Pp. 228–244 in *Sexual Deviance*, edited by John H. Gagnon and William Simon. New York: Harper & Row.

Adam, Barry D. 1978. *The Survival of Domination: Inferiorization and Everyday Life*. New York: Elsevier.

Adam, Barry D. 1985. "Structural Foundations of the Gay World." *Comparative Studies in Society and History* 27(4):658–671.

Adam, Barry D. 1987. *The Rise of a Gay and Lesbian Movement*. Boston: Twayne Publishers.

ADVOCATE, The. 1991. "News in Brief: International." *The ADVOCATE: the National Gay and Lesbian Newsmagazine* (584, 27 August):29.

ADVOCATE, The. 1991. "News in Brief: International." *The ADVOCATE: the National Gay and Lesbian Newsmagazine* (585, 10 September):29.

ADVOCATE, The. 1991. "Foreign Flicks." *The ADVOCATE: the National Gay and Lesbian Newsmagazine* (587, 8 October):96.

ADVOCATE, The. 1991. "News in Brief: International." *The ADVOCATE: the National Gay and Lesbian Newsmagazine* (592, 17 December):29.

ADVOCATE, The. 1992. "News in Brief: International." *The ADVOCATE: the National Gay and Lesbian Newsmagazine* (604, 2 June):27.

ADVOCATE, The. 1992. "World View." *The ADVOCATE: the National Gay and Lesbian Newsmagazine* (604, 2 June):28.

ADVOCATE, The. 1992. "World View." *The ADVOCATE: the National Gay and Lesbian Newsmagazine* (605, 16 June):33.

ADVOCATE, The. 1992. "News in Brief: the World." *The ADVOCATE: the National Gay and Lesbian Newsmagazine* (606, 30 June):32.

ADVOCATE, The. 1992. "World View." *The ADVOCATE: the National Gay and Lesbian Newsmagazine* (606, 30 June):32.

ADVOCATE, The. 1992. "World View." *The ADVOCATE: the National Gay and Lesbian Newsmagazine* (608, 30 July):33.

ADVOCATE, The. 1992. "World View." *The ADVOCATE: the National Gay and Lesbian Newsmagazine* (608, 30 July):33.

ADVOCATE, The. 1992. "World View." *The ADVOCATE: the National Gay and Lesbian Newsmagazine* (609, 13 August):30.

ADVOCATE, The. 1992. "News in Brief: the World." *The ADVOCATE: the National Gay and Lesbian Newsmagazine* (611, 8 September):30.

ADVOCATE, The. 1992. "World View." *The ADVOCATE: the National Gay and Lesbian Newsmagazine* (614, 20 October):32.

ADVOCATE, The. 1992. "World View." *The ADVOCATE: the National Gay and Lesbian Newsmagazine* (615, 3 November):34.

ADVOCATE, The. 1992. "World View." *The ADVOCATE: the National Gay and Lesbian Newsmagazine* (615, 3 November):34.

ADVOCATE, The. 1992. "News in Brief: the World." *The ADVOCATE: the National Gay and Lesbian Newsmagazine* (616, 17 November):31.

ADVOCATE, The. 1993. "1992: the Year in Review." *The ADVOCATE: the National Gay and Lesbian Newsmagazine* (620, 12 January):45.

ADVOCATE, The. 1993. "World View." *The ADVOCATE: the National Gay and Lesbian Newsmagazine* (623, 23 February):32.

Aldrich, Howard E. 1979. *Organizations and Environments.* Englewood Cliffs, NJ: Prentice-Hall.

Ammassari, Paolo. 1994. "Ecology and the Quality of Social Life." Pp. 43–49 in *Ecology, Society and the Quality of Social Life,* edited by William V. D'Antonio, Masamichi Sasaki, and Yoshio Yonebayashi. New Brunswick, NJ: Transaction Publishers.

Amnesty International U.S.A. 1994 *Breaking The Silence: Human Rights Violations Based on Sexual Orientation.* New York: Amnesty International Publications.

Arato, Andrew. 1991. "Social Movements and Civil Society in the Soviet Union." Pp. 197–214 in *Perestroika from Below: Social Movements in the Soviet*

Union, edited by Judith B. Sedaitis and Jim Butterfield. Boulder, CO: Westview Press.

Babbie, Earl R. 1973. *Survey Research Methods*. Belmont, CA: Wadsworth Publishing Company.

Babbie, Earl R. 1982. *Social Research for Consumers*. Belmont, California: Wadsworth Publishing Company.

Babbie, Earl R. 1989. *The Practice of Social Research, Fifth Edition*. Belmont, California: Wadsworth Publishing Company.

Barringer, Felicity. 1994. "When G-Notes Are Small Change." *The New York Times*, October 16, p. 4:5.

Barshay, Jill. 1993. "Russia's Gay Men Step Out of Soviet-Era Shadows." *The New York Times*, 10 February, p. A3.

Bell, Alan P. 1975. "Research in Homosexuality: Back to the Drawing Board." *Archives of Sexual Behavior* 4(4, July):421–431.

Bell, Alan P. and Martin S. Weinberg. 1978. *Homosexualities: a Study of Diversity Among Men and Women*. New York: Simon & Schuster.

Bell, Alan P., Martin S. Weinberg, and Sue Kiefer Hammersmith. 1981. *Sexual Preference: Its Development in Men and Women*. Bloomington, IN: Indiana University Press.

Bell, Wendell and Marion D. Boat. 1957. "Urban Neighbourhood Types and Informal Social Relations." *American Journal of Sociology* 62(January):391–398.

Bell, Wendell and Maryanne T. Force. 1956. "Urban Neighbourhood Types and Participation in Informal Social Relations." *American Sociological Review* 21(February):25–34.

Berger, Bennett M. 1988. "Disenchanting the Concept of Community." *Society* 25(6, September/October):50–52.

Berger, Peter L. and Thomas Luckmann. 1967. *The Social Construction of Reality: a Treatise in the Sociology of Knowledge*. Garden City, NY: Anchor Books.

Bérubé, Allan. 1983. "Marching to a Different Drummer: Lesbian and Gay GIs in World War II." Pp. 88–99 in *Powers of Desire: the Politics of Sexuality*, edited by Ann Snitow, Christine Stansell, and Sharon Thompson. New York: Monthly Review Press.

Bieber, Irving. 1962. *Homosexuality: A Psychoanalytic Study*. New York: Basic Books.

Blumstein, Philip and Pepper Schwartz. 1983. *American Couples: Money, Work, Sex*. New York: William Morrow.

Breton, Raymond. 1964. "Institutional Completeness of Ethnic Communities and the Personal Relations of Immigrants." *American Journal of Sociology* LXX (2, September):193–205.

Berzon, Betty and Robert Leighton. 1979. *Positively Gay*. Millbrae, CA: Celestial Arts.

Bronski, Michael. 1984. *Culture Clash: the Making of Gay Sensibility*. Boston: South End Press.

Bullough, Vern L. 1976. *Sexual Variance in Society and History*. Chicago: University of Chicago Press.

Bullough, Vern L. 1979. *Homosexuality: a History*. New York: Wylie.

Burgess, Ernest W. 1949. "The Sociologic Theory of Psychosexual Behavior." In *Psychosexual Development in Health and Disease*, edited by Paul H. Hoch and Joseph Zubin. New York: Grune & Stratton.

Burgin, Diana Lewis. 1992. "Sophia Parnok and the Writing of a Lesbian Poet's Life." *Slavic Review* 51(2, Summer):215–231.

Burke, Peter J. 1991. "Identity Processes and Social Stress." *American Sociological Review* 56(6, December):836–849.

Burton, P. 1977. "Gennady Trifonov." *Gay News* (119, 19 May-1 June).

Cain, Roy. 1991. "Stigma Management and Gay Identity Development." *Social Work* 36(1, January):67–73.

Callender, Charles and Lee M. Kochems. 1983. "The North American Berdache." *Current Anthropology* 24:443–456.

Cass, Vivienne C. 1979. "Homosexual Identity Formation: a Theoretical Model." *Journal of Homosexuality* 4(3, Spring):219–235.

Cass, Vivienne C. 1983-84. "Homosexual Identity: a Concept in Need of Definition." *Journal of Homosexuality* 9 (2–3, Winter/Spring), 105–126.

Chalidze, Valery. 1977. *Criminal Russia: Essays on Crime in the Soviet Union*. Translated by P. S. Falla. New York: Random House.

Chauncey, George, Jr. 1994. *Gay New York: gender, urban culture, and the making of the gay male world, 1890–1940*. New York: Basic Books.

Chua-Eoan, Howard G. 1991. "Coming Out in Moscow: Soviet Gays Battle Stalin's Ghost for Civil Rights." *International Time*, 26 August, 41.

Connell, R. W. 1992. "A Very Straight Gay: Masculinity, Homosexual Experience, and the Dynamics of Gender." *American Sociological Review* 57(6, December):735–751.

Costlow, Jane T., Stephanie Sandler and Judith Vowles, eds. 1993. *Sexuality and the Body in Russian Culture*. Stanford, CA: Stanford University Press.

References

Cox, Stephen and Cynthia Gallois. 1996. "Gay and Lesbian Identity Development: a Social Identity Perspective." *Journal of Homosexuality* 30(4):1–30.

Craven, Paul and Barry Wellman. 1973. "The Network City." *Sociological Inquiry* 43(3–4):57–88.

Crites, Thomas Richard. 1976. "Coming Out Gay." Pp. 142–154 in *The Social Psychology of Sex*, edited by Jacqueline P. Wiseman. New York: Harper & Row.

Damron, Bob. 1992. *Bob Damron's Address Book '92*. 28th Edition. San Francisco: The Damron Company.

Dank, Barry M. "Coming Out in the Gay World" *Psychiatry* 34 (1971) 1880–97

Dark, Tessa. 1984. "A Close Look at Gay Survival Behind the Iron Curtain." *GLC Voice*, 1 October, 10.

Darrow, William W.; Jaffe, Harold W.; Thomas, Pauline A.; Haverkos, Harry W.; Rogers, Martha F.; Guinan, Mary E.; Auerbach, David M.; Spira, Thomas J.; and Curran, James W. 1986. "Sex of Interviewer, Place of Interview, and Responses of Homosexual Men to Sensitive Quesions," *Archives of Sexual Behavior* 15(1): 79–88.

DeCecco, John P. and Michael G. Shively. 1985. *Origins of Sexuality and Homosexuality*. New York: Harrington Park Press.

De Jong, Ben. 1982. "'An Intolerable Kind of Moral Degeneration': Homosexuality in the Soviet Union." *Review of Socialist Law* 4:341–357.

Delph, Edward William. 1978. *The Silent Community: Public Homosexual Encounters*. Beverly Hills, CA: Sage Publications.

D'Emilio, John. 1983a. "Capitalism and Gay Identity." Pp. 100–113 in *Powers of Desire: the Politics of Sexuality*, edited by Ann Snitow, Christine Stansell and Sharon Thompson. New York: Monthly Review Press.

D'Emilio, John. 1983b. *Sexual Politics, Sexual Communities: the Making of a Homosexual Minority in the United States, 1940–1970*. Chicago: The University of Chicago Press.

D'Emilio, John. 1984. "Making and Unmaking Minorities: the Tensions Between Gay Politics and History." *New York University Review of Law and Social Change* 14:915–922.

D.J.P. 1990. "Moscow Gays Come Out." *Radio Free Europe/Radio Liberty Daily Report*, 19 February.

Dorf, Julie and Masha Gessen. 1991. "Notes from the Revolution." *Tema International* (2):2–9.

Dorf, Julie and Masha Gessen. 1992. "From Moscow with Homo Love." *OutLook: National Lesbian & Gay Quarterly* (15, Winter):48-54.

Doyal, Len and Ian Gough. 1991 *A Theory of Human Need*. New York: The Guilford Press

Duberman, Martin Bauml, Martha Vicinus, and George Chauncey, Jr., eds. 1989. *Hidden from History: Reclaiming the Gay and Lesbian Past*. New York: New American Library.

DuCett, Paul. 1986. "Gays in the USSR: a Traveler Seeks the Good Life Behind the Iron Curtain." *Bay Windows: New England's Largest Gay and Lesbian Newspaper*, 4(49, 4-10 December):1, 11-13.

Dynes, Wayne R. 1987. *Homosexuality: A Research Guide*. New York: Garland Publishing.

Ebert, Alan. 1977. "Sex in the Soviet Union: Sublimate or Siberia." *The ADVOCATE: the National Gay and Lesbian Newsmagazine* (215, 4 May):11-12.

Effrat, Marcia Pelly. 1973. "Approaches to Community: Conflicts and Complementarities." *Sociological Inquiry* 43(3-4):1-32.

Ehrenstein, David. 1981. "Three Directors: Sergei Paradzhanov, an Exile from His Art." *The ADVOCATE: the National Gay and Lesbian Newsmagazine* (313, 19 March):4-5.

Engelstein, Laura. 1992. "There is Sex in Russia—and Always Was: Some Recent Contributions to Russian Erotica." *Slavic Review* 51(4, Winter):786-790.

Engelstein, Laura. 1996. "Soviet Policy toward Male Homosexuality: Its Origins and Historical Roots." *Journal of Homosexuality* 29(2, Winter):786-790.

Essig, Laurie. 1991. "A Circle of Queerdom: Homosexuality as a Politically Organizing Identity in the United States and Russia." Paper prepared for coursework in the Department of Sociology, Columbia University. 20 December.

Essig, Laurie. 1996. *Sex, Self, and Other: the Production and Performance of Queer in Russia, 1989-94*. Doctoral Dissertation. Columbia University.

Evans, Meredydd. 1990. "Getting to Glasnost and Beyond: a Look at Homosexuality in the Soviet Union." Unpublished Senior Thesis written at Columbia University. April.

Faderman, Lillian. 1991. *Odd Girls and Twilight Lovers: a History of Lesbian Life in Twentieth-Century America*. New York: Columbia University Press.

Fehér, Ferenc, Agnes Heller, and György Márkus. 1983. *Dictatorship Over Needs: an Analysis of Soviet Societies*. Oxford, England: Basil Blackwell.

References

Ferrari, Marianne. 1992. *Ferrari's Places of Interest: Worldwide Gay & Lesbian Guide*. Phoenix, AZ: Ferrari Publications.

Feyerabend, Paul K. 1975. *Against Method: outline of an anarchistic theory of knowledge*. London: NLB.

Field, Mark G. 1988. "Soviet Society and Communist Party Controls: A Case of Constricted Development." Pp. 119-146 in *Understanding Soviet Society*, edited by Michael Paul Sacks and Jerry G. Pankhurst. Boston: Unwin Hyman.

Fischer, George. 1966. "Current Soviet Work in Sociology." *The American Sociologist* 1(3, May):127-132.

Fisher, Wesley A. 1980. *The Soviet Marriage Market: Mate-Selection in Russia and the USSR*. New York: Praeger.

Friedman, Sonya. 1992. "Homosexuality in Russia: Interview with Roman Kalinin." Half-hour talk-show segment. *Sonya Live in L.A.*, 8 January. Cable News Network (CNN).

"G." 1984. "The Secret Life of Moscow." Pp. 199-207 in *The Christopher Street Reader*, edited by Michael Denneny, Charles Ortleb and Thomas Steele. New York: Wideview/Perigee.

Gagnon, John H. and William Simon. 1973. *Sexual Conduct: the Social Sources of Human Sexuality*. Chicago: Aldine.

Gagnon, John H. and William Simon, eds. 1967. *Sexual Deviance*. New York: Harper & Row.

Gay Community News, The. 1991. "International News: Latvia" *The Gay Community News* 18(12, December):10.

Gay Paper. 1992 "Rep. Frank to Lead Group in Effort to Free Russian Gays." *Gay Paper*, 4 December, 38.

Gerhart, Genevra. 1974 *The Russian's World: Life and Language*. New York: Harcourt Brace Jovanovich.

Gerth, Hans Heinrich and C. Wright Mills. 1953. *Character and social structure: the psychology of social institutions*. New York: Harcourt, Brace.

Gessen, Masha. 1990a. "We Have No Sex: Soviet Gays and AIDS in the Era of Glasnost." *OutLook: National Gay & Lesbian Quarterly* (Summer 1990).

Gessen, Masha. 1990b. "On the Theme: Talking with the Editor of the Soviet Union's First Gay and Lesbian Newspaper." *OutLook: National Lesbian and Gay Quarterly*, Summer, 55-59.

Gessen, Masha. 1990c. "Moscow Activists Push for Gay Glasnost." *The ADVOCATE: the National Gay and Lesbian Newsmagazine*, 18 December, 50.

Gessen, Masha. 1991a. "Comrade in Arms." *OutLook: National Lesbian & Gay Quarterly*, 3(3):67–71.

Gessen, Masha. 1991b. "Soviet Queers Fight Coup: Gay Newspaper Became Printing Plant for Russian Resistance." *The ADVOCATE: the National Gay and Lesbian Newsmagazine* (586, 24 September):50.

Gessen, Masha. 1991c. "Russian Lesbians Define Their Own Agenda." *The ADVOCATE: the National Gay and Lesbian Newsmagazine* (591, 3 December):46–47.

Gessen, Masha. 1993a. "Red Army of Lovers." *Out Magazine* (5, April/May):56–61.

Gessen, Masha. 1993b. "The Gay Gulag: a Survivor Recalls His Nightmare Years in a Soviet Prison." *The ADVOCATE: the National Gay and Lesbian Newsmagazine* (623, 23 February): 44.

Gessen, Masha. 1993c. "Ballet-Russe: Sex-law Reform: Nobody's Priority." *The ADVOCATE: the National Gay and Lesbian Newsmagazine* (633, 13 July): 31.

Gessen, Masha. 1994. *The Rights of Lesbians and Gay Men in the Russian Federation: An International Gay and Lesbian Human Rights Commission Report* (San Francisco: IGLHRC)

Gillette, John M. 1926. "Community Concepts." *Social Forces* 4(4, June):677–689.

Goffman, Erving. 1959. *The Presentation of Self in Everyday Life*. Garden City, NY: Doubleday.

Goffman, Erving. 1963. *Stigma: Notes on the Management of Spoiled Identity*. New York: Simon & Schuster, Inc.

Goldenberg, Sheldon and Valerie A. Haines. 1992. "Social Networks and Institutional Completeness: from Territory to Ties." *Canadian Journal of Sociology / Cahiers Canadiens De Sociologie* 17(3):301–312.

Goode, Erich and Richard Troiden. 1975. *Sexual Deviance and Sexual Deviants*. New York: William Morrow.

Goode, William J. 1957. "Community Within a Community: the Professions." *American Sociological Review* 22(April):194–200.

Goodwin, Joseph P. 1989. *More Man Than You'll Ever Be: Gay Folklore and Acculturation in Middle America*. Bloomington, IN: Indiana University Press.

Grahn, Judy. 1984. *Another Mother Tongue: Gay Words, Gay Worlds*. Boston: Beacon Press.

Granovetter, Mark S. 1973. "The Strength of Weak Ties." *American Journal of Sociology* 78:1360-1380.

Grau, Rawley. 1992. "Black and White and Read all Over." *Baltimore Alternative*, December, 3. Article about letter to the newspaper from a lonely Russian man.

Greenberg, David F. 1988. *The Construction of Homosexuality*. Chicago: The University of Chicago Press.

Greer, Scott. 1956. "Urbanism Reconsidered: a Comparative Study of Local Areas in a Metropolis." *American Sociological Review* 21(February):19-25.

Guide, The. 1992. "VoiceMale Personals: International." *The Guide: Gay Travel, Entertainment, Politics, & Sex* 12(7, July):143-144. Boston: Fidelity Publishing.

Hannan, Michael T., and John Freeman. 1977. "The Population Ecology of Organizations." *American Sociological Review* 82:929-964.

Harry, Joseph. 1974. "Urbanization and the Gay Life." *The Journal of Sex Research* 10(3, August):237-247.

Harry, Joseph. 1982. *Gay Children Grown Up: Gender Culture and Gender Deviance*. New York: Praeger.

Harry, Joseph and William B. DeVall. 1978. *The Social Organization of Gay Males*. New York: Praeger.

Hart, John and Diane Richardson. 1981. *The Theory and Practice of Homosexuality*. London: Routledge & Kegan Paul.

Hawley, Willis D. and Frederick M. Wirt, eds. 1968. *The Search for Community Power*. Englewood Cliffs, NJ: Prentice-Hall.

Henry, Jules. 1958. "The Personal Community and Its Invariant Properties." *American Anthropologist* 60(October):827-831.

Herdt, Gilbert. 1987. *The Sambia: Ritual and Gender in New Guinea*. New York: Holt, Rinehart & Winston.

Herdt, Gilbert, ed. 1984. *Ritualized Homosexuality in Melanesia*. Berkeley: University of California Press.

HHES (Housing and Household Economic Statistics Division). 1995. "Table 2a. Households Owning Asset Types, by Selected Characteristics: 1991." *Asset Ownership of Households: 1993*. Washington, DC: United States Bureau of the Census.

Hillery, George A., Jr. 1955. "Definitions of Community: Areas of Agreement." *Rural Sociology* 20(2, June):111-123.

Hillery, George A., Jr. 1959. "A Critique of Selected Community Concepts." *Social Forces* 37(3, March):237-242.

Hillery, George A., Jr. 1969. *Communal Organizations: a Study of Local Societies.* Chicago: University of Chicago Press.

Hocquenghem, Guy. 1978. *Homosexual Desire.* Translated by Daniella Dangoor. London: Allison & Busby.

Hooker, Evelyn. 1963. "The Adjustment of the Male Overt Homosexual." Pp. 141-161 in *The Problem of Homosexuality in Modern Society*, edited by Henrik M. Ruitenbeek. New York: E. P. Dutton & Co.

Hooker, Evelyn. 1965. "Male Homosexuals and Their 'Worlds'." Pp. 83-107 in *Sexual Inversion: the Multiple Roots of Homosexuality*, edited by Judd Marmor. New York: Basic Books.

Hooker, Evelyn 1967 "The Homosexual Community," pp.167-184 in: *Sexual Deviance,* John H. Gagnon & William Simon, eds. (New York: Harper & Row)

Hoult, Thomas Ford. 1969. *Dictionary of Modern Sociology.* Totowa, NJ: Littlefield, Adams, & Co.

Humphreys, Laud. 1970. *Tearoom Trade: Impersonal Sex in Public Places.* Chicago: Aldine.

Humphreys, Laud. 1971. "New Styles in Homosexual Manliness." *Trans-Action*, March-April, 38-46, 64-65.

Humphreys, Laud. 1972. *Out of the Closets: the Sociology of Homosexual Liberation.* Englewood Cliffs, NJ: Prentice-Hall.

Hunter, Floyd. 1953. *Community Power Structure: a Study of Decision-Makers.* Garden City, NY: Anchor Books.

Indiana, Gary. 1990. "The Boys in the Baltic: Gay 'Liberation' Comes to the Soviet Union." *The Village Voice*, 26 June.

International Gay and Lesbian Human Rights Commission (IGLHRC). 1992a. "HIV+ Gay Man Imprisoned Under Russian Article 115." *IGLHRC Action Alert*, February.

International Gay and Lesbian Human Rights Commission (IGLHRC). 1992b. "Lithuanian Gays Imprisoned Under Article 122." *IGLHRC Action Alert*, February.

International Gay and Lesbian Human Rights Commission (IGLHRC). 1993. "Lithuania Decriminalizes Homosexuality." *IGLHRC Action Alert*, July/August.

International Gay and Lesbian Human Rights Commission (IGLHRC). 1995. "Latvian State Security Service Beat Gays." *IGLHRC Action Alert*, IV(4), December.

References

Janowitz, Morris. 1952. *The Community Press in an Urban Setting.* New York: The Free Press.

Kaiser, Charles. 1997. *The Gay Metropolis: 1940-1996.* Boston: Houghton Mifflin.

Kalton, Graham. 1983. *Compensating for Missing Survey Data.* Research Report Series. Ann Arbor, MI: Survey Research Center, Institute for Social Research, University of Michigan.

Karlen, Arno. 1971. *Sexuality and Homosexuality.* New York: W. W. Norton.

Karlen, Arno. 1978. "Homosexuality: the Scene and Its Students." Pp. 223-248 in *The Sociology of Sex: an Introductory Reader*, Revised Edition, edited by James M. Henslin and Sagarin Edward. New York: Schocken Books.

Karlinsky, Simon. 1976. "Russia's Gay Literature & History (11th-20th centuries)." *Gay Sunshine: A Journal of Gay Liberation.* (29/30, Summer/Fall).

Karlinsky, Simon. 1977. "Russia's Gay Literature, Part II: Controversy." *Gay Sunshine: A Journal of Gay Liberation.* (31, Winter).

Karlinsky, Simon. 1979. "The Case of Gennady Trifonov." *Christopher Street*, January, 65.

Karlinsky, Simon. 1982. "Gay Life Before the Soviets: Revisionism Revisited." *The ADVOCATE: the National Gay and Lesbian Newsmagazine* (339, 1 April):16.

Karlinsky, Simon. 1984. "The Case of Gennady Trifonov." Pp. 207-210 in *The Christopher Street Reader*, edited by Michael Denneny, Charles Ortleb and Thomas Steele. New York: Wideview/Perigee.

Karlinsky, Simon. 1989. "Russia's Gay Literature and Culture: the Impact of the October Revolution." Pp. 347-364 in *Hidden from History: Reclaiming the Gay & Lesbian Past*, edited by Martin Bauml Duberman, Martha Vicinus and George Chauncey, Jr. New York: New American Library.

Karlinsky, Simon. 1991. "Unearthing Russia's Gay Past." *The ADVOCATE: the National Gay and Lesbian Newsmagazine* (591, 3 December):48-49.

Katz, Jonathan N. 1976. *Gay American History: Lesbians and Gay Men in the U.S.A.* New York: Thomas Y. Crowell.

Keller, Bill. 19890. "Shevardnadze Stuns Kremlin by Quitting Foreign Ministry and Warning of 'Dictatorship'." *The New York Times*, December 21, Late edition, p. A-1.

Keller, Suzanne. 1968. *The Urban Neighborhood: a Sociological Perspective.* New York: Random House.

Kinsey, Alfred C., Wardell B. Pomeroy and Clyde E. Martin. 1948. *Sexual Behavior in the Human Male*. Philadelphia: W. B. Saunders.

Kinsey, Alfred C., Wardell B. Pomeroy, Clyde E. Martin and Paul H. Gebhard. 1953. *Sexual Behavior in the Human Female*. Philadelphia: W. B. Saunders.

Kon, Igor. 1993. "Sexual Minorities." Pp. 89–115 in *Sex and Russian Society*, edited by Igor Kon and James Riordan. Bloomington: Indiana University Press.

Kon, Igor S. 1995. *The Sexual Revolution in Russia: From the Age of the Czars to Today*. Translated by James Riordan. New York: The Free Press.

Kramer, Judith. 1970. *The American Minority Community*. New York: Crowell.

Krieger, Susan. 1983. *The Mirror Dance: Identity in a Women's Community*. Philadelphia: Temple University Press.

Lapidus, Gail W. 1989. "State and Society: Toward the Emergence of Civil Society in the Soviet Union." Pp. 121–147 in *Politics, Society, and Nationality Inside Gorbachov's Russia*, edited by Seweryn Bialer. Boulder, CO: Westview Press.

Lauritsen, John and David Thorstad. 1974. *The Early Homosexual Rights Movement (1864– 1935)*. New York: Times Change Press.

Lee, John Alan. 1979. "The Gay Connection." *Urban Life* 8(2, July):175–198.

Lee, John Alan. 1981. "Forbidden Colors of Love: Patterns of Gay Love." Pp. 128–139 in *Single Life: Unmarried Adults in Social Context*, edited by Peter J. Stein. New York: St. Martin's Press.

Lee, Terence. 1968. "The Urban Neighborhood as a Socio-Spatial Schema." *Human Relations* 21(August):241–267.

Levin, Eve. 1989. *Sex and Society in the World of the Orthodox Slavs, 900–1700*. Ithaca, NY: Cornell University Press.

Levine, Martin P., ed. 1979a. *Gay Men: the Sociology of Male Homosexuality*. New York: Harper & Row.

Levine, Martin P. 1979. "Gay Ghetto." Pp. 182–204 in *Gay Men: the Sociology of Male Homosexuality*, edited by Martin P. Levine. New York: Harper & Row.

Leznoff, Maurice. 1956. "Interviewing Homosexuals" *The American Journal of Sociology* 62:202–4.

Leznoff, Maurice and William A. Westley. 1956. "The Homosexual Community." *Social Problems* 3:257–263.

Lorimer, James and Myfanwy Phillips. 1971. *Working People: Life in a Downtown City Neighborhood*. Toronto: James, Lewis, & Samuel.

Lynd, Robert S. and Helen M. Lynd. 1929. *Middletown: a Study in Contemporary American Culture*. New York: Harcourt Brace.

MacDonald, Heather. 1992. Kiev Blue. In *The 4th Annual New York International Festival of Lesbian and Gay Film*. World premiere of a documentary film. New York: Garden Films.

Mamonova, Tatyana. 1989. *Russian Women's Studies: Essays on Sexism in Soviet Culture*. Oxford: Pergamon Press

Marmor, Judd, ed. 1980. *Homosexual Behavior: a Modern Reappraisal*. New York: Basic Books, Inc.

Martin, John L. and Laura Dean. 1990. "Developing a Community Sample of Gay Men for an Epidemiologic Study of AIDS." *American Behavioral Scientist*, 33(5):546–561.

Martin, Del and Phyllis Lyon. 1972. *Lesbian/woman*. San Francisco: Glide Publications.

Masters, William H. and Virginia E. Johnson. 1966. *Human Sexual Response*. Boston: Little, Brown.

Masters, William H. and Virginia E. Johnson. 1979. *Homosexuality in Perspective*. Boston: Little, Brown.

Mayhew, Leon. 1990. "The Differentiation of the Solidary Public." Pp. 294–322 in *Differentiation Theory and Social Change: Comparative and Historical Perspectives*, edited by Jeffrey C. Alexander and Paul Colomy. New York: Columbia University Press.

McAdam, Doug. 1982. *Political Process and the Development of Black Insurgency 1930–1970*. Chicago: University of Chicago Press.

McCann, James C. 1973. "Human Ecology." Pp. 419–431 in *Society Today*, Second Edition, edited by Rodney Stark. Del Mar, CA: CRM Books.

McIntosh, Mary. 1968. "'The Homosexual Role'." *Social Problems* 16:182–192.

McWhirter, David P. and Andrew M. Mattison. 1984. *The Male Couple: How Relationships Develop*. Englewood Cliffs, NJ: Prentice-Hall, Inc.

Miller, Brian. 1978. "Adult Sexual Resocialization: Adjustment toward a Stigmatized Identity." *Alternative Lifestyles* 1:207–34.

Mills, C. Wright. 1959. *The Sociological Imagination*. New York: Grove Press.

Minton, Henry L. and Gary J. McDonald. 1983–84. "Homosexual Identity Formation as a Developmental Process." *Journal of Homosexuality* 9(2–3, Winter/Spring): 91–104.

Moses, A. Elfin and Robert O. Hawkins, Jr. 1982. *Counseling Lesbian Women and Gay Men*. St. Louis, MO: The C. V. Mosby Company.

Murray, Stephen O. 1980. "The Institutional Elaboration of a Quasi-Ethnic Community in Canada." Pp. 31–43 in *Homosexuality in International*

Perspective, edited by Joseph Harry and Man Singh Das. New York: Advent Publishers.

Murray, Stephen O. 1984. *Social Theory, Homosexual Realities*. Gai Saber Monograph No. 3. New York: Gay Academic Union.

Murray, Stephen O. 1987. *Male Homosexuality in Central and South America*. Gai Saber Monograph No. 5. New York: Gay Academic Union.

Nestle, Joan. 1984. "The Fem Question." Pp. 232–241 in *Pleasure and Danger: Exploring Female Sexuality*, edited by Carol S. Vance. Boston: Routledge & Kegan Paul.

Neuwirth, Gertrude. 1969. "A Weberian Outline of a Theory of Community: Its Application to the 'Dark Ghetto'." *British Journal of Sociology* 20(2):148–163.

Newton, Esther. 1972. *Mother Camp: Female Impersonators in America*. Englewood Cliffs, NJ: Prentice-Hall.

Nicholls, Stephen. 1998. "Black nights for Moscow's gays." *Sydney Morning Herald Online*, www.smh.com.au/daily/content/980214/world/world8.html

Nisbet, Robert A. 1953. *The Quest for Community*. London: Oxford University Press.

NOGLSTP. 1990. "Gay Statisticians: How Do You Poll the Community?" *NOGLSTP Bulletin*, January/February, 1.

Nungesser, Lon G. 1983. *Homosexual Acts, Actors, and Identities*. New York: Praeger.

Olsen, Mancur. 1965. *The Control Logic of Collective Action; Public Goods and the Theory of Groups*, Cambridge, MA: Harvard University Press.

Park, Robert E. 1952. *Human Communities*. Glencoe, IL: The Free Press.

Perrow, Charles. 1967. "A Framework for the Comparative Analysis of Organizations." *American Sociological Review* 32:194–2089.

Person, Ethel Spector. 1980. "Sexuality as the Mainstay of Identity: Psychoanalytic Perspectives." *Signs: Journal of Women in Culture and Society* 5(4, Summer):605–630.

Phillips, Derek. 1969. "Social Class, Social Participation and Happiness: a Consideration of Interaction, Opportunities and Investment." *Sociological Quarterly* 10(Winter):3–21.

Pipes, Richard. 1968. *The Formation of the Soviet Union: Communism and Nationalism, 1917–1923*. New York: Atheneum.

Plummer, Kenneth. 1975. *Sexual Stigma: an Interactionist Account*. Boston: Routledge & Kegan Paul.

Plummer, Kenneth. 1981. *The Making of the Modern Homosexual*. London: Hutchinson.

Ponse, Barbara. 1978. *Identities in the Lesbian World: the Social Construction of Self*. Westport, CO: Greenwood Press.

Rayfield, Donald, ed. 1985. *The Confessions of Victor X*. New York: Grove Press.

Redfield, Robert. 1941. *The Folk Culture of the Yucatan*. Chicago: University of Chicago Press.

Reiss, Albert J. 1961. "The Social Integration of Queers and Peers." *Social Problems* 9:102–119.

Riddle, Dorothy I. and Stephen F. Morin, eds. 1978. *Psychology and the Gay Community*. Special Issue of the Journal of Social Issues, Vol. 34, No. 3 (Summer). Ann Arbor, MI: Society for the Psychological Study of Social Issues.

Robinson, Harlow. 1991. "'*Molchanie—eto smert*' or 'Keeping Russia Clean': Recent Developments in the Gay and Lesbian Movement in Russia." Paper presented at 23rd National Convention of the American Association for the Advancement of Slavic Studies. Miami, Florida, 22–25 November.

Rosenberg, M. Michael and Jack Jedwab. 1992. "Institutional Completeness, Ethnic Organizational Style and the Role of the State: the Jewish, Italian and Greek Communities of Montreal." *Canadian Review of Sociology and Anthropology / Review Canadienne Sociolgie Et Anthropologie* 29(3):266–287.

Rossi, Peter H., J. D. Wright, and A. B. Anderson. 1983. *Handbook of Survey Research*. New York: Academic Press.

Rubin, J. 1993. "Gay Political Movement Takes Place in Russia." *Associated Press report* (16 August).

Sagarin, Edward, editor. 1971. *The Other Minorities*. Waltham, MA: Xerox.

Sagarin, Edward. 1978. "Sex Research and Sociology: Retrospective and Prospective." Pp. 249–277 in *The Sociology of Sex: an Introductory Reader*, Revised Edition, edited by James M. Henslin and Edward Sagarin. New York: Schocken Books.

Sandomirsky, Vera. 1951. "Sex in the Soviet Union." *The Russian Review* 10(3, July):199–209.

Savin-Williams, Ritch C. 1990. *Gay and Lesbian Youth: Expressions of Identity*. New York: Hemisphere Publishing Corporation.

Scagliotti, John, executive producer. 1986. *Before Stonewall: The Making of a Gay and Lesbian Community*. Documentary film.

Schluter, Daniel P. 1991. "Catch as Catch Can: Sampling and Representativeness Among Sexual Minorities in the USSR." Paper presented at the Conference on Methodological Problems in Minority Research. Tallinn, Estonia, USSR: Institute of History, Estonian Academy of Sciences.

Schluter, Daniel P. 1992a. "Social Institutions in the Ex-Soviet Gay World: Fraternity Without Community." Paper presented at the Columbia University Seminar on Homosexualities. New York, NY, 5 March.

Schluter, Daniel P. 1992b. "Movement Toward a Lesbian & Gay Community in the Former USSR." Paper presented at the 1992 Annual Meeting of the Society for the Study of Social Problems (SSSP). Pittsburgh, PA, 18-20 August.

Schluter, Daniel P. 1993. "ГОЛУБЫЕ И РОЗОВЫЕ: Gay & Lesbian Life in the Former USSR, Data from a 1991 Survey." Paper presented at the 25th National Convention of the American Association for the Advancement of Slavic Studies (AAASS). Honolulu, HI, 19-22 November.

Schuvaloff, George. 1976. "Gay Life in Russia." *Christopher Street* 1(3, September):14-22.

Scott, W. Richard, and John W. Meyer. 1983. "The Organization of Societal Sectors." Pp. 129-154 in *Organizational Environments: Ritual and Rationality*, edited by John W. Myer and W. Richard Scott. Beverly Hills: Sage.

Shalin, Dmitri N. 1978. "The Development of Soviet Sociology, 1956-1976." *Annual Review of Sociology*, 4:171-191.

Shalin, Dmitri N. 1990. "Sociology for the Glasnost Era: Institutional and Substantive Changes in Recent Soviet Sociology." *Social Forces*, 68(4):1019-1039.

Shaw, Clifford and Henry D. McKay. 1942. *Juvenile Delinquency and Urban Areas*. Chicago: University of Chicago Press.

Sheatsley. 1983. "Questionaire Construction and Item Writing." Chapter 6. In *Handbook of Survey Research*, edited by P. H. Rossi, J. D. Wright and A. B. Anderson. New York: Academic Press.

Shlapentokh, Vladimir. 1987. *The Politics of Sociology in the Soviet Union*. Boulder, CO: Westview Press.

Skocpol, Theda. 1979. *States and Social Revolutions: a comparative analysis of France, Russia, and China*. Cambridge: Cambridge University Press.

Skolander, Bjoern. 1997. "Kazakstan: Decriminalization of sodomy." http://www.qrd.org/qrd/world/asia/kazakstan/decriminalization.of.sodomy-10.29.97.

References

Socarides, Charles W. 1968. *The Overt Homosexual.* New York: Grune & Stratton.

Spada, James. 1979. *The Spada Report: the Newest Survey of Gay Male Sexuality.* New York: New American Library.

Specter, Michael. 1995. "Gay Russians Are 'Free' Now But Still Stay in Fearful Closet. *New York Times* (8 July):A-1,4.

Stacey, Margaret. 1969. "The Myth of Community Studies." *British Journal of Sociology* 20(2):134–147.

Stein, Maurice R. 1964. *The eclipse of community: an interpretation of American studies.* Princeton, NJ: Princeton University Press.

Stern, Mikhail. 1980. *Sex in the USSR.* Translated by Mark Howson and Cary Ryan. New York: Times Books.

Strubbe, Bill. 1991. "Pink Triangles in Red Square." *The Guide: Gay Travel, Entertainment, Politics, & Sex* 11(10, October):20–24. Boston: Fidelity Publishing.

Sudman, Seymour. 1976. *Applied Sampling.* New York: Academic Press.

Sudman, Seymour and Norman Bradburn. 1983. *Asking Questions: A Practical Guide to Questionnaire Design.* San Francisco: Jossey-Bass.

Suttles, Gerald D. 1968. *The Social Order of the Slum.* Chicago: University of Chicago Press.

Suttles, Gerald D. 1972. *The Social Construction of Communities.* Chicago: University of Chicago Press.

Sylvester, R. 1977a. "From Russia with Love." *Christopher Street*, March.

Sylvester, R. 1977b. "Gennady Trifonov." *Gay Sunshine* (32, Spring).

Theodorson, George A. and Achilles G. Theodorson. 1969. *A Modern Dictionary of Sociology.* New York: Thomas Y. Crowell Company.

Thompson, Mark, ed. 1987. *Gay Spirit: Myth and Meaning.* New York: St. Martin's Press.

Tilly, Charles. 1973. "Do Communities Act?" *Sociological Inquiry* 43(3–4):209–240.

Tilly, Charles, Louise Tilly, and Richard Tilly. 1975. *The Rebellious Century, 1830–1930.* Cambridge, MA: Harvard University Press.

Troiden, Richard R. 1974. "Homosexual Encounters in a Highway Rest Stop." Pp. 211–228 in *Sexual Deviance and Sexual Deviants*, edited by Erich Goode and Richard R. Troiden. New York: William Morrow.

Troiden, Richard R. 1979. "Becoming Homosexual: a Model of Gay Identity Acquisition." *PSYCHIATRY* 42(November):362–373.

Troiden, Richard R. 1985. "Self, Self-Concept, Identity, and Homosexual Identity: Constructs in Need of Definition and Differentiation." *Journal of Homosexuality* 10(3/4, Winter):97–109.

Troiden, Richard R. 1988. *Gay and Lesbian Identity: a Sociological Analysis.* Dix Hills, NY: General Hall, Inc.

Troiden, Richard R., and Goode, Erich. 1975. "Homosexual Encounters in a Highway Reststop," Pp. 211–228 in *Sexual Deviance and Sexual Deviants* Troiden, Richard R, and Goode, Erich, eds. New York: William Morrow.

Tuller, Dave. 1991. "Gay Liberation Russian Style: Gays and Lesbians Are Coming Out and Organizing Across the Vast Country." *The ADVOCATE: the National Gay and Lesbian Newsmagazine* (591, 3 December):42–44.

Tuller, Dave and Gessen Masha. 1991. "Gays Behind Bars: Russian Gays Still Live with the Everyday Threat of Imprisonment or Forced Psychiatric Treatment." *The ADVOCATE: the National Gay and Lesbian Newsmagazine* (591, 3 December):38–40.

Tuller, David. 1992a. "It's Still Winter for Russia's Gays." *L.A. Times*, 30 January.

Tuller, David. 1992b. "New Country, Old Problems: Lithuanian Gays Say Repression Didn't Lift with the Iron Curtain." *The ADVOCATE: the National Gay and Lesbian Newsmagazine* (609, 13 August):44–45.

Tuller, David. 1996. *Cracks in the Iron Closet: Travels in Gay & Lesbian Russia.* Boston: Faber & Faber.

Vidich, Arthur J. and Joseph Bensman. 1958. *Small Town in Mass Society: Class, Power and Religion in a Rural Community.* Garden City, NJ: Anchor Books.

von Hagen, Mark L. 1984. *Talk on Gay Life in the USSR.* Stanford University.

Warner, W. Lloyd and Paul S. Lunt. 1941. *The Social Life of a Modern Community.* New Haven, CT: Yale University Press.

Warren, Carol A. B. 1972. "Observing the Gay Community." Pp. 139–163 in *Research on Deviance*, edited by Jack D. Douglas. New York: Random House.

Warren, Carol A. B. 1974. *Identity and Community in the Gay World.* New York: John Wiley & Sons.

Warren, Roland L. 1963. *The Community in America.* Chicago: Rand McNally.

References

Webber, Melvin. 1963. "Order in Diversity: Community Without Propinquity." Pp. 23–54 in *Cities and Space: the Future Use of Urban Land*, edited by L. Wingo. Baltimore: Johns Hopkins University Press.

Webber, Melvin M. 1964. "The Urban Place and the Nonplace Urban Realm." Pp. 79–153 in *Explorations Into Urban Structure*. Philadelphia, PA: University of Pennsylvania Press.

Webster's. 1970. *Webster's Seventh New Collegiate Dictionary*. Springfield, MA: G. & C. Merriam Company.

Weeks, Jeffrey. 1985. *Sexuality and its Discontents: Meanings, Myths, & Modern Sexualities*. London: Routledge & Kegan Paul.

Weeks, Jeffrey. 1986. *Sexuality*. Edited by Peter Hamilton. Key Ideas Series. Chichester/London: Ellis Horwood Limited/Tavistock Publications.

Weinberg, Martin S. 1970 "Homosexual Samples: Differences and Similarities" *Journal of Sex Research* (6), 312–25.

Weinberg, Martin S. and Colin J. Williams. 1974. *Male Homosexuals: Their Problems and Adaptations*. Oxford: Oxford University Press.

Weinberg, Martin S. and Colin J. Williams. 1975. "Gay Baths and the Social Organization of Impersonal Sex." *Social Problems* 23:124–136.

Weinberg, Thomas S. 1978. "On 'Doing' and 'Being' Gay: Sexual Behavior and Homosexual Male Self-Identity." *Journal of Homosexuality* 4(2, Winter):143–156.

Weinberg, Thomas S. 1983. *Gay Men, Gay Selves: the Social Construction of Homosexual Identities*. New York: Irvington Publishers, Inc.

Wellman, Barry. 1979. "The Community Question: the Intimate Networks of East Yorkers." *American Journal of Sociology* 84(5):1201–1231.

Whyte, Wiliam Foote. 1955. *Street Corner Society*. Chicago: University of Chicago Press.

Williams, Christopher. 1995. "Singing the Blues: the Russian Gay Movement in the 1990s." *Perversions: the International Journal of Gay and Lesbian Studies* 4(Spring):128–148.

Wirth, Louis. 1929. *The Ghetto*. Chicago: University of Chicago Press.

Wockner, Rex. 1989. "U.S.S.R. Plans to OK Gay Sex." *TWN - Florida's Most Complete Gay & Lesbian Information & Entertainment Source Since 1977*, 23 (August):33.

Wockner, Rex. 1991. "Moscow/Leningrad Events Called 'Soviet Stonewall'." *Outlines*, (September).

Wockner, Rex, Compiler. 1992a. "Russian Gays Remember AIDS Losses." *Frontiers: the Nation's Gay Newsmagazine* 11(15, 20 November):24.

Wockner, Rex, Compiler. 1992b. "Around the World: Lithuania." *Baltimore Alternative*, (December):12.

Wockner, Rex, Compiler. 1992c. "Around the World: Russia." *Baltimore Alternative*, (December):12.

Wockner News Service. 1998. "Kyrgyzstan." *GLPCI Parents' Network, a publication of the Gay and Lesbian Parents Coalition International* (January 18, 1998), *http://www.glpci.org*.

Young, Michael and Peter Willmott. 1957. *Family and Kinship in East London*. London: Routledge & Kegan Paul.

Zorbaugh, Harvey W. 1929. *The Gold Coast and the Slum*. Chicago: University of Chicago Press.

References

RUSSIAN-LANGUAGE SOURCES

«1/10». 1992. "Хроника нечистого дела". «1/10», № 1(2), 1 января. ["Chronicle of a Dirty Deed". *1:10 (One in Ten)*, No. 1(2), January 1.]

Айзенштадт, Яков. 1986. "Разбойные Нападения На Гомосексуалистов". Стр-ы. 196-199 в «Арготе Русской Гомосексуальной Субкультуры: Материалы К Изучению», создаватель – Владимир Козловский. Benson, VT: Chalidze Publications. [Ayzenshtadt, Yákov. 1986. "Marauding Attacks on Homosexuals", Pp. 196-199 in: *The Argot of the Russian Homosexual Subculture: Materials for Research*, edited by Vladímir Kozlóvskiy. Benson, VT: Chalidze Publications.]

ВЦИОМ (Всесоюзный центр изучения общественного мнения). 1990. «Общественное мнение в цифрах: Информационное издание ВЦИОМа», № 9(16), апрель. [VTsIOM (All-Union Center for the Study of Public Opinion). 1990. *Public Opinion in Figures: An Informational Publication of VTsIOM*, 9(16), April.]

Гейгес, Адриан и Суворова, Татьяна. 1990. «Любовь–вне плана (Sex & перестройка): Интимная жизнь и положение женщин в СССР». Москва: Собеседник. [Geiges, Adrian and Suvórova, Tatyána. 1990. *Love is not in the Plan (Seks i Perestróyka): Intimate life and the situation of women in the USSR*. Moscow: Interlocutor.]

Горячева, Июлия. 1991. "Сексуальная революция в Петербурге и Москве". «Независимая газета», 13 августа, Стр. 6. [Goryácheva, Iyúlia. 1991. "Sexual Revolution in Petersburg and Moscow", *The Independent Newspaper*, August 13, P.6.]

Госкомстат СССР (Государственный комитет СССР по статистике). 1990. «Социальное развитие СССР: статистический сборник». Москва: Финансы и статистика. [Goskomstát SSSR (USSR State Committee on Statistics). 1990. *The Social Development of the USSR: Statistical Collection*. Moscow: Finances and Statistics.]

Госкомстат СССР (Государственный комитет СССР по статистике). 1991. «Народное хозяйство СССР в 1990г.: статистический ежегодник». Москва: Финансы и статистика. [Goskomstát SSSR (USSR State Committee on Statistics). 1991. *The National Economy of the USSR in 1990: Statistical Yearbook*. Moscow: Finances and Statistics.]

Гражданкин, А.К. и Зоркая, Н.А. 1990. "Исследование 'Каналы передачи опыта'", «Общественное мнение в цифрах: Информационное издание ВЦИОМа», № 9(16 – апрель), Стр-ы. 8-9. [Grazhdánkin, A. K. & Zórkaya, N. A. 1990. "Research: 'Channels for the Transmission of Knowledge'", *Public Opinion in Figures: An Informational Publication of VtsIOM*, No. 9(16, April), Pp.8-9.]

Ермаков, Д. 1991. "Поймали 'сексуального шпиона'?". «Труд», 9 июля, стр. 4. [Yermakóv, D. 1991. "'Sex Spy' Caught?". *Trúd (Labor)*, July 9, p.4.]

Исаев, Дмитрий Дмитриевич. 1989. "Патологические девиации сексуального поведение у подростков мужского пола", Автореферат диссертации на соискание учённой степени кандидата медицинских наук. Ленинград: Ленинградский научно-исследовательский психоневрологический институт имени В. М. Бехтерева. [Isáyev, Dmítriy Dmítriyevich. 1989. "Pathological Deviations in Sexual Behavior among Male Adolescents", *Author's Abstract of Dissertation for the academic degree Doctor of Medical Sciences*. Leningrad: The Leningrad V.M. Békhterev Psychoneurological Scientific Research Institute.]

Козловский, Владимир. 1986а. «Арготъ Русской Гомосексуальной Субкультуры: Материалы К Изучению». Benson, VT: Chalidze Publications. [Kozlóvskiy, Vladímir. 1986a. *The Argot of the Russian Homosexual Subculture: Materials for Research*. Benson, VT: Chalidze Publications.]

Козловский, Владимир. 1986б. "Гомосексуалисты И Властъ", Стр-ы.147-168 в «Арготъ Русской Гомосексуальной Субкультуры: Материалы К Изучению», создаватель – Владимир Козловский. Benson, VT: Chalidze Publications. [Kozlóvskiy, Vladímir. 1986b. "Homosexuals and Power", Pp. 147-168 in: *The Argot of the Russian Homosexual Subculture: Materials for Research*, edited by Vladímir Kozlóvskiy. Benson, VT: Chalidze Publications.]

Козловский, Владимир. 1986в. "Энциклопедии о гомосексуализме", Стр-ы. 169-179 в «Арготъ Русской Гомосексуальной Субкультуры: Материалы К Изучению», создаватель – Владимир Козловский. Benson, VT: Chalidze Publications. [Kozlóvskiy, Vladímir. 1986v. "The Encyclopedias on Homosexuality", Pp.169-179 in: *The Argot of the Russian Homosexual Subculture: Materials for Research*, edited by Vladímir Kozlóvskiy. Benson, VT: Chalidze Publications.]

Козловский, Владимир. 1986г. "Разговоры с Гомосексуалистом и Лесбиянкой", Стр-ы. 211-228 в «Арготъ Русской Гомосексуальной Субкультуры: Материалы к Изучению», создаватель – Владимир Козловский. Benson, VT: Chalidze Publications. [Kozlóvskiy, Vladímir. 1986g. "Conversations with a Homosexual and a Lesbian", Pp. 211-228 in: *The Argot of the Russian Homosexual Subculture: Materials for Research*, edited by Vladímir Kozlóvskiy. Benson, VT: Chalidze Publications.]

Кон, Игорь. 1989. "Гомосексуализм", Стр-ы. 155-158 в «50/50: Опыт Словаря Нового Мышления», создаватели – Юрий Афанасьев и Марк Фелло. Москва: Прогресс. [Kón, Ígor. 1989. "Homosexuality", Pp. 155-158 in: *50/50: Learning from the Lexicon of New Thinking*, edited by Yúri Afanásyev and Mark Fello. Moscow: Progress.]

Кон, Игорь. 1990. "Левшу не переучишь", «Аргументы и факты», № 50, Стр-ы. 6-7. [Kón, Ígor. 1990. "You Can't Re-Train a Lefty", *Arguments and Facts*, No. 50, Pp. 6-7).]

Кон, Игорь Семёнович. 1988. «Введение в Сексологию» Москва: Медицина. [Kón, Ígor Semyónovich. *An Introduction to Sexology*. Moscow: Medicine.]

Кон, Игорь Семёнович. 1991. "Opening Remarks" at the 10th World Conference of Sexology, Amsterdam. [Kón, Ígor Semyónovich]

Кузнецов, Эдуард. 1986. "Странный народ", «Мордовский марафон» [Kuznyétsov, Eduárd]"A Strange People"]. from the book [*Mordvinian Marathon*], (Jerusalem, 1979).

Кузьмынский, К. 1983. "Койфман Из Провинции", «Новая газета», 16-22 апреля, Стр. 24. [Kuzmínskiy, K. 1983. "Koifman from the Provinces", *The New Paper*, April 16-22, p. 24.

Левада, Ю. А. и Левинсон, А. Г. 1990. "Исследование 'Социальные Дистанции'", «Общественное мнение в цифрах: Информационное издание ВЦИОМа» № 9(16 – апрель), Стр. 11. [Levada, Yu. A. & Levinsón, A. G. "Research: 'Social Distances'", *Public Opinion in Figures: an Informational Publication of VtsIOM*, No. 9(16, April, P. 11.]

Левинсон, Алексей. 1991. "Опрос: Репрессивный [*sic*: Репрессированный] Секс", «Известия», 8 марта, Стр. 7. [Levinsón, Alekséy. 1991. "Survey: Repressive [*sic*: Repressed] Sex", *Izvéstiya* (*The News*), March 8, p.7.]

Московский комсомолец 1987. "Кавалеры приглашают кавалеров", «Московский комсомолец», 24 марта ["(Male) Suitors Invite (Male) Suitors", *The Moscow Komsomol [Committee of Soviet Youth] Member*, March 24.]

Правда. 1990. "Дальше ехать некуда", «Правда», 15 ноября, Стр. 4. ["(There's) Nowhere Left to Go", *Právda* (*The Truth*), November 15, p.4.]

Пономарёв, Прокуратор города Москвы. 1991. [Ponomaryóv, Prosecutor, City of Moscow]. "Letter from the State Prosecutor of Moscow to the Vice-President of the Moscow City Council", Document No. 32-24-163-90, 18 January.

Прохоров, А. Ф. 1972. «Большая Советская Энциклопедия, Третье Издание (Том 7-ой)». Москва: Издательство «Советская Энциклопедия». [Prokhorov, A. F. 1972. *The Big Russian Encyclopedia, Third Edition* (Volume 7). Moscow: Soviet Encyclopedia Press.]

РИСК. 1991. "Сочи. Террор милиции" «РИСК / Равенство ● Искренность ● Свобода ● Компромисс», январь, Стр. 4. [RISK. 1991. "Sochi: Police Terror" *RISK: Equality ● Honesty ● Freedom ● Compromise*, January, p. 5.]

Розановъ, Василій В. 1913(1990). «Люди лунного свѣта: Метафизика христіанства» («Люди лунного света: Метафизика христианства») Репринтное воспроизведение второго издания. Москва: Издательство «Дружба народов». [Rozanov, Vasíliy Vasílyevich. 1913 (1990). *People of the Moonlight: the Metaphysics of Christianity*, Reprint of the Second Edition. Moscow: "Friendship of the Peoples" Press.]

Рубинов, Анатолий Захарович. 1991. «Интимная Жизнь Москвы». Москва: Экономика. [Rubínov, Anatóliy Zakhárovich. 1991. *The Intimate Life of Moscow*. Moscow: Economics.]

Саломони, Антонелла. 1989. "Гомосексуализм", Стр-ы. 158-160 в «50/50: Опыт Словаря Нового Мышления», создаватели – Юрий Афанасьев и Марк Фелло. Москва: Прогресс. [Antonella Salomoni. 1989. "Homosexuality", Pp. 158-160 in: *50/50: Learning from the Lexicon of New Thinking*, edited by Yúri Afanásyev and Mark Fello. Moscow: Progress.]

Черноморская здравница. 1991. "Притворился нашим один аспирант из США". «Черноморская здравница», 10 июля, Стр. 1. [The Black Sea Healthworker. 1991. "A Graduate Student From the USA Made Like One of Us". *The Black Sea Healthworker*, July 10, p.1.]

Шлютер, Даниэл. 1993. "Наш с вами народ... На грани будущего". «Ты», январь, Стр-ы. 83-93. [Schluter, Daniel. 1993. "(Yours and) Our People... on the Brink of the Future". *Thou*, January, Pp. 83-93.]

Щербаков, Сергей. 1991. "Как Это Начиналось При Тоталитаризме". «РИСК / Равенство ● Искренность ● Свобода ● Компромисс», № 1, Стр. 3. [Shcherbakóv, Sergéy. 1991. "How It Began Under Totalitarianism". *RISK: Equality ● Honesty ● Freedom ● Compromise*, No. 1, p. 3.]

Index

activism, 30, 34, 40, 44, 48, 126, 127, 129, 139, 145, 172
activist organizations, 101, 143, 148, 164
anti-sodomy statutes, 31, 34, 41, 52, 87, 119-122, 144, 145, 155-157
   history of, 117-122
   article 121.1, 122, 123, 130, 163
   enactment in Imperial Russia and the Soviet Union, 119-122
   enforcement in the USSR, 122-124
article 121, 122, 123, 130, 163
autonomy, 24, 25, 117, 155

bánya, 102-106
basic human needs, 23, 24

civil society, 32, 33, 138
collective action, 20, 126-129, 132, 150
   insurgent consciousness and, 128-129
   organizational readiness and, 129
   political opportunities and, 127-128

"coming out", 6, 76-79, 80, 157, 159, 163, 171
   to family and friends, 77-78
   to heterosexual others, 77
   to one another, 79
   to oneself, 76
communication and community, 6, 17, 19, 20, 28, 75, 129, 135, 138
community, 1, 3, 5-8, 11-28, 30-32, 34, 35, 75, 84, 101, 112, 126, 127, 129, 134, 135, 137-147, 149, 150, 160, 163-165, 167, 169, 172, 173
   defined, 6, 9, 13-28
   territorial basis of, 17
   communication and, 19, 20, 138
   as invention, 23-25, 30-32
   institutional completeness and, 26-27
   forms of, 18-19
   typology of, 14-16
   versus other forms of social organization, 19-22
"community concept", 12, 17, 140, 149
community of interest, 18-19
"communityness", 12, 16, 18, 140
constricted development, 12, 33, 146-147

dácha, 111
decriminalization, 120, 156–158
disco, *discothéque*, 107, 167, 168
discrimination, 34, 43, 44, 80, 132, 133, 144, 145, 156, 158–160, 163, 168, 170

ecological-level institutions, 87, 151
  anti-sodomy statutes, 31, 34, 41, 52, 87, 119–122, 144, 145, 155–157
  human rights, 154–158
  improvements in, 151–160
  public opinion, 158–160

fraternity, 3, 6, 7, 11, 21, 27, 28, 32, 35, 137, 138, 140–142, 144, 147, 149, 150, 163, 170, 173
  defined, 6, 9, 27–28
  versus community, 19–28, 138–140, 147

gay activism, 30, 48, 126, 127, 129, 139, 145, 172
gay activist organizations, 101, 123, 129–133, 143, 161–164
  reform/assimilationist groups, 132
  revolutionary/separatist groups, 132–133
  success of, 30, 34, 40, 48, 108, 117, 122, 127, 130, 134, 161, 163, 166
gay bar, 101
gay bashing, 34, 43, 124, 126
gay beach, 50, 98–100
gay community, 31–32
"gay ghetto", 46, 110
gay identity, 69, 76, 79, 129
gay people, 7, 31, 35, 63, 75, 76, 79, 90, 98, 102–104, 108–110, 112, 142, 148, 154

gay places, 35, 87–89, 92, 93, 95, 97, 98, 100, 101, 103–111, 126, 166, 168–169, 173
  the *bánya*, 102–105
  gay beach, 98–101
  the *pléshka*, 89–92
  public toilets, 93–99, 103
  train, bus, and subway stations, 96, 98
gay press, 145–146, 165
gay publications, 145, 163–166
gay subculture, 4, 6, 9, 30, 32, 76, 100, 160, 167
gay world, 3, 5, 7, 30, 31, 40, 53, 61, 84, 87–89, 111, 112, 137, 139, 147
glásnost, 4, 5, 33, 39, 122, 123, 125, 138, 150
"*golubóy*", 76
group-level institutions, 8, 31, 117, 129, 143, 147, 150, 160
  gay activist organizations, 101, 129–133, 143, 161–164
  gay places, 126, 166, 168, 169
  gay publications, 145, 163–166

health, 41, 60, 104, 117, 144
human needs, 12, 22–24, 154
human rights, 30, 51, 130, 154, 156, 160, 173

identification, 7, 19, 43, 45, 54, 69–79, 80, 84, 108, 140–142, 157, 169
  and "coming out", 70–71, 79–81
  defined, 9, 70
  and social risk, 141–142
identity, 3, 7, 20, 28, 29, 31, 40, 43, 52, 69–80, 82–84, 126, 129, 138, 141, 143, 146, 147, 149, 159
  as "being" versus "doing", 73–75

Index

as the application of labels, 72–73
aspects of, 72–75
defined, 6, 8–9
development of, 79–85
gay, 69, 76, 79, 129
prerequisites of, 70–72
imputation of missing data, 61–62
individual-level institutions, 7, 31, 170–172
institution, social, 11, 22–24, 26, 34, 35, 69, 101, 102, 117, 128, 139–141, 147, 152
defined, 6, 9
as invention, 23, 30
fraternal institutions, 5, 6, 11, 139–141
communal institutions, 6, 17, 102–104, 108, 110, 139
institutional completeness, 12, 26–28, 31, 140
and community, 26–27
institutionalization, 6, 7, 22, 30, 32, 34, 39, 73, 117, 118, 140, 150, 169
as habitualized action, 22–23
and community, 23–25

"kitchen culture", 109, 128

new thinking, 33, 39, 122, 138

on the "theme", 44, 130, 145, 164

participant observation, 39, 40
perestróyka, 4, 5, 33, 39, 96, 122, 123, 125, 128, 138, 150–152
personal problems, 17, 41, 140
pléshka, 89–94, 97, 98, 103, 106, 169
private places fashioned to accommodate gay needs, 88, 96, 108–111, 150
private apartments, 109–111
dáchas, 111

public bathhouse, 102–105, 112
public beach, 98–100
public opinion, 124, 125, 158–160, 170
public parks, 89, 93
public places appropriated for gay purposes, 88, 89–101
the *pléshka*, 89–92
public parks and woods, 92–93
public toilets, 93–96
train, bus, and subway stations, 96–98
public beaches, 98–101
public toilets, 89, 94–96, 98, 112

reform/assimilationist groups, 132, 144
representativeness, 43, 44–46, 55, 59, 60, 62, 84, 101, 142
revolutionary/separatist groups, 132, 144
rule of law, 34, 152

sample, 7, 43–47, 51–63, 74, 76, 80, 84, 89, 91, 95, 105–108, 110, 126, 134
sample characteristics, 53–60
by age, 57–58
by educational level, 58–59
by ethnicity (nationality), 56–57
by gender, 59
by place of residence and origin, 55–56
by recruitment source, 53–55
sample recruitment, 46–52
sampling, 13, 40, 44–52, 55, 60–63, 76
snowball, 47–49
targeted, 49–52
semi-private and partly-public places subverted for gay uses, 88, 101–108
bars and discos, 107–108
the *bánya* or public bathhouse, 102–105

  cafés and restaurants, 105–107
  hotel rooms, 108
social category, 20–21, 70–72, 79, 141, 150
  versus social group, 20–21, 138
  and community, 138
social construction, 28–30
  of homosexuality, 29
  of sexuality, 28
social constructionism, 12, 23–24, 28, 29, 140
  versus essentialism, 23–24
social group, 25, 26, 40, 70, 79, 134, 138, 140, 144, 147, 149, 150, 163
social institution (*see also* institution), 22–24, 69, 101, 102, 128, 139–141
social issues versus personal problems, 140–141, 144
social movement, 126, 134, 150, 156
societal attitudes toward homosexuality, 124–126, 158–160, 170
sodomy, 31, 34, 35, 41, 52, 87, 117–123, 130, 131, 141, 144, 145, 155–157
  defined, 119–120, 123
  legal restrictions on (*see* anti-sodomy statutes)
stigma, 3, 20, 34, 69, 71, 79, 132, 172
survey questionnaire, 41–44, 76
  development of, 42
  questions in, 43

voluntary associations, 6, 8, 15, 27, 52, 139